Architecture For Dummies®

Cheat Sheet

Is This Architecture Any Good?

How can you tell if a work of architecture is any good? It's simple. You know a work of architecture is good if you can answer "yes" to the following questions:

- Does it express its function in a visually intriguing way?
- Does it complement or contrast with its surroundings?
- Is it well built?
- Does it continue to age well?
- Does it have the ability to surprise, inspire, delight, or disturb you?
- Is it simply unforgettable?

Architectural Vocabulary

You're standing in front of the Parthenon or another great monument. The tour guide next to you starts talking about "orders." You're ready to put in your lunch request until you realize that she's referring to the architecture. Quick, what is she talking about?

- **arch:** a structure spanning an opening that is supported from the sides.
- **buttress:** a support on the outside of a wall that helps to stabilize a vault or roof.
- **column:** a vertical post divided into a base, a shaft, and a capital at the top.
- **dome:** a curved, semispherical roof structure that is circular in plan.
- **entasis:** a slight, outward curvature in a column that corrects an optical illusion and gives the appearance of being straight.
- **facade:** the face or exterior architectural treatment of a building.
- **gable:** the triangular portion of a wall under the end of a pitched roof.
- **hypar:** short for *hyperbolic paraboloid,* a type of shell structure with downwardly and upwardly curved surfaces.
- **Ionic:** a type of classical architecture with scroll-like decorations, called *volutes,* on the column capital.
- **jamb:** the vertical side of a doorway or window.
- **keystone:** a wedge-shaped unit at the top of an arch.
- **lintel:** a horizontal beam spanning the top of a door or window.
- **minaret:** a slim tower that is part of a mosque and is used to call the faithful to prayers.
- **orders:** styles of classical architecture developed by the ancient Greeks and Romans; they include the Doric, Ionic, and Corinthian.
- **portico:** a porch with a roof supported by a row of columns.
- **quoin:** a large stone at the corner of an exterior wall.
- **rustication:** roughly surfaced stonework on exterior walls; popular during the Renaissance.
- **shaft:** the section of a column between the base and the capital.
- **tracery:** curvy ornament in the upper part of a Gothic window.
- **uplift:** raising of a structure in response to structural forces.
- **vault:** an arched ceiling or roof.
- **wythe:** a continuous band of brick or stone that is one unit in thickness.
- **ziggurat:** a type of stepped pyramid used as a temple in ancient Mesopotamia.

Architecture For Dummies®

Cheat Sheet

Oscars for Architects

Of all the awards related to architecture, the most prestigious is the Pritzker Prize. Established in 1979 by Jay and Cindy Pritzker, the cash ($100,000) prize is funded by the Pritzkers' Hyatt Hotel Foundation and given annually to honor a body of work by a living architect. Candidates are selected through a process modeled after the Nobel Prize, with secret voting by an international panel of judges. The awards ceremony is held at architecturally significant sites around the world. Here is the list of the Pritzker Prize winners:

- 1979 — Philip Johnson, United States
- 1980 — Luis Barragan, Mexico
- 1981 — James Stirling, Great Britain
- 1982 — Kevin Roche, United States
- 1983 — I.M. Pei, United States
- 1984 — Richard Meier, United States
- 1985 — Hans Hollein, Austria
- 1986 — Gottfried Boehm, Germany
- 1987 — Kenzo Tange, Japan
- 1988 — Gordon Bunshaft, United States, and Oscar Neimeyer, Brazil
- 1989 — Frank Gehry, United States
- 1990 — Aldo Rossi, Italy
- 1991 — Robert Venturi, United States
- 1992 — Alvaro Siza, Portugal
- 1993 — Fumihiko Maki, Japan
- 1994 — Christian de Portzamparc, France
- 1995 — Tadao Ando, Japan
- 1996 — Rafael Moneo, Spain
- 1997 — Sverre Fehn, Norway
- 1998 — Renzo Piano, Italy
- 1999 — Norman Foster, Great Britain
- 2000 — Rem Koolhaas, Netherlands
- 2001 — Jacques Herzog and Pierre De Meuron, Switzerland

A Few Big Names in the Architecture Game

To understand architecture's evolution, it's important to become acquainted with some of the stars who pushed design in new directions.

- **Imhotep:** The first architect known by name, this ancient Egyptian created the world's first stone monument, a tomb for King Zoser.
- **Ictinus and Callicrates:** This team of Greek architects spent more than a decade perfecting the Parthenon, the most influential building of all time.
- **Hadrian:** A Roman emperor and architecture buff, Hadrian propelled design and engineering to new heights with the Pantheon.
- **Abbot Suger:** This French monk was influential in developing the soaring architecture of Gothic cathedrals.
- **Filippo Brunelleschi:** One of the first architects of the Italian Renaissance, Brunelleschi designed the dome of Florence Cathedral.
- **Christopher Wren:** This English classical architect is more famous for rebuilding St. Paul's Cathedral than for the 51 new churches he designed in London.
- **Karl Friedrich Schinkel:** Versatile in classical and Romantic styles, this German master designed one of the world's first museums.
- **Louis Sullivan:** A skyscraper pioneer, Chicago architect Louis Sullivan decorated his modern structures in leafy ornament.
- **Frank Lloyd Wright:** The most famous American architect of the twentieth century rooted his organic architecture in the land.
- **Le Corbusier:** Born Charles Edouard Jeanneret, this Swiss-French genius used glass, steel, and concrete to invent a modern language for buildings and cities.

For Dummies: Bestselling Book Series for Beginners

Architecture FOR DUMMIES®

by Deborah K. Dietsch

Foreword by Robert A. M. Stern
Dean of the Yale School of Architecture

Wiley Publishing, Inc.

Best-Selling Books • Digital Downloads • e-Books • Answer Networks • e-Newsletters • Branded Web Sites • e-Learning

Architecture For Dummies®
Published by
Wiley Publishing, Inc.
909 Third Avenue
New York, NY 10022
www.wiley.com

About the Author

Deborah K. Dietsch is a Washington, D.C.-based writer who specializes in architecture and design. She is the author of *Classic Modern: Midcentury Modern at Home* and *Dream Pools.* Additionally, she frequently writes for *The Washington Post* and various magazines.

Dietsch received a Master of Architecture degree and a Master of Science in Historic Preservation degree from Columbia University. After working for several New York architecture firms, she began a career in journalism.

From 1989 to 1997, Dietsch was the editor-in-chief of *Architecture* magazine. Under her tenure, the magazine received dozens of editorial and design awards and critical praise from the profession. She subsequently joined the *South Florida Sun-Sentinel* as the newspaper's art and architecture critic.

Over the past decade, Dietsch has helped judge many design competitions for civic, academic, and commercial buildings. She has served as an advisor to the U.S. General Services Administration in selecting architects for a new federal courthouse in Orlando, Florida, and research laboratories at the National Institutes of Health. The American Institute of Architects awarded her an honorary membership in recognition of her contributions to the architecture field.

Dedication

To all my architect friends — who keep me enthused about the art and craft of building.

Author's Acknowledgments

Many thanks to all the smarties who helped make this Dummies book possible. I'm grateful to Bob Stern, whose thoughtful Foreword adds a grace note to the book. His teaching, writing, and passion for architecture continue to inspire me. A huge thanks to Barry Bergdoll of the Department of Art History & Archaeology at Columbia University, whose wise comments improved my text. Architects Charles Brickbauer and Andrea Leers deserve credit for taking their red pens to several chapters. I am also indebted to my agent Diane Maddex of Archetype Press, who urged me to undertake this project, and to editor Sherri Fugit for her dedication and support.

Publisher's Acknowledgments

We're proud of this book; please send us your comments through our Dummies Online Registration Form located at www.dummies.com/register/.

Some of the people who helped bring this book to market include the following:

Acquisitions, Editorial, and Media Development

Project Editor: Sherri Fugit

Acquisitions Editor: Tracy Boggier

Copy Editor: Greg Pearson

Technical Editors: Barry Bergdoll, Beth Blostein

Editorial Manager: Jennifer Ehrlich

Editorial Assistant: Nívea C. Strickland

Cover Photos: © Joe Sohm, Chromosohm / Stock Connection / PictureQuest

Production

Project Coordinator: Bill Ramsey

Layout and Graphics: Kelly Hardesty, Clint Lahnen, Barry Offriga, Betty Schulte, Jeremey Unger

Proofreaders: David Faust, Andy Hollandbeck

Indexer: TECHBOOKS Production Services

Special Help

Christine Meloy Beck, Marcia L. Johnson, Tonya Maddox

General and Administrative

Wiley Consumer Reference Group

Business: Kathleen Nebenhaus, Vice President and Publisher; Kevin Thornton, Acquisitions Manager

Cooking/Gardening: Jennifer Feldman, Associate Vice President and Publisher; Anne Ficklen, Executive Editor; Kristi Hart, Managing Editor

Education/Reference: Diane Graves Steele, Vice President and Publisher

Lifestyles: Kathleen Nebenhaus, Vice President and Publisher; Tracy Boggier, Managing Editor

Pets: Kathleen Nebenhaus, Vice President and Publisher; Tracy Boggier, Managing Editor

Travel: Michael Spring, Vice President and Publisher; Brice Gosnell, Publishing Director; Suzanne Jannetta, Editorial Director

Wiley Consumer Editorial Services: Kathleen Nebenhaus, Vice President and Publisher; Kristin A. Cocks, Editorial Director; Cindy Kitchel, Editorial Director

Wiley Consumer Production: Debbie Stailey, Production Director

Contents at a Glance

Table of Contents

Chapter 11: Revivals Everywhere: The Classical and Gothic Are New Again 127

Chapter 12: Here Comes the Industrial Age: Prefab Is Here to Stay 141

Part IV: Eastern Architecture: A Survey of the Most Important Structures

Foreword

· ·

*A*rchitecture is an artistic and practical expression of the real world — it is the art of building in the service of individuals and institutions. It is the art of construction, not deconstruction; of representation, not communication; it is the solidity of the here-and-now. Architecture is important. It is the setting for life. Despite the reality of architecture, or perhaps because of it, architecture is a field whose very nature is endlessly questioned by its own practitioners and appointed experts — theorists and critics, who, to avoid confronting the simple but profound circumstances of architecture, try to judge it by criteria outside itself, whether from literature or science or the social sciences, or whatever. It's a process of avoidance that reminds me of the Paul Simon song, *Fifty Ways to Leave Your Lover.* But architecture can stand on its own. Some architects and a few critics stick by it, even exult in it. Deborah Dietsch is one of these people — one who has the capacity to convey architecture's meanings in clear terms. I first met Deborah Dietsch when she was a student at Columbia University, where she was the first ever to earn a Master of Architecture and a Master of Science in Historic Preservation in the same year. She went on to become editor of one of America's foremost professional journals. Deborah is a passionate advocate for responsible building; a journalist, not an ideologue; and a teacher, not a preacher. Who better, then, to sweep away the cobwebs spun by the theoreticians to reveal the simple but fascinating lessons of architecture than Deborah?

— Robert A. M. Stern

Dean of the Yale School of Architecture, Robert A. M. Stern is a practicing architect, a teacher, and a writer with a dozen books to his credit. He is best known to the public for *Pride of Place: Building the American Dream,* a documentary television series that aired on PBS in 1986.

Introduction

Chances are, unless you're reading this book in the middle of nowhere, you are experiencing architecture right now. You're probably sitting inside a room, surrounded by walls, a floor, a ceiling, windows, and doors. These commonplace elements make up the buildings where people live, work, and play. In the hands of a talented designer, they are transformed into the art of architecture.

The creations drawn by architects affect us more directly than other art forms. You don't have to look at a painting or attend a concert, but you do have to interact with architecture on a daily basis. Architecture is unique in its capability to blend utility and beauty.

Most people don't understand architecture or what architects do. And with good reason. Architecture, especially contemporary architecture, can feel forbidding, inscrutable, and cold. Talking about its stylistic development can sound effete, and discussion of its methods and materials of construction can make it seem too technical.

In contrast to painting or sculpture, it's harder to look at architecture and take it all in. You can wander around a building and walk through room after room without comprehending the structure's overall design. Trying to understand architecture from plans and other types of drawings can also be confusing if you don't know what you're looking at.

Unless you've hired an architect at some point, you probably have no clue as to how he or she works. If you've ever read *The Fountainhead* or watched the movie, you probably think architects are do-it-my-way-or-else egotists who make all the design decisions and won't let you move the furniture. They appear to be artsy types who wear bow ties and trendy glasses and are only a tiny bit more practical than sculptors and painters. The structures they design are more expensive than those put up by a builder. At the same time, architects' creations are often criticized — sometimes undeservedly so — for their leaky roofs and drafty windows.

Architects and critics also tend to use obscure jargon when talking about architecture. They snobbishly pride themselves on their "archi-speak" as they identify each drawing and detail. Pity the poor client who asks where to find the front door.

Although the image of the architect as an impractical, inarticulate snob is sometimes accurate, it is largely a myth.

It's true that Frank Lloyd Wright insisted on controlling every piece of furniture — if the owners dared to rearrange the rooms, he changed them back to the way they were. (His buildings also leaked.) And yes, architect-designed buildings tend to cost more, but they typically last longer and sell at higher prices than speculative buildings. The language of architecture can also be incomprehensible, but that's because it is extremely precise in its identification of each tiny detail.

Today's architects are a more diverse group than in the past, capable of producing a wide range of designs for every conceivable purpose. Sure, the profession is more conservative than the art world (a building has to withstand a lot more over time than does a typical work of art), but the field is changing as interest in architecture continues to grow, and the public demands more from their built environments.

More people understand and appreciate architecture than in the past thanks to increasing public awareness of the building arts. Newspapers and magazines devote more space to covering the subject than ever before. (Some even employ architecture critics who write in plain English.) Television shows and museum exhibitions are also exposing more people to the contributions of architects. And chain stores such as Target, mail-order catalogs, and Internet sites now routinely sell furniture and products designed by architects.

This book is dedicated to boosting your ability to experience the joys of architecture. The magical way that light and shadow animate a façade, the tactile delight of touching cool tile or rough stone, and the clatter of footsteps across a cavernous room are only a few of architecture's sensory pleasures.

About This Book

With enough exposure to architecture, anyone can become an expert. The secret is to experience buildings — not through magazines, books, lectures, or photographs but by soaking up the real thing, the physicality of space.

A few years ago, I drove from Chicago, Illinois, to Racine, Wisconsin, to visit Wright's Johnson Wax headquarters, a modern building I had known only through photos. I remember being shocked at how small its famous mushroom-shaped columns were and how cozy its open workroom felt. The photos — taken without a person in sight, as so many images of architecture are — made the building seem so much more monumental and austere.

While this book can't capture a building in three dimensions, it can help you understand architecture and give you the confidence to talk about the subject — even to an architect. It tells you how to start looking at architecture, it explains the essentials of structure and style, and it identifies some of the greatest architects and architecture.

How This Book Is Organized

This book is intended to be a reference book, written in an accessible style for the beginner. It also provides useful information for those who know something about architecture and want to brush up on their history — or discover a few fun facts. Of course, not every architectural style and nuance is discussed, and some architects aren't mentioned that could have been. (To be truly comprehensive, this book would have to be almost as big as a building!) But all the great architects are included, along with some contemporary designers whose place in architectural history is less certain.

Part I: Knowing and Appreciating Architecture

Is it a building or architecture? For the novice, it's hard to tell the difference. This section defines architecture through its essential attributes — function, structure, and beauty — and explains the importance of each. It provides a list of requirements that must be met before architecture can be considered good or bad, and it gives you tips on viewing a building so that you can discover its assets for yourself. A list of design fundamentals helps you analyze a building's style no matter what its age, and various terms are identified for different types of walls, roofs, windows, and doorways.

Part II: Nuts and Bolts: Looking at How Architecture Is Designed and Built

This part deals with the process of designing and constructing a building — from the architect's first sketch to the construction of the walls and roof. It begins with an analysis of how architects use functional requirements to shape recognizable buildings and to invent new building types. The evolution of an architectural design is traced from sketches to final blueprints, with an explanation of each drawing used to document the building. If you decide to consider your own building project, this part also has tips on hiring an architect that can help ease the process.

After the design is completed, it must be translated into bricks and mortar (or any other material). A chapter on basic structural principles helps you understand the different ways architecture withstands loads and forces to achieve stability, permanence, and beauty.

Part III: Western Architecture: A Survey of the Most Important Structures

Since the dawn of civilization, people have built shelter against the sun, wind, and rain. This part begins with the earliest nomadic structures and stone monuments and ends with the latest architecture built for the digital age. It steers you through all the styles in between, concentrating on European and American examples. Presented throughout is a wide range of building types — from houses and castles to cathedrals, palaces, and museums.

Because architecture is dependent on structure and materials to create a visual language, each chapter explains the development of the construction technologies that made each style possible. Stylistic progress is traced through important historical buildings and architects' lasting contributions to the field.

Part IV: Eastern Architecture: A Survey of the Most Important Structures

Most books on architecture concentrate on the Western world while ignoring the achievements of Asia and the Middle East. This book is different because it explains the exciting architectural treasures found in China, Japan, India, and Islamic countries. The concise history in this part shares many Eastern splendors with you, explaining the centuries-old building traditions that made them possible.

In Part IV, you get information about the design and construction of pagodas, stupas, and mosques. You also discover the far-reaching influence of this exotic architecture on the West.

Part V: Arranging the Present and Saving the Past

The history of architecture is the history of human settlements. This part explores the contribution of architecture to the evolution of cities, from the ancient villages of Mesopotamia to the modern-day metropolises of Paris and New York. This part also presents different types of urban planning and growth and shows how they parallel the development of architectural styles.

Renewed appreciation of cities in recent decades has led architects to preserve and adapt individual buildings and entire neighborhoods. I include a chapter about historic preservation to give you an idea of preservation's history and growing significance within the architectural field.

Part VI: The Part of Tens

Turn to this part when you want a quick synopsis of the ten greatest buildings of all time. I put together this list, with buildings that you can still visit, to represent many of the stylistic developments covered in Parts III and IV. Or, if you're thinking about hiring an architect, you may want to soak up the information in Chapter 21. You can also pick up some interesting facts that you won't find in most history books about architecture and architects through the ages.

Icons Used in This Book

Throughout this book, you can find icons to help guide you through the material.

This icon alerts you to interesting tips on architecture that you should pay attention to.

Whenever special architecture terms, such as trabeated and triglyph, are presented, this icon tells you to take notice.

This icon is placed next to information related to building construction and technology.

When you see this symbol next to a description of a building, you can safely assume that a photo of the architecture is in this book's color insert — the next best thing to viewing the structure in person!

The evolution of architecture is filled with interesting twists and turns. This icon alerts you to historical facts that are important to your understanding of the field.

Where to Go from Here

Step out of your house or office and explore the world of architecture. Start with the buildings around you. Look at the way they rise from the ground, face the street, and touch the sky. You may discover an ornate molding or an interestingly shaped window that you've never noticed before.

If you aren't confident about investigating architecture on your own, call your local historical society or chapter of the American Institute of Architects for help. (Consult www.aiaonline.com to get started.) They often sponsor guided tours and public events aimed at boosting architectural awareness.

After you learn more about architecture, you'll discover that it is as subjective as any art form. One person's favorite building is another's carbuncle. (That's what Britain's Prince Charles called the proposed modern addition to the National Gallery in London.) Sometimes it's fun to look at ugly and ordinary buildings — such as shopping malls or casinos — just to figure out how they work and why they are so despised by most architects.

The more you study architecture, the more you'll appreciate its form, function, materials, and construction. When you are familiar with the amazing ways that structures and spaces come alive, you'll never look at a building the same way again!

Part I

Knowing and Appreciating Architecture

The 5th Wave   By Rich Tennant

I really felt it was time for traditional lighthouse architecture to evolve.

In this part . . .

If you've ever wondered about what architects do, this part gives you a short summary. An introduction to the language of architecture explains the special terms used to identify the different types of doors, windows, roofs, and other components that contribute to a particular style.

Chapter 1

Knowing When a Building Is Just a Building and When It's Architecture

In This Chapter

▶ Comparing buildings and architecture

▶ Discovering the fundamental elements of architecture

▶ Viewing great architecture

*W*e live, work, and play in buildings every day. Architecture is an important part of our lives, helping us shape the natural environment for human needs.

From ancient temples to modern skyscrapers, architecture has constantly evolved to reflect the accomplishments of civilizations in all corners of the world. It records our cultural, social, and political ambitions in three dimensions. You need only glance at the imposing ruins of the Roman Forum (see Chapter 8) to comprehend the imperial pride of ancient Rome, enter the magnificent space of Chartres Cathedral (see Chapter 9) to feel the religious fervor of medieval Europe, or gaze up at the Empire State Building (see Chapter 13) to view an instant picture of modern American enterprise.

Each one of these buildings represents the era in which it was built. To understand the symbolic meaning of architecture, you have to relate the structure and style of a building to a particular period of history. As you come to understand the basics of architecture, you will find it easier to determine the era in which a particular building was built.

The Beauty of Form Meets Function

A building provides shelter from the elements. But architecture does more than just provide shelter. Architecture responds to the needs of its users and rises to the level of art. Like sculpture, architecture is a three-dimensional visual expression of form, material, and color. French architect Le Corbusier (see Chapter 14) described it as a magnificent play of masses brought together by light. But architecture isn't merely giant sculpture to be looked at — it serves a practical purpose. Even the most creative architect has to consider where to place the doors, stairs, and bathrooms.

Unlike paintings and sculpture, which can be viewed nearly anywhere, architecture is connected to a particular place. It relates to the specifics of geography, climate, and surroundings. After Arabian Muslims invaded Africa and Spain (see Chapter 18), for example, they drew upon local materials and architectural motifs from indigenous buildings when designing their mosques and palaces.

Called "the mother of the arts," architecture serves as both a place for viewing art and a backdrop on which to create it. It provides settings for appreciating paintings and sculpture and watching dance and theater in comfortable sur-roundings. For centuries, architecture has led sculptors, painters, and other artisans to decorate its surfaces. It's hard to imagine a Gothic cathedral, for instance, without gargoyles, gilded altarpieces, or stained-glass windows.

Why Is Architecture Important?

Architecture has a profound effect on our lives. Working in an office filled with sunlight or in a windowless cubicle changes our habits and our moods for better or worse. As Winston Churchill once observed, people shape their buildings and afterwards their buildings shape them.

Architecture has a wider cultural significance than being merely useful. It per-manently records a civilization's aesthetic tastes, material resources, political and social aspirations, and sheer will in brick, stone, steel, and glass.

When you look at architecture, you can learn a lot about the people who built it. The Great Pyramids outside Cairo (see Chapter 7) convey the ancient Egyptians' belief in immortality. The great dome of Florence Cathedral (see Chapter 10) reveals the logical mind of the Renaissance scholar. The grand mansions of Newport, Rhode Island (see Chapter 11) show off the wealth and extravagance of the Gilded Age tycoons.

A unique blend of beauty and utility, architecture reflects advancements in both art and science. Modern European buildings of the late nineteenth and early twentieth century, for example, were highly influenced by the Industrial Revolution. Their open spaces and large windows were also made possible by the latest developments in structural engineering and building technology (see Chapters 12 and 13), while echoing the spare lines of abstract art created during the same period (see Chapter 14).

What Makes Architecture Good?

Ancient Roman architect Vitruvius insisted that three fundamental principles are essential to architecture. His formula still holds true. A building must balance all three to be considered architecture. These three fundamental principles are

- **Function:** This refers to how a building is used. Whether a building is used as a house, a store, or a museum, it must accommodate practical requirements for every purpose within its walls. A building without function may be beautiful, but it's sculpture, not architecture. Artist Richard Serra, for example, creates room-sized steel enclosures that are structurally daring and mysteriously beautiful, but you can't live in one.

- **Structure:** This refers to how a building stands up. Whether it consists of steel columns, wood studs, or brick walls, the framework must resist gravity and the loads placed upon it. But to be architecture, it must do more. It must create beauty from structural necessity — this is what differentiates architecture from engineering.

- **Beauty:** This refers to the visual and sensory appeal of buildings. It is what Vitruvius called "delight." Architectural delight can be found in a neatly patterned brick wall, a vaulted stone ceiling, or a tiny window emitting a stream of sunlight. Beauty is the ultimate test of good architecture. Without beauty, a highly functional building is merely utilitarian without rising to the realm of architecture. It's the difference between a suburban tract house and Frank Lloyd Wright's masterpiece, Fallingwater (see Chapter 14).

What is considered beautiful and what is considered ugly changes over time. The Kennedy Center in Washington, D.C., designed by Edward Durrell Stone, a leading architect of his day, was considered the height of architectural beauty when it opened in 1971. Today, it's ridiculed for its boxy shape, gigantic lobbies, and modernistic decorations.

Sometimes an architectural style that was once considered beautiful will fall out of favor, only to be rediscovered decades later. In Miami Beach, the city's once thriving Art Deco hotels fell into disrepair in the 1970s and 1980s after years of neglect. After preservationists pointed out the merits of these architectural treasures, the hotels were renovated to become hip tourist destinations. Art Deco (see Chapter 13) has once again become synonymous with the beauty of Miami Beach.

Truly outstanding works of architecture never fail to wow us with their spatial power. Such structures as Stonehenge (see Chapter 7) and the Parthenon (see Chapter 8) are still admired for their monumentality even though they are thousands of years old.

How to Spot Good Architecture

How can you tell if a building is good architecture? You can be pretty sure that a building is good architecture if you can answer "yes" to the following questions:

- ✔ **Does it express its function in a meaningful and visually interesting way?** For example, an airport may be aerodynamically streamlined to resemble flight, a museum may be sculpted into abstract shapes to represent the contemporary art inside, or an institution that values collaboration among its employees may consist of buildings grouped around a shared courtyard.

- ✔ **Does it complement or contrast with its surroundings?** Good architecture does not end at its walls. The design of an individual building should relate to its environment in a unique way. Some of the best buildings aren't very noticeable right away — they use the same materials and shapes as neighboring structures but tweak them in new ways. Other buildings introduce a completely different vocabulary to call attention to the form and the function of a particular structure.

- ✔ **Is it well built?** Architecture should be made to last. It's easy to discern a flimsy building from a solid one — hollow doors, shaky floors, and crooked walls give it away. But the difference between average and excellent architecture is harder to discern: It often hinges on, well, the hinges. Small details such as door hardware, windowsills, stair railings, and even baseboards can make or break the architecture. As modern architect Mies van der Rohe once said, "God is in the details." That's why the best architects always insist on designing every tiny thing — and then whine about clients who won't spend money on the design.

- ✔ **Does it age well?** Good architecture has an essential character that remains steadfast even though the building's use and the needs of its inhabitants may change. New York's Grand Central Terminal, for example, was built with large halls for passengers waiting to board trains.

Although busy commuters no longer sit in these rooms — the interior has been changed with new stores and restaurants — Grand Central still imparts the same magnificence as it did when it first opened in 1913.

✔ **Do the building's spaces surprise, inspire, mystify, delight, or disturb?**
Good architecture solicits a visceral reaction. A tranquil courtyard filled with plants and fountains soothes our senses, while a dark, underground passageway may fill us with dread. An equally spaced row of monumental columns appeals to our sense of balance, and angled walls, floors, and ceilings that look about to tumble over impart danger and disorientation.

Understanding the complexity of architecture can seem daunting. To understand this complexity, you must find out about the science of structures, the craft of building, and the art of space-making, as well as the terminology of architecture. The terminology can be maddeningly obscure, but the rewards that come from understanding it are great. You will be able to appreciate not only your immediate surroundings but also iconic buildings throughout history. Buildings and cities are more likely to improve in the future if more people become knowledgeable about architecture.

Where Can You See Architecture?

From an old Victorian house in your neighborhood to the brand-new museum downtown, you can find interesting architecture almost anywhere. But to understand the truly great buildings — the earth-shattering kind that changed civilization — you have to travel to Europe, Asia, and other far-flung places. To get you started, this book offers a brief history of Western and Eastern architecture that highlights outstanding structures around the globe. In addition, Chapter 22 gives you a list of the most outstanding buildings from each period to visit.

Never pass up an opportunity to visit a landmark in the city that you are visiting. Many an architecture buff has knocked on the door of a perfect stranger just for the chance to walk through an interesting building. (Most owners of great architecture are only too happy to show off their prized possession.)

Your ability to appreciate architecture will grow as you experience buildings firsthand. No photograph can capture the thrill of stepping into the cavernous space of an ancient temple or mosque, or of ascending to the top of a skyscraper for a breathtaking view. The more you learn about architecture, the more you will notice the similarities and differences among structures from different eras. You'll awaken to the beauty of proportions, rhythms, solids, and voids. (These elements are all discussed in Chapter 2.) You'll discover how to appreciate the walls, floors, and ceilings — and even the doorknobs — of the buildings around you.

If You Do Go . . .

Wear the most comfortable shoes you can find — experiencing architecture requires tons of walking. You'll be trekking across streets, through room after room, and up and down many flights of stairs. Take a camera — conventional, video, or digital — to record what you've seen. Or even a sketchbook. Most architects never travel without one. Drawing a building yourself forces you to see how the basic elements of architecture are put together to create a style — see Chapter 3 for more details. Before you go, consult a guidebook to figure out where to see the most interesting buildings. Many cities offer guided walking tours of historic areas for a small fee. Be prepared for a few surprises — sometimes the most interesting architecture isn't on the tour.

LINGO

What is an architect?

An *architect* is different from an engineer and an interior designer because he or she is responsible for creating both the exteriors and interiors of a building — not just the structure or the decoration of the rooms.

The great architects of the past were often great artists — Michelangelo not only painted the Sistine Chapel, but he also added the dome to St. Peter's Cathedral and designed the buildings of the Piazza del Campidoglio in Rome. French master Le Corbusier composed abstract paintings and furniture, as well as modern houses and cities.

The architects of the past were also more closely involved with the construction process.

Medieval European architects worked alongside masons, sculptors, and artisans when building cathedrals. The first architect of the Renaissance, Filippo Brunelleschi, supervised the firing of brick and carved turnips to demonstrate the type of masonry joints that he wanted.

Today, an architect is a highly specialized professional who leads a team of designers and consultants, such as engineers, to create projects for clients (see Chapter 5 for more on the design process). An architect, like a doctor or lawyer, must meet certain educational requirements and pass an examination to obtain a license to practice architecture (see Chapter 5).

Chapter 2

How to Look at a Building

*L*ooking at architecture — no matter what the building's style or age — requires an understanding of the basic elements of design. Architects shape space by using solids, voids, scale, massing, proportion, rhythm, color, texture, and light. By understanding these design fundamentals, you can appreciate the form of architecture in all its nuances and recognize how it has changed over time. Nothing ever stays the same, and architecture is certainly no exception. However, the fundamentals always stay the same, and knowing the fundamentals is how you build your own foundation (yeah, pun intended!) for appreciating architecture. Dig in!

Space: Solids and Voids

Rigid elements — walls, floors, and roofs that enclose cavities such as rooms, windows, and doorways — form the building. The relationships among these solids and voids are what create architectural space. Each space is distinguished from the others through the placement, size, shape, and materials of its enclosure. This variation is what gives every building its distinctive character.

Mirror images: Symmetry

Designing one side of a space to mirror the opposite side is called *symmetry*. You can see an example of symmetry in Figure 2-1. The dividing line between the identical halves is called an *axis*. The balanced arrangement of elements gives symmetrical buildings a feeling of formality, harmony, and dignity. It's easy to understand our affinity for this type of architecture: Symmetry reflects the bilateral form of the human body. The country homes designed by Italian architect Andrea Palladio during the late Renaissance (see Chapter 10) are good examples of architectural symmetry. They are composed of a central block flanked by porches and wings of equal size — like the arms of a torso.

Symmetry, however, is not always applied to a whole building: You may find it in only one part. For example, the living room may be symmetrical, with equally spaced walls, doorways, and windows, while the dining room and kitchen may be of different sizes and shapes. The living room is an example of *local symmetry,* which is used to balance an irregular arrangement of spaces. When shaped into a multi-sided symmetrical form such as an octagon, the room becomes an example of *radial symmetry,* or equal parts that radiate around a center.

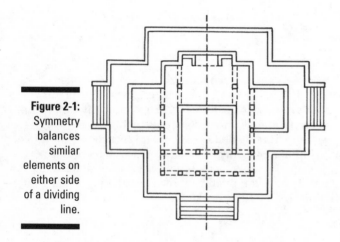

Figure 2-1:
Symmetry balances similar elements on either side of a dividing line.

Imbalance and tension: Asymmetry

Architectural elements that are unevenly spaced so that they don't balance each other create *asymmetry.* A door that is placed off center in a wall or an irregular pattern of windows across a façade are two examples of asymmetry. This unbalanced arrangement of elements gives architecture a feeling of informality and movement — and sometimes a note of surprise. The Victorians liked asymmetry, which they believed gave buildings a ruggedness in harmony with nature. Modernists such as German-born architect Mies van der Rohe (see Chapter 14) also liked asymmetry. He positioned freestanding walls and glass panels at irregular intervals to make space feel like it flowed between the indoors and outdoors.

When openings, such as windows and doors, or solid elements, such as chimneys and domes, are positioned asymmetrically within symmetrical enclosures, they establish a tension that often makes a building more dynamic. For example, when architect Christopher Wren (see Chapter 10) designed the Royal Naval Hospital in Greenwich, England, in the eighteenth century, he placed a pair of domes at the ends of his symmetrical blocks rather than in the centers. Their tall, rounded shapes provide a vertical emphasis and accent, directing the eye through the middle of the vast building complex to the Queen's House in the distance.

A room's length, width, and height also determine the quality of its space. A small room with a flat ceiling feels more claustrophobic than the same size room with a curved ceiling. Wide, low spaces also create a spatial experience that is horizontal rather than vertical; Frank Lloyd Wright's Prairie-style houses, for example, direct the view horizontally and out into the landscape (See chapter 14.) On the other hand, a space topped by a vault or dome directs the view upward to accentuate the room's height. A long rectangular or oval space leads the eye toward the end of the room, while a round or square room directs the eye to the center.

Scale and Proportion: Size Matters

Each architectural element — whether it's a door, a window, or a brick — shares a relationship with every other element in the building. The size of each component in relation to the size of the other components is called *scale*.

Scale: It's all relative

Scale refers not only to the relative size of one element to another within the building but also to the entire building's size in relation to its surroundings. By manipulating scale, an architect can make a building feel imposing or intimate. For example, tall columns that extend two stories higher than a three-story exterior wall are large in scale relative to the size of the wall. By scaling the columns so tall, the architect makes the three-story building appear more monumental than it would appear without them.

Determining scale requires comparing the size of one element against a standard point of reference. The term *out of scale* infers that one part of the architecture is too big or too small for its surroundings or the other elements of its design. One obvious example of this concept is a 40-story glass tower amid a low-rise neighborhood of brick homes. Another example might be the inflated keystone applied by Postmodernist Michael Graves to the top of his Portland Building (see Chapter 15), a government office building in Portland, Oregon. Breaking the rules with oversized elements, however, is not always inappropriate. Like the keystone in Graves's Portland Building, overscaled elements can add verve and excitement to a design. In designing the Staatsgalerie in Stuttgart, Germany, British architect James Stirling added large, brightly colored handrails that might be considered greatly out of scale to emphasize the dynamics of movement along and through the building. Visual scale, unlike size, is relative, not absolute.

Architectural plans are drawn to *mechanical* or *architectural scale*. Every increment of the drawn lines in the architectural plans (⅛ inch, for example) corresponds to a real measurement in space (1 foot, for example). Of course, the drawing might also be scaled so that every 1/16-inch mark equals 1 foot.

Scale is created from elements that are proportioned according to various dimensions. *Proportion* is a quantified relationship among the parts of an element, as well as the relationship of that element to the whole.

Dust off your math, because balanced proportions require understanding the correspondence between two ratios in which the first of the four numbers divided by the second number equals the third divided by the fourth ($4 \div 2 = 10 \div 5$). What do these ratios have to do with architecture? For a designer, they help in figuring out the same relationship between the measurements of the windows and the measurements of the exterior walls so that the building looks and feels harmonious.

Proportional systems: The pursuit of perfection

Although there is no absolute and uniform proportioning system, architects have continuously attempted to work out systems for sizing elements to ensure a pleasing appearance in their buildings. They have determined certain relationships between width and height and applied them to sizing a door or window — or the space between the two — as well as to calculating the number of elements in a façade.

Renaissance architect Leonardo da Vinci captured the proportions of the human body in his famous drawing of an outstretched figure of man (see Figure 2-2). In the twentieth century, modern Swiss-born architect Le Corbusier (see Chapter 14) also used a human figure as the basis for building dimensions. He called the system *Le Modulor* and tried to persuade the building industry to use it as a standard.

Some proportions were based on the *golden section* (or *golden mean*) — a system that Renaissance theorists thought to be divine. With this system, the architect determines her dimensions for building elements by dividing a line into two unequal parts so that the relationship between the smaller and larger sections is the same as the relationship between the larger section and the whole; the ratio between these sections is about 5 to 8. See Figure 2-3.

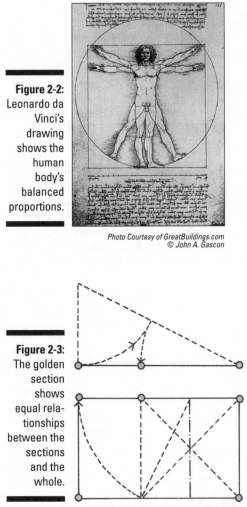

Figure 2-2: Leonardo da Vinci's drawing shows the human body's balanced proportions.

Photo Courtesy of GreatBuildings.com
© John A. Gascon

Figure 2-3: The golden section shows equal relationships between the sections and the whole.

HISTORICAL NOTE

Let anatomy be your guide!

Some of the oldest proportioning systems are based on the size of the human body and the relationship between the body's parts. Ancient Greek and Roman architects used their bodies as inspiration for vertical supports called columns (see Chapter 8): The top of a column (called a *capital*), for example, was a metaphor for the human head; the main part of the column was the body; and the block, or *plinth,* on which the column rested, acted like the feet.

Weight and Mass: It Ain't Heavy, It Just Looks That Way

Building materials exert a great impact on the public's perception of architecture. Weighty units such as stone or brick convey permanence, durability, and strength. Renaissance architects often built palaces with the lower stories faced in rough-cut stones. This design technique helped them to look strong and impenetrable.

Smooth and transparent surfaces seem lighter and more delicate. Modern architects such as Le Corbusier (see Chapter 14) faced their buildings in stucco and glass to make the exterior walls seem to "float" off the heavy concrete structures beneath. The appearance of a building, however, doesn't necessarily represent the true quality of its construction. Think about this: A brick wall appears substantial. But when it is covered in stucco, the same wall looks much lighter, even though the combination of brick and stucco weighs more than bricks alone.

It's a material world

Materials can also be used to express attributes that are the opposite of those conveyed by the material's weight and mass. Heavy materials such as stone can be cut to express the luminosity of translucent glass. The windows of the Beinecke library at Yale University, designed by Skidmore, Owings, and Merrill, are covered with thin sheets of alabaster, a type of marble that glows in light. Lightweight materials such as dark-colored glass, on the other hand, look opaque and can convey more solidity and mass.

Additive and subtractive massing: Give a little, take a little

Composing three-dimensional shapes or volumes into a building design is called *massing*. Architects often begin a project by assembling rough blocks of cardboard or clay into what is called a *massing model*. The model allows them to study the shapes and the silhouette of a building before they develop the details.

The result may be an accumulation of masses — a design approach that is known as *additive*. This grouping of building blocks is based on a unit or module that is repeated. For hundreds of years, Japanese architects (see Chapter 16) used the additive approach to design traditional wooden houses based on the size of a 3-x-6-foot straw floor mat called a *tatami*. In the nineteenth century, European architects used this design approach to create *picturesque massing* (see Chapter 11): They would surround the main building block with towers and lower wings to produce an irregular silhouette.

Another type of massing calls for removing parts of a building from a solid block — this design approach is called *divisive* or *subtractive*. Baroque buildings are typical of this approach. A good example of a building that was built with subtractive massing is San Carlo alle Quattro Fontane in Rome, a chapel designed by Francesco Borromini (see Chapter 10). Within the straight enclosure of this small chapel, Borromini sculpted the space with undulating walls and an oval domed ceiling. On the exterior, alternating concave and convex curves seem to be carved from the building front. The rounded shapes seem to sway and swerve to create a sense of dynamic movement.

High-tops and low-tops

Building masses may be low to the ground to create a horizontal emphasis and harmony with the earth. The earth-hugging houses designed by Frank Lloyd Wright (see Chapter 14) are a good example of this approach. Building masses may also stand vertically upright and soar to the sky to create an uplifting spirit, as in the pinnacles and towers of Gothic cathedrals.

The Elements of Design

German poet Johann Goethe once said that architecture is "frozen music." This phrase aptly captures the rhythmic arrangement of elements in a building.

Regularly spaced windows, doors, and columns tap out a measured, stately pace. Renaissance architects preferred this orderly rhythm to represent the logic and reason behind their geometric forms. Overlapping, irregular, and asymmetrically placed building elements, on the other hand, pulse in a syncopated beat. A contemporary example of this style is the Guggenheim Museum in Bilbao, Spain, designed by Los Angeles architect Frank Gehry (see Chapter 21). Its collage of rippling metal shapes expresses the improvised feeling of modern jazz.

Interior space can also be arranged into rhythmic variations. The architectural sequence of small, low spaces leading to bigger, higher ones builds to a climax much like a musical crescendo.

The technique of organizing spaces according to their visual or functional importance is called *hierarchy*. Rooms shared by many people — libraries, courtrooms, or hotel lobbies, for example — are often given more prominence within a building than private spaces used by individuals, such as offices, judges' chambers, or bedrooms. Public rooms are made larger in size and stature through monumental effects ranging from giant columns and domes to bold colors and materials.

In designing the University of Virginia, for example, Thomas Jefferson (see Chapter 11) developed a clear hierarchy to help represent his ideas about learning at the "academical village." On either side of a lawn, he placed two-story pavilions for both classrooms and teachers' living accommodations. Connecting these small buildings are colonnades and one-story rooms for students. Jefferson placed the library at the end of the lawn and designed it to look like the Roman Pantheon (see Chapter 8) to symbolize its importance to higher learning and campus life.

Color me functional: Texture and color

Smooth and rough surfaces, and bright and pale colors further differentiate the various parts of a building. Gothic Revival architects (see Chapter 11) were particularly adept at these contrasts. They would often shape brick walls, stone trim, painted cast-iron columns, and stained-glass windows into colorful, textured fantasies.

Modernists also enjoyed using color and texture. Le Corbusier (see Chapter 14), who began his career as a painter, often injected bright blues and reds into his spare white architecture. Mies van der Rohe (see Chapter 14) made his minimalism appear luxurious through textured partitions made of colored marbles, exotic woods, and sumptuous velvets.

Color and texture can be applied to emphasize the functional and structural roles of a space or element. Public spaces, for example, may be painted in a brighter tone than private rooms, or walls may be contrasted in smooth plaster and knotty wood. Varying color and texture can also make different areas seem heavier, lighter, smaller, larger, warmer, or cooler.

Color in architecture is often associated with regional traditions. Walls of Mediterranean houses are covered in yellow, orange, and white stucco, while the walls of houses in rural Scandinavia are clad in red-painted wood. Mexican architect Luis Barragan carried on this tradition, as he colored his simple stucco buildings in brilliant shades of cobalt blue, fuchsia, and red in a manner similar to the vernacular buildings of his native country.

From stone to neon: Ornament

Decorative flourishes have always served to add visual detail, human scale, and sensual delight to architecture. Classical temples are festooned with sculpture (see Chapter 8), Gothic cathedrals sprout gargoyles (see Chapter 9), and Chinese palaces are adorned with ornate carvings (see Chapter 16).

Some ornamentation articulated a didactic purpose: Romanesque churches (see Chapter 9), for example, instructed parishioners in Christian doctrines through murals and sculptures. Other styles of decoration helped to ease the acceptance of new building types. In designing early skyscrapers in the 1890s, Chicago architect Louis Sullivan (see Chapter 13) developed a system of ornamentation to dignify each part of his towers and symbolically connect them to the landscape: grounded heavy base, light middle, and ornamented top meeting the sky. In the twentieth century, decoration fell on hard times. It was called irrelevant, dishonest, and even criminal by architects pursuing streamlined, abstract designs (see Chapter 14).

Recent decades, however, have witnessed a return to decoration. In the 1980s, postmodernists such as Charles Moore and Michael Graves (see Chapter 15) jazzed up plain walls with sculpture, brackets, and garlands. Today, electronic signs and video monitors mounted on buildings are replacing the static ornaments of the past with kinetic, changeable images.

Let there be light — and sound

Light, whether natural or artificial, is essential to any building. It is what shapes the form of architecture and brings it to life. The placement of windows in a wall or of a skylight in the roof affects the amount of daylight streaming into the building by day, as well as the illumination patterns seen on the wall at night.

The amount of daylight that a building lets in also effects the mood of the space. Evenly distributed, bright light drains a space of shadows and depth. Focused, dim light, on the other hand, calls attention to the recesses and projections in a room. The Pantheon, for example, is suffused in daylight from the *oculus* — the round opening — high at the top of its dome. As the day progresses, the pattern and intensity of light changes to illuminate the niches at the sides of the room in different ways. In their churches, Baroque and Rococo architects hid windows and skylights behind walls and ceilings to illuminate spaces in mysterious, indirect light that looked like it was coming from the heavens.

The location and intensity of artificial light fixtures — incandescent, fluorescent, halogen, and metal halide, for example — also effect the spatial feeling. The artificial lights can produce effects ranging from a warm glow to an irritating glare. Light shining through large walls of glass at night can make the architecture seem to disappear altogether.

Sound also plays a role in architecture. Listening to organ music in the vast interior of a cathedral or the gurgling of a fountain in a garden courtyard can enhance the experience of space. The size, shape, and materials of a room contribute to the quality of the sounds heard in the room. Hard surfaces, such as stone, reflect sound, while soft materials, such as fabric, absorb it. The science of determining these reflections and reverberations is called *acoustics*. When designing performance halls and other sound-sensitive environments, architects often consult specialists in sound called *acousticians* (say that three times fast!).

There goes the neighborhood: Site and context

Location is another important factor in design. Rural buildings, for example, must consider how they relate to a site's land contours and natural features. Many architects use topography as a starting point for their designs. One of the most famous examples of this architectural approach is Fallingwater, the house designed by Frank Lloyd Wright (see Chapter 14) to cantilever over a stream in Bear Run, Pennsylvania. Wright called his architecture "organic," because many of his buildings seem to grow from the ground. In fact the stone walls of the building were quarried on site and, to meet Wright's specifications, horizontally arranged according to the stratified rock layer from which they came.

Rural designs are often influenced by regional traditions — indigenous building methods that have grown over time. A good example of this type of rural design is Sea Ranch, a 1960s condominium complex, located north of San Francisco that was designed by Charles Moore. Its redwood siding and shed-like shapes are based on wooden farm buildings in the area.

Urban architecture, on the other hand, is designed in relationship to *context,* or existing structures and streets that surround new buildings. Architecture inserted into the middle of a block calls for one kind of design, while a building on the corner requires another type of design. A new building's design may draw upon the scale and materials of neighboring structures for inspiration. This harmonious relationship is called *contextual design,* and it is often encouraged in historic districts such as Greenwich Village in New York or Georgetown in Washington, D.C. (see Chapter 20).

Buildings can also be contextual without the need to adhere to a uniform style. Daniel Burnham's plan for the development of Michigan Avenue in Chicago called for guidelines that controlled building heights and window patterns so that stylistically different buildings could live harmoniously with one another.

In an attempt to establish contrast, an architect may design a building so that it differs from its surroundings. A good example of this type of design is the Schroeder house in Utrecht, Holland (see Chapter 14). Dutch architect Gerrit Rietveld designed the house in the same scale as the surrounding row of brick houses, yet his design stands out because of its colorful, cubist exterior.

In order to understand the concepts of design, you must experience architecture — not just study photographs of it. When you feel the protection (or the disorientation) of a space, touch the texture of a stair railing, watch the light fade from a window, hear the sound of someone walking across the room, or smell the scent of potted plants or musty old books, you experience sensual delights that can't be conveyed by two-dimensional images.

A visit to a building often changes your perception of a design. For example, the Barcelona Pavilion, designed by Mies van der Rohe, is a pioneering piece of modern architecture that was long known only through black-and-white photos. It was designed as a temporary structure for a 1929 fair that lasted only seven months. The building was dismantled after the fair was over. For nearly half a century, the structure was only appreciated through drawings and photos. When the marble and glass structure was re-created in the 1980s on the fairgrounds in Barcelona, visitors were amazed to discover just how colorful and kaleidoscopic its interiors really are when compared to the static photographic images.

Chapter 3

Building Your Architectural Vocabulary

In This Chapter

▶ Examining architectural style

▶ Understanding the language of architecture

▶ Recognizing the essential elements of style

▶ Using architectural terms

*T*o understand architecture, you must understand the lingo. Each element of a building is identified by a very particular term. You may refer to a roof as a roof, but to be more precise, it may be a mansard, a gambrel, or a butterfly. Mounted within its slope may be a cricket, a dormer, or an eyebrow. Knowing this architectural vocabulary helps you recognize the style and the date of a building.

Defining Architectural Style

Style is what gives a building character. Style comes from the way that the fundamental elements of architecture — scale, massing, color, light, and so on (see Chapter 2) — are constructed in materials and details. A coarsely textured stone wall with deep doorways, for example, expresses a heavy permanence that is opposite in character or style from the fragile transparency of a glass wall with sliding doors.

Some styles depend on materials for their identity. The German Baroque style, for example, is associated with light-colored stucco (see Chapter 10); International Style modernism is synonymous with steel and glass (see Chapter 14). Some architectural styles become a new style simply by using a different material. Early American architects, for example, translated the stone architecture of neoclassical English and French buildings into brick and wood, creating the Federal style (see Chapter 11).

Style as symbolism: The language of architecture

Certain styles evoke certain attributes. The classical orders (see Chapter 8) signify decorum, stability and permanence so they are often used on museums and banks. Their roots in the ancient republics of Greece and Rome also make them a logical choice for government buildings. Gothic architecture, with its pointed arches, spires, and sculptural gargoyles is associated with medieval cathedrals and monastic cloisters and is still used for churches and college buildings. See Chapter 9 for more about that. It was deemed "picturesque" by eighteenth- and nineteenth-century architects who applied a simplified version of the style to cottages and country houses.

Style can both resuscitate tradition and revolt against it. Renaissance architects revived the ornamentation of the Greeks and Romans, while modernists stripped their buildings bare (see Chapter 14). Some styles are short-lived, such as the streamlined, zigzagging lines of Art Deco, which was popular during the late 1920s and early 1930s (see Chapter 13). Others, such as the classical tradition, have endured for hundreds of years and spawned countless variations on the style, from Baroque palaces to early American churches to suburban tract houses. See Chapter 8 for more about classical stuff.

An Architect's style and language don't always beget time and place

Different styles often coexist at the same time. This was particularly true in the nineteenth and early twentieth centuries, when architects recycled a wide variety of historic styles, including Greek, Egyptian, Byzantine, Gothic, Romanesque, and Renaissance styles. In a 1913 essay, Ralph Adams Cram identified seven "tendencies," or styles that were present during the early twentieth century:

- Classicism
- Beaux-Arts French Modern
- Colonial
- High Gothic
- Medieval Revival
- Steel-framed modernism
- California Arts and Crafts

The coexistence of traditional and modern styles is still present in architecture today.

Some are still nostalgic

Even when a particular style is in vogue, some architects will totally ignore it and continue designing in a different vein. In 1937, for example, Philip Goodwin and Edward Durrell Stone shaped the Museum of Modern Art in New York to reflect the latest International Style modernism; that same year, John Russell Pope designed the National Gallery of Art in Washington, D.C., in the age-old classical tradition with columns, pediments, and rotunda.

Some like to switch around

Not every architect sticks to a consistent style for every building. In the early 1800s, Prussian architect Karl Friedrich Schinkel used classical columns and pediments for public buildings, such as a museum and an opera house, but used the Gothic style for churches. From the late nineteenth through the early twentieth centuries, New York architects McKim, Mead, and White similarly favored classical architecture for public buildings, such as train stations and public libraries, but switched to Shingle, French Renaissance, and Colonial styles for country houses.

Some are rebels in architecture

Some architects break the rules of an accepted tradition and in doing so they invent a new fashion. Italian Renaissance architect Andrea Palladio copied the architecture of Roman temples for country houses and then added extended symmetrical wings to the sides (see Chapter 10). This Palladian style was copied for two centuries in Europe and America. American architect Frank Lloyd Wright stretched the classical house into the landscape and flattened the roof to create the Prairie style (see Chapter 14). Mies van der Rohe put steel elements on the outside of his glassy high-rises and changed the face of the skyscraper (see Chapter 13).

God is in the details (and other secrets)

Details play an important role in establishing a style: They are literally the nuts and bolts of construction. A building is assembled from hundreds of details, ranging from the intersection between a wall and a ceiling to roof gutters, windowsills, and railings. The manner in which these elements are combined can make or break a style.

A wall with a crown molding and baseboard, for example, appears more traditional than an unadorned wall that extends straight to the floor and has no details. The crown molding and baseboards look right at home in a classical setting but completely out of place in a modern interior.

"God is in the details," German-born architect Mies van der Rohe (see Chapter 14) is famous for saying. He meant that the spirit of a building — somber, lively, monumental, or cozy — comes from the way that each architectural element is shaped and put together in a consistent way. Mies's own architecture reflected this philosophy. Though minimalist, his modern buildings were finely crafted of luxurious materials and refined details.

Talkin' the talk

Architectural style is often compared to language. The grammar of style is formed by the "words" of walls, windows, doors, roofs, and other elements arranged into three-dimensional "sentences" that form the building. Just as styles change, so does the language of architecture. The best architects invent new grammar by coming up with new arrangements of architectural elements that are unexpected and different from the buildings of the past. Frank Lloyd Wright, for example, constantly changed his architectural grammar and his style. He abandoned the horizontal lines of his Prairie houses for curved forms, culminating in his revolutionary Guggenheim Museum in New York (see Chapter 4).

The language of architecture can be pretty obscure. A *jerkinhead* isn't a derogatory term for a lousy designer, but is part of a hipped roof. A *cyma recta* may sound like a part of the human anatomy, but it refers to a molding with a concave curve at the top and a convex curve at the bottom. (Its twin is a *cyma reversa,* which is a molding with a convex curve at the top and concave curve at the bottom.) An *amortizement* is the sloping top on a buttress or pier, not a method of paying down your mortgage.

Even familiar words have different meanings when it comes to architecture. The word *soldier* is often used to refer to an enlisted person sent to war, but in a building, it refers to a vertically laid brick. A *barge* doesn't only refer to a boat; it also refers to the board at the edge of a roof gable. A *boss* is the person you work for, as well as the ornamental knob covering the intersection of ribs in a ceiling vault. If an architect uses the term *fornication,* he or she is probably talking about a curved roof covering (*fornix* is Latin for "vault"), not someone's love life.

After you're familiar with the language of architecture, you can understand its various dialects. For example, the classical language expressed by Italian Renaissance architect Donato Bramante is far more delicate than the monumental version used by ancient Greeks and Romans, and more restrained than the curvy classicism of later Baroque architecture. All these classical forms are worlds away from the playful decorative classicism used by contemporary architects such as Michael Graves (see Chapter 15). For the Disney headquarters in Burbank, California, Graves translated the graceful female figures holding up the Erechtheion on the Athens Acropolis into Snow White's Seven Dwarfs. Recognizing this visual pun is part of the fun of architecture.

Essential Elements of Architecture

To get comfortable with the language of architecture, you need to appreciate the form of architecture and recognize the ways that it has changed over time. The following sections offer some examples of the basic elements of architecture.

Architecture's crowning glory: Roofs

Roofs protect a building from rain and snow and are one of the most basic elements of architecture. Over the centuries, they have evolved from simple, triangular shapes called *gables* into more elaborate designs. The following list gives examples of roof types:

- **Hipped or hip roof:** This early type of roof has sloping ends and sides that meet in a horizontal line or ridge at the top. It was used in medieval buildings in both Europe and Asia.

- **Pavilion roof:** This roof is shaped like a pyramid and is used to cover a square structure. It was applied to the defense towers of the ancient palace built by Roman Emperor Diocletian for his retirement.

- **Barrel vault:** This semi-circular roof was often built in stone or brick. The Romans invented it (see Chapter 8) as a way of covering over the tops of two arches. The barrel vault became a basic element of Romanesque churches built in Europe in the eleventh and twelfth centuries (see Chapter 9).

- **Gambrel roof:** This roof combines two different pitches below a ridge at the top: a short upper gable and a long lower slope (see Figure 3-1). It was widely used in American architecture of the 1700s.

- **Cricket:** This small peaked element is used on a sloping roof to divert rainwater around a chimney.

- **Mansard roof:** This roof combines two differently sloped parts. At the bottom of the roof are steeply pitched, almost vertical sloped sections. Nearer the top are shallower sloping parts that form a hip roof shape (see Figure 3-2). The mansard roof was named after French architect Francois Mansart, and it became fashionable in Paris during the seventeenth century. (You probably recognize it from certain fast-food restaurants.)

- **Butterfly roof:** This inverted roof type looks like a "V" and is formed from inwardly angled slopes. The design resembles the shape of butterfly wings and became popular during the 1950s (along with cars with big tailfins).

✔ **Flat roof:** This roof type appears to have no slope and became popular in European architecture of the early twentieth century (see Chapter 14). Modern architects like the flat roof because it makes their buildings look more abstract. This type of roof, however, is rarely flat; it usually has a slight pitch to allow rainwater to drain off the roof (see, function is always important!).

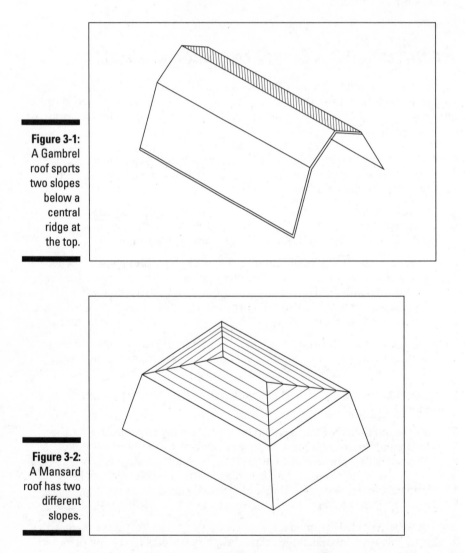

Figure 3-1: A Gambrel roof sports two slopes below a central ridge at the top.

Figure 3-2: A Mansard roof has two different slopes.

A blank (or decorated) canvas: Walls

Smooth or rough, decorated or plain, walls serve to enclose, divide, or protect a space. An exterior wall is referred to as a *façade,* meaning the face of the building. The top part of an exterior wall that rises above the roof to form a low barrier is called a *parapet*. A wall shared by adjacent structures is called a *party wall*. The part of the wall that is buried within the ground to support a building is called a *foundation wall*.

Large, continuous surfaces, walls create the canvas on which doors, windows, moldings, and ornamental details are composed. (A wall having no openings is called a *blind* wall.) Walls may be constructed of brick, stone, wood, concrete, or glass. They may be covered in stucco, siding, or paint. They can be shaped into planes that are straight, curved, or angled. Here are some examples:

- **Rusticated wall:** This type of wall is made of stones that are typically rough and raised off the wall surface. It was used to face the ground floors of Renaissance palaces to make them look impenetrable.

- **Half-timbered wall:** This timber-framed wall is designed with portions of the wooden structure left exposed. The spaces in between are then filled in with brick, stone, or plaster. The short piece of wood inserted between the timbers to strengthen the frame is called a *nog;* the brick used to fill the spaces between the timbers is referred to as *nogging*. Half-timbered walls were common in sixteenth-century European houses and identified with Tudor-style houses.

- **Clapboard wall:** This wall is made up of wood siding laid horizontally. It typifies the homes built by English settlers in the American colonies during the seventeenth century.

- **Board and batten siding:** This wall type consists of wide boards erected vertically, with their joints covered with narrow strips of wood called *battens*. It was used in the American Carpenter Gothic houses of the Victorian era.

- **Wainscoting:** This term refers to the wood paneling covering the lower portion of an interior wall. The lower part of an interior wall that is treated in a different material than the upper part is called a *dado*.

- **Stucco wall:** One of the oldest means of protecting and decorating an exterior wall is to cover it in *stucco,* which is made of cement, sand, and lime mixed with water. Once applied to the wall, stucco can be finished to create many textured effects. German Baroque architects of the seventeenth and eighteenth centuries liked painting the stucco walls of their churches in pastel colors to make them seem more ethereal.

- **Glass wall:** The transparent window wall came into common use in the late nineteenth and early twentieth centuries with advancements in plate glass manufacturing (see Chapter 12). Frames of cast-iron and then steel were used to hold the glass panels in place. By the mid-twentieth century, sliding, floor-to-ceiling walls of glass were common features of American suburban homes, creating a seamless boundary between indoors and outdoors. Glass walls in modern office towers are often called *curtain walls*, indicating their non-structural role in enclosing the building.

Let there be light: Windows

Openings in walls were small and unglazed until medieval times when they were filled in with pieces of glass held together by lead. Over the centuries, windows have assumed various arrangements, called *fenestration,* and increased in size. (Some walls are covered entirely in glass as described in the previous section.) Here is a brief summary of windows through the ages:

✔ **Lancet window:** This window was created from narrow openings with pointed arches and became popular for Gothic buildings (see Chapter 9). The tops of these windows were often filled with decorative stonework called *tracery.* Rounded ornament or a *foil* was also used in various forms; a cloverleaf shape of three foils is called a *trefoil;* four foils form a *quatrefoil.*

✔ **Palladian window:** This type of window, featuring a rounded arch flanked by narrower, rectangular openings, was named after the sixteenth-century Italian architect Andrea Palladio, who often used it in his country house designs. It came into vogue during the Renaissance. (Palladio actually lifted this motif from another Italian architect, Sebastiano Serlio. It is often referred to as a *Serlian window.*) You can see one in Figure 3-3.

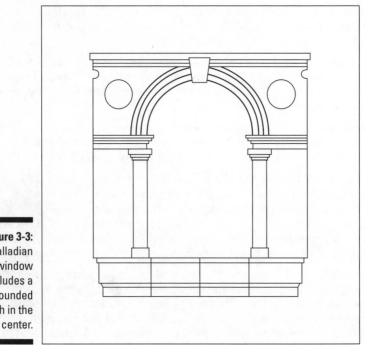

Figure 3-3:
A Palladian window includes a rounded arch in the center.

✔ **Oeil-de-boeuf (ox-eye):** This small window is round or oval in shape (like an eye) and often used as a design accent within a wall. The ox-eye design was used on the upper stories of Baroque churches during the seventeenth and eighteenth centuries to illuminate the top of a room and create the effect that the sunlight was coming down from heaven.

✔ **Double-hung window:** This type of window is commonly found in houses and is made of two vertically sliding frames, called *sashes,* in which the glass is set. These windows are often divided by slender vertical pieces of wood called *mullions* that frame the panels of glass. A window that has only one movable sash is called a *single-hung* window. A window that has two frames that move horizontally is called a *sliding sash.*

✔ **Dormer window:** This window type projects out from a sloping roof to light a top floor or attic and is usually covered by a mini-roof. A *lutheran* is another name for a dormer with a roof of its own. A low, rounded version of a dormer, called an *eyebrow,* became fashionable for romantic houses designed in the Romanesque Revival and Shingle styles in the late nineteenth century.

✔ **Bay window:** This window projects from the surface of a wall to let in light from three sides. Inside the building, a bay window often forms an alcove with a deep ledge used as a seat. It became a popular feature of Arts-and-Crafts-style houses (see Chapter 14) during the late nineteenth century. A bay window supported from below by wooden brackets or brickwork is called an *oriel.* A bay window that curves outward is referred to as a *bow* window.

✔ **Ribbon window:** This window type is made up of a horizontal band of windows. It was popular in the Modern architecture of the 1920s. Swiss-born French architect Le Corbusier considered ribbon windows, or *fenetre en longeur,* an essential part of his avant-garde architecture.

✔ **Casement window:** This window type has vertical frames that are hinged on the sides and swing outward. A casement that is hinged at the top is called an *awning window;* when hinged at the bottom, it's referred to as a *hopper window.* A window made up of horizontal glass louvers that pivot outward is called a *jalousie.*

Making an Entrance: Doorways

When it comes to architecture, doors are some of the simplest elements of a building. These flat panels of wood, glass, or metal are hinged on one side and shaped into rectangles or even circles. What makes a door special is the decorative frame or *surround* around its top and sides. The vertical side of a doorframe is called a *jamb;* the top of the doorframe is called the *head.* The horizontal piece on the floor at the bottom of the doorframe is called a *sill* or *threshold;* when raised off the floor, it's called a *saddle.* Post-and-lintel doorways are the most ancient doorways (see Chapter 6). The Mycenaean Lion Gate (see Chapter 7) and the entrances to Greek temples were formed from stone vertical posts supporting horizontal beams (or *lintels*) and were rectangular in shape.

- **Arched doorways:** Doors to medieval cathedrals were deeply sunk into curved supports called *arches* (see Chapter 8). Arched doorways of twelfth-century Romanesque churches were rounded in shape; Gothic arched doorways of the thirteenth century were pointed.

- **Pedimented doorways:** Placing a triangular shaped stone element called a *pediment* over the vertical supports of a building became popular in ancient Greece and Rome (see Chapter 8). Ancient architects often used pediments filled with sculpted decoration to call attention to the building face containing the main entrance. Renaissance architects revived the pediments of ancient Greece and Rome and used them over doorways and windows. They gave these triangular elements a new twist by gracefully curving their two sides, adding decoration to the point at the top, and adding curved supports at the bottom.

- **Venetian door:** This type of door has a shape similar to a Palladian window (see earlier section on windows). Above the door is a semicircular window called a *fanlight* and at the sides are long windows called *sidelights*.

- **French door:** This door type incorporates two panels that open from the center and is often filled with glass. It became popular in France during the seventeenth century. The grand palace of Versailles outside Paris (see Chapter 10) is full of French doors.

- **Sliding doors:** In the fifteenth century, Japanese architects created doors from sliding wall panels covered in paper at the top and wood at the bottom. Called *shoji screens,* these designs led to sliding panels entirely filled with translucent paper.

Modern architects of the twentieth century translated this idea into sliding doors of wood and glass. When the door actually slides *into* the wall, it's called a *pocket door*. Sliding doors of glass became popular for houses beginning in the 1950s as a means of joining indoor living spaces to outdoor patios.

Part II

Nuts and Bolts: Looking at How Architecture Is Designed and Built

The 5th Wave   By Rich Tennant

"My brother and I built the barn, but his son, who's an architect, helped us with the silo."

In this part . . .

This part outlines the step-by-step process an architect uses to create a building and get it built. You get the inside track about architects and what qualifications to look for as well as what to expect after the contract is signed. Also, I include the main types of architectural drawings to explain how to read a blueprint and how to understand a building's design before construction even begins.

The ways that buildings are conceived and constructed are explained through historical examples. Basic structural principles are defined so that you can understand how architecture stands up — no matter how heavy its materials may be. It ain't heavy — it's just architecture!

Chapter 4

How Buildings Are Born

....

....

*T*he study of architecture is the study of society. Every building — from a small house to a vast sports stadium — reflects the needs and desires of the people who commission its design. In the prosperous decades following World War II, for example, corporate chieftains erected skyscrapers to represent the economic clout of their organizations. During the digital revolution, software inventors had custom-designed mansions built to show off their wealth. Today, government officials construct embassies that protect people against the increasing threat of international terrorism.

In the Beginning: The Program

Every structure — whether it's a high-rise, a house, or an embassy — requires a list of practical requirements called a *program*. The program, which is determined by the client, outlines every function of the building, from the boardrooms to the bathrooms. The architect translates the program into linked spaces that often express the building's purpose. The symmetrical shape of the U.S. Capitol, for example, reflects America's bicameral government, with the House of Representatives on one side of the building and the Senate on the other.

Out with the old and in with the new

An architect often organizes a program according to a building design that has already become tried and true. Early Christian churches, for example, followed the configuration of an ancient Roman meetinghouse called a *basilica* (see Chapter 8). When a new type of building is being developed, however, the architect is required to rethink the familiar and propose new spatial arrangements to satisfy the program and the client's image for the building.

A good example of this spatial reinvention is Dulles International Airport outside Washington, D.C. Finnish-born architect Eero Saarinen designed it in the late 1950s, when airports were still a new type of building. Instead of designing a single building, Saarinen divided the airport into two parts: a main terminal with ticket counters, lounges, and restaurants, and a secondary terminal with gates on the tarmac. Passengers are transported between the two terminals by custom-designed vehicles called mobile lounges. As the gateway to the airport, the main terminal is designed with a soaring curved roof to symbolize the movement of flight.

From program to type

Unusual designs pave the way for the further development of architecture for a specific purpose. When architectural form becomes accepted by society through repeated use, it is called a *building type*. The history of architecture traces the evolution of building types, which have become more diverse with the passage of time. Some familiar building types include the medieval cathedral, the Baroque palace, the Victorian railroad station, and the modern skyscraper. The invention of these building types all came about through a long period of design experimentation and refinement. Architects still tinker with the designs of building types — even ones that have been valid for centuries — as a way of making a statement about the culture of their times.

Different Building Types and the Evolution of Style

New building types, which mirror the changes in society, evolve over years — even centuries — rather than spring full-blown from a single concept. Their design may stem from earlier structures that serve completely different purposes.

From many ideas comes one building type

A new building type can spring from the design ideas of several architects working on the same building over decades. In 1792, for example, William Thornton drew up his scheme for the U.S. Capitol by copying the architecture of English mansions and French schools, which, in turn, were inspired by ancient Roman temples. Architect Benjamin Latrobe, who devised decoration based on American plants such as corn, tobacco, and magnolia trees, subsequently refined Thornton's design. Charles Bulfinch, who designed the Capitol rotunda, then followed Latrobe. Thomas U. Walter enlarged Bulfinch's rotunda in the 1850s with a cast-iron dome. Walter may have modeled his design on French and Russian churches. All of these experiments led to a new type of government building and a powerful symbol of America's democracy that served as a model for state capitols.

Everybody's welcome: Private galleries morph into public museums

Some building types began as smaller, private rooms that were slowly turned into larger, public spaces. The museum is a good example of this trend. In fact, the term *museum,* first used in the Renaissance, referred to collections of artwork that were displayed in long corridors or galleries in palaces, castles, and other royal structures. The collections served as entertainment for aristocrats and their invited guests. In sixteenth-century Florence, Italy, for example, the Medici family's holdings were displayed on the top floor of the Uffizi (begun in 1560), a royal palace and office building (*uffizi* means "offices"), and could be visited by request; centuries later, the building was transformed into a public museum. (The Uffizi is shown in Figure 4-1.)

By the nineteenth century, rulers were commissioning architecture specifically for their art collections. In 1816, Ludwig I, the crown prince of Bavaria, began building a museum in Munich called the Glypothek to show off his holdings of sculpture to the public. The Glypothek was soon followed by public museums in Germany and other European countries. By the late 1800s, America was exhibiting art publicly in grand civic structures; New York's Metropolitan Museum of Art and Boston's Museum of Fine Arts both opened in 1870.

A day at the Improv: Improvisation and specialization

Early building types evolved from improvised structures that housed several functions under one roof. In thirteenth-century Italy, for example, town halls, housing law courts, and government offices were built over open markets. By the fourteenth century, markets demanded larger buildings of their own. The town hall took on its own distinctive identity as a tower built over a fortress-like block. A good example of this town hall building type is the Palazzo Vecchio in Florence, completed in 1314.

For centuries the number of building types was very small. As historian Nikolaus Pevsner points out in his book, *A History of Building Types,* Western architecture through the mid-eighteenth century "is almost entirely made up of churches and castles and palaces." It was not until the nineteenth century that a wide variety of building types emerged in response to the changing needs of society during the Industrial Revolution. As commerce, transportation, and industry flourished during the 1800s, banks, department stores, train stations, factories, and other new buildings were born. These specialized buildings required not only new functional layouts but new styles to go with them, as well.

Technical innovations in building materials also played an important role in the evolution of building types. Cast iron, first used in bridges, was eventually applied to the construction of large exhibition halls, department stores, and office buildings (see Chapter 12). In the 1890s, taller office buildings and hotels became possible because of new developments in structural systems, elevators, and plumbing (see Chapter 13). After World War II, further advances in steel and glass construction led to skyscrapers that rose to new heights.

Figure 4-1:
The Uffizi
Palace in
Florence,
Italy.

Photo courtesy of GreatBuildings.com © John A. Gascon.

Planning guides for building types

The growing complexity of building types in the nineteenth century prompted the publication of planning guides to help architects work out a design that was both practical and beautiful. Jean-Nicolas-Louis Durand, a professor at the École Polytechnique in Paris, published one of the most famous planning guides, *Lessons of Architecture,* in 1802. Durand's book advised architects to plan the building first and then design its exterior. "Architects should concern themselves with planning and with nothing else," Durand wrote. He recommended ways to subdivide or multiply spaces and provided an assortment of standard architectural features, such as columns, arches, and windows that could be combined to achieve a visually pleasing façade. In a second volume, he offered blueprints for different buildings, such as lighthouses, theaters, and tombs.

Using the Past to Design the Future

Most nineteenth-century architects, however, preferred to express a building's purpose in a more individualistic way. They selectively chose elements from historic architecture to align new buildings with the glories of the past. In designing the Houses of Parliament, for example, architects Charles Barry and Augustus Pugin applied elements from Gothic cathedrals to create an uplifting, moral image for the British government. Their architecture of towers and spires popularized the neo-Gothic style for all types of buildings — from university campuses to skyscrapers and hotels.

Over time, certain styles have become associated with specific buildings: Columns and pediments borrowed from ancient Greek and Roman temples, for example, became common for banks and civic structures in the early 1800s — and they still are. Such traditional elements help make a new building appear more substantial and familiar to its users. Early New York skyscrapers, for example, were decorated with Gothic-style arches, pinnacles, and ornament to link them with the past.

Building types continue to evolve through many variations. Museums evolved from salon-style galleries with picture moldings in the nineteenth century to whitewashed spaces devoid of decoration in the twentieth century. In recent decades, museum architecture has shifted from neutral spaces to idiosyncratic architecture that often overshadows the art on display.

The boxy Museum of Modern Art in New York, for example, seems bland compared to the wildly curvaceous Guggenheim in Bilbao, Spain (see Chapter 21 for more on this contemporary landmark).

When progress goes awry

Progress hasn't always improved building types. Early hospitals were as grand as palaces, with domes, porticoes, and patient wings arranged around courtyards for access to fresh air. A good example of these early hospitals is the Royal Naval Hospital in Greenwich, England. Architect Christopher Wren designed the hospital for retired seamen beginning in 1694. The vast complex took 40 years to complete, with its construction involving several architects. It's hard to imagine a hospital as a beautiful and influential piece of architecture, but Wren's stately design certainly does qualify as such.

Today, hospitals are anything but magnificent. Medical discoveries have led architects to compress patient wards, operating rooms, labs, and such into sealed antiseptic blocks with few redeeming architectural features. Much of the design is concentrated on efficient space-planning and building systems that help health-care professionals do their work while preventing the spread of infectious agents (Wren didn't have to worry about that!).

Not just an architect: The new specialties

Contemporary architecture has become so specialized for certain functions that today's architects often concentrate on producing one or two building types — airports and sports arenas, for example. This narrowly focused practice is very different from the past, when one architect was called upon to undertake all sorts of buildings. In the 1870s and 1880s, for example, Bostonian Henry Hobson Richardson designed churches, courthouses, houses, libraries, and department stores — all of them groundbreaking designs.

A truly great architect will challenge conventions to create an exceptional piece of architecture — and forever change the way that people view a building type. Frank Lloyd Wright, for example, revolutionized the museum with his spiraling design of the Guggenheim Museum in New York. Before this building opened in 1959, museums were organized with rectangular galleries linked by hallways. Wright seized the idea of turning the hallway into a large ramp and focusing the entire museum around it. Winding up through the building like a giant corkscrew, the ramp exhibits the visitors as much as it does the artwork. You can see this in Figure 4-2. Pretty cool!

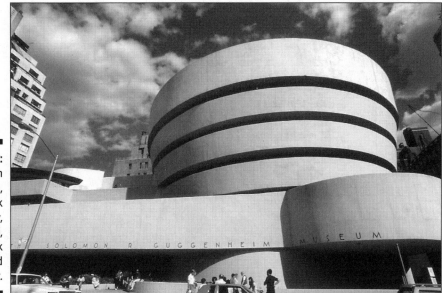

Figure 4-2:
Guggenheim
Museum,
New York
City,
1943-1959,
by Frank
Lloyd
Wright.

Photo Courtesy of and © Solomon R. Guggenheim Museum.

Chapter 5

Just What Do Architects Do, Anyway?

• •

In This Chapter

▶ Understanding Architects' changing roles through history

▶ Finding out the necessary professional qualifications

▶ Winding through an architect's typical workday

▶ Working with the architect

• •

So, you think that being an architect looks fun and easy? Think again. The job demands a combination of creative, technical, and management talents. Architecture is often referred to as a "Renaissance" profession, requiring its practitioners to be well versed in the sciences and the arts. Basically, architects have to be good at everything.

The job of the architect has always been to provide shelter from the elements. Before anything else, a building must keep inhabitants safe and dry. Creating a protective environment, however, is only the first of the architect's many responsibilities. Here are just a few of the architect's tasks:

✔ Take the client's long list of functional needs and draw up an arrangement of interconnected spaces

✔ Shape building materials into permanent structures that enclose the spaces, admit light, and make sure the building doesn't fall down (see Chapter 6)

✔ Reach beyond structural and functional necessities to create a design statement that's beautiful and stirs the emotions.

In fulfilling this last requirement, architects have come to be called "form-givers." Spaces, in turn, must be organized and shaped to meet a variety of functional needs. At the same time, architecture must rise above mere structural and utilitarian necessity to achieve beauty and make an impression.

These daunting tasks require the architect to possess a combination of organizational, technical, and creative talents. Basically, architects have to be good at everything. Architecture is often referred to as a "Renaissance" profession, requiring its practitioners to be well versed in the sciences and the arts. And that's not all architects have to do. Today's architects must possess business and management skills. They have to drum up work; consult with engineers, landscape architects, lighting designers, and other specialists; supervise design and construction teams; and oversee budgets and project schedules. (Architects say it also helps to have the skills of a psychiatrist when calming nervous clients.) So, add Project Manager to that long list of diverse requirements.

The Roles They Are A-Changin'

In ancient times, architects and builders were one and the same. Roman architect Marcus Virtruvius Pollio (see Chapter 8) wrote in his influential book, *Ten Books on Architecture,* that architects should possess knowledge of both the theoretical and practical aspects of construction. However, the architects of ancient times were subservient to the owner, who claimed the design of the building as his own. Credit for the beauty and structural ingenuity of the Pantheon, for example, went to Roman emperor Hadrian — not to the architect.

You don't learn experience, you live it: The Middle Ages

During the Middle Ages, architects were called *master builders.* They acted as designer, supervisor, and contractor for cathedrals and castles (see Chapter 9). They learned their craft through on-the-job training with stonecutters, carpenters, and other artisans before rising to the rank of master. Not until Renaissance Italy did the architect become wholly responsible for the artistic aspect of a building and have his name associated with the project. The owner, meanwhile, assumed the role of patron or financial supporter, and prided himself on fostering the most talented designer.

Blue-blooded and blue collar: The eighteenth century

During the eighteenth century, architecture became a subject studied in books and at school. You weren't considered educated unless you knew something about buildings and their design. Aspiring architects traveled throughout Europe and farther afield, sketching and soaking in famous architectural sights. From their drawings of ancient Greek and Roman temples and other historic monuments, European and American architects of the 1700s and early 1800s created new buildings for their own times (see Chapter 11).

During the eighteenth century, two distinct types of architects emerged.

- ✔ **The gentleman architect** was well educated in architectural theory. This architect designed buildings in his spare time while pursuing another career. He was the guy that you see in all of those old European paintings standing in his library wearing a powdered wig, breeches, and white stockings.

  A good example is President Thomas Jefferson. He owned a vast collection of books about architecture and completed many impressive buildings, including his Virginia home, Monticello (see the color insert for a photo).

- ✔ **The builder-architect** was trained practically and was more closely tied to masons and carpenters. The builder-architects were the guys who liked Scotch, got their hands dirty, and told stories about Daniel Boone and North American Indians. Several early American architects followed this model, including Asher Benjamin who, in 1797, wrote the first book about architecture to be published in America. His writings and drawings of Greek Revival buildings had an enormous influence on American architecture.

As the Industrial Revolution took off, the gap between the design and construction aspects of a project continued to increase as structures became more sophisticated. In fact, building technology increased to the point where an engineer was added to the building team. Engineers were responsible for the entire design in some cases and created awesome metal-and-glass structures, much to the chagrin of architects (see Chapter 12).

Now they're getting fancy: The nineteenth century

During the nineteenth century, architects separated themselves from amateur designers and the building trades. They were distinguished by their knowledge of printed sources, such as treaties from ancient Rome and the Renaissance, and their ability to draw. The grand tour of the European continent was an important part of their education. You were just a big nobody if you didn't do it. Many young architects studied the classical buildings of Italy and Greece and other continental styles of architecture, which, in turn, inspired their own designs.

Where are the women?

It's still a man's world in the architecture profession. According to a recent survey conducted by the American Institute of Architects, 13 percent of registered architects are women. Only 9 percent of these women head their own firms. In Europe, women comprise fewer than 16 percent of all architects.

Women have made important contributions to architectural history. San Francisco architect Julia Morgan designed San Simeon, the lavish California estate owned by William Randolph Hearst. German designer Lilly Reich helped Mies van der Rohe create his pioneering modern buildings. Prairie architect Marion Mahony drew many of Frank Lloyd Wright's most memorable buildings and went on to design the new capital city of Canberra, Australia, as well as the capitol building with her husband Walter Burley Griffin.

Some contemporary female architects have beaten the odds and gained international acclaim: London-based Zaha Hadid, Italian Gae Aulenti, Itsuko Hasegawa of Japan, and American Maya Lin. In the United States, leading female architects include Denise Scott Brown of Philadelphia; Bostonians Andrea Leers and Jane Weinzapfel; Los Angelenos Katherine Diamond and Rebecca Binder; Chicagoans Margaret McCurry and Carol Ross Barney; Elizabeth Plater Zyberk and Laurinda Spear of Miami; and Deborah Berke, Laurie Hawkinson, Marilyn Taylor, and Billie Tsien of New York.

Tonight's episode of Architecture Theatre . . .

Like today's pop stars, the turn-of-the-last-century architects were showmen who paid careful attention to the location and design of their offices and to how they dressed when they consulted with clients. For example, Boston architect Henry Hobson Richardson established a studio that resembled an artist's atelier and purposely situated it in suburban Brookline, Massachusetts, so that clients would have to travel a distance to see him. When clients arrived at his studio, Richardson greeted them in a monk's robe and sounded a temple gong to summon his office boy. (I wonder if his clients also used the gong to let him know when they didn't like one of his designs!) Visitors were made to feel like pilgrims in his exotic retreat.

Modern architects also cultivated an artsy style: Frank Lloyd Wright donned capes and pork-pie hats; Louis Kahn sported bow ties; and Le Corbusier wore owlish round glasses (they were copied by Philip Johnson and others).

Such image-building strategies are still a part of architectural practice. To be successful, most architects must be first-rate marketers and business people while still conveying the artistic air of inspired creators. Everybody's got a gimmick these days!

How Architects Get to Be Architects

Contemporary American architects are licensed or registered to practice by the state within which they work. Licensure requirements include a professional degree in architecture, a period of practical training called an *internship*, and a passing grade on a state-administered test called the *architect registration examination*.

There are several types of professional degrees in architecture:

✔ One type is a 5-year Bachelor of Architecture degree, intended for students who are entering the program from high school or have no previous architecture training.

✔ Another type is a 2-year Master of Architecture degree for students who already have an undergraduate degree in architecture.

✔ Some universities also offer a 3- or 4-year Master of Architecture program for students with a degree in a discipline other than architecture.

Graduates of these programs are required to complete an internship before taking the registration exam and becoming licensed. The registration exam covers a broad body of architectural know-how, from building technology to history. Those who pass the exam and meet all standards established by their state registration board are licensed to practice architecture in that state.

HISTORICAL NOTE

Becoming a profession

By the mid-nineteenth century, architecture had become an organized profession. The Royal Institute of British Architects (RIBA) was formed in 1837 to advance the "esteemed" art and science of architecture and its positive effect on towns and cities. The American Institute of Architects, founded in 1857, followed the RIBA's example.

Architectural education in America and Europe was strongly influenced by the École des Beaux Arts in Paris. The French academy, established in the seventeenth century, favored the study of ancient Greek and Roman architecture. The academy encouraged students to produce symmetrical designs and elaborate, two-dimensional watercolor renderings of their building projects. This method was adopted by American schools of architecture, beginning with the first one at the Massachusetts Institute of Technology in 1865. It led to *Beaux-Arts Classicism,* an architectural style that was widely applied in America from about 1880 to 1930 in such buildings as the New York Public Library and Grand Central Terminal.

Hiring an architect

The most common way to choose an architect to design your house or workplace is to rely on referrals from people who have already hired an architect. Local chapters of the American Institute of Architects can help suggest qualified architects. Many of the chapters also hold seminars about selecting and working with an architect.

After you have narrowed down your list of architects, visit their offices, tour past projects, and talk with their former clients to help you make your final decision. Don't underestimate chemistry — you are going to have to communicate with the architect over months and even years.

Most architects don't charge a fee for the initial meeting, although some bill an hourly rate to determine whether their potential client is really serious. There is no set fee structure for designing a building. Most architects base their compensation on a percentage of the total construction costs. For smaller projects, some charge an hourly rate.

The length of the design and construction process varies with the size and complexity of the building. Think of the process as custom-made clothing; it may be more expensive and take longer than shopping in a department store, but the tailor-made design will fit your needs better.

Many states require continuing education to maintain licensure. Requirements vary by state, but they usually involve attending workshops, university classes, and conferences for a certain number of hours. Many architects are members of the American Institute of Architects, a group that sets professional standards but does not license architects. (You can be a state-registered architect and legally practice architecture without being a member of the AIA.)

What Architects Really Do from 9 to 5

Each project begins with a *program,* or a list of necessary functions and desirable features to be housed inside the building, that is submitted by the building owner or client (see Chapter 4 for details). The program defines the building's type — house, office, store, and so on — and breaks down the building's functions into areas and their square footage. This initial phase of a project is often referred to as *programming.* Sometimes the architect will map out the program with a *bubble diagram,* a sketch representing the relationships between each function. For example, an office may be drawn as a cluster of circles with each circle representing a work cubicle, a conference room, or a reception area. This graphic is then refined into a more precise layout.

Architects and clients often use programs to discuss what a building should represent and what it should look like. For a corporation, the architecture may be shaped to represent the identity of the organization. A headquarters designed with classical columns, for example, may send a message of tradition, while a building with a soaring glass tower may express modernity.

Searching for a design

After the program is set, the architect begins laying out the functions, selecting materials and finishes, and determining how the building will look. This phase of the project is called *schematic design.* Periodically, the architect meets with the owner to discuss the design concepts and material selections for certain parts of the building and then revises the scheme accordingly. This phase, called *design development*, can take weeks or months to complete, depending on the size and complexity of the building. Although some architects stubbornly cling to their first idea, most architects keep refining their designs to meet the specific requirements of the client and site. Many architects use their persuasive powers to convince the client to agree to their design vision and to spend the big bucks to build it.

Expressing ideas: Models and plans

The architect's ideas are represented through *models* — miniature buildings in cardboard, wood, or clay — and drawings. Many models and drawings are generated throughout each phase of a building project.

Drawings convey a lot of information about architectural style. By just looking at a drawing, you can usually tell the historical period of the building. The cross-shaped plan of a Gothic cathedral, for example, is clearly distinctive from the asymmetrical, pinwheel plan of a Frank Lloyd Wright house.

Most people associate architectural drawings with *blueprints,* paper copies that turn blue when the original drawing is fed through the blueprint machine (computers have replaced this early photographic process, which was invented in 1842). The architectural drawings that make up a set of blueprints follow standard formats to illustrate and document the three-dimensional spaces of a building in two dimensions. The drawings are drawn to *scale* — a proportional measurement determining the relationship of the drawing to the actual building. For example, a plan may be drawn with a ⅛-inch increment for every foot of real space.

Get a new plan, Stan

The most basic type of architectural drawing is a floor plan. You can see one in Figure 5-1. *Floor plans* are horizontal depictions of the building that show the arrangement of rooms, walls, windows, and doors on each level of the building. Drawing a floor plan is like cutting horizontally through the building and looking at this slice from above. Some architects start their building projects with a floor plan, which they consider the "generator" of the entire design.

Typically, an architect draws a floor plan for each level of the building, as well as a site or plot plan that identifies the location and orientation of the building or buildings on a property.

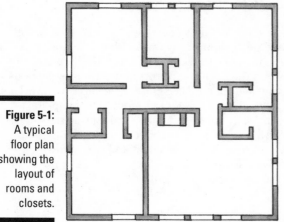

Figure 5-1:
A typical floor plan showing the layout of rooms and closets.

How it all stacks up: Section drawings

Architectural designs may also be represented through section drawings. *Section drawings* are vertical slices through the building that show the height of rooms and staircases, and the thickness of the walls, roof, and interior façades. Section drawings for buildings with more than one story show the relationship of spaces stacked on different floors. Walls, columns, and other solid surfaces are usually indicated in heavy black or hatched lines called *poché*. See Figure 5-2.

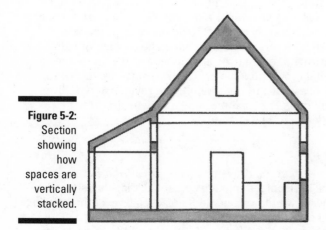

Figure 5-2:
Section showing how spaces are vertically stacked.

Fun with spatial relationships: Elevation drawings

Drawings of walls undistorted by perspective are called *elevation drawings.* You can see one of these in Figure 5-3. They show the arrangement of doors, windows, and other elements within the vertical plane of an exterior or interior wall. Elevation drawings are particularly useful for determining relationships between wall surfaces and windows rather than expressing the visual experience of the building.

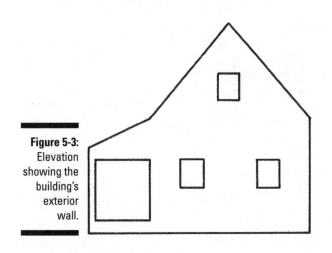

Figure 5-3:
Elevation showing the building's exterior wall.

The third dimension: Perspective drawings

A drawing that conveys the three-dimensional qualities of a building — the way you actually might see it — is called a *perspective drawing.* Perspective drawings, which were invented during the Renaissance, are constructed to resemble our field of vision and create a sense of depth and distance. See Figure 5-4. Today, architects often create perspective drawings on a computer with three-dimensional modeling programs.

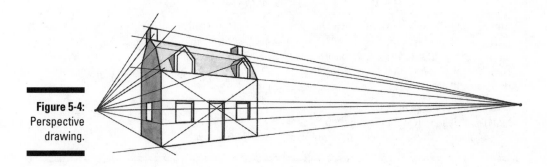

Figure 5-4:
Perspective drawing.

Some other types of three-dimensional drawings are orthographic, axonometric, and isometric projections. They represent a building or an object in space through the projection of lines that are perpendicular or inclined to the picture plane. These drawings make the building or object look foreshortened (see Figure 5-5). The difference between an axonometric projection and an isometric projection can be seen in the angles used to create their foreshortening effects.

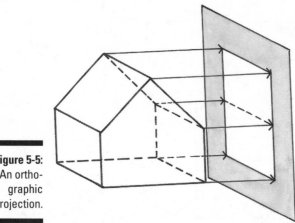

Figure 5-5:
An ortho-
graphic
projection.

Perspectives and models are often used to help the client understand the building design because they capture the experience of occupying a space better than plans, section drawings, elevation drawings, and projection drawings.

Vogue: Architectural fashions

Architectural models and drawings are more than just tools of representation: They are an art form in and of themselves. In recent decades, models and drawings have become hot collectibles and part of museum collections.

Styles of drawing change — much like architectural styles change. In the nineteenth century, architects drew on linen and painted in watercolors with breathtaking realism. Modern architecture ushered in tracing paper, a transparent plastic called Mylar, and erasable ink. *Parallel rules* — bars that move up and down on cables — replaced T-squares on drafting tables. Today, drafting tables are disappearing as architects do their drawing and designing on computer.

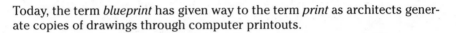

Let's make it legal: Working drawings

When a design is finalized, the sketched plans, sections, and elevations of the building are then turned into more finished documents called *working drawings.* These drawings indicate the measurements and materials of each architectural element. Diagrams of lighting, electrical, and mechanical systems and details of cabinets and other elements often supplement them. Copies of these drawings are called *blueprints.* Today, architects generate these copies through computer printouts.

Today, the term *blueprint* has given way to the term *print* as architects generate copies of drawings through computer printouts.

A set of working drawings serves as a legal document of the architect's intentions and instructs the builders about how to construct the architecture. To make the working drawings legal, the set is stamped with the architect's state-issued registration number and signed by the architect.

Most buildings require many sheets of drawings to cover every aspect of construction.

Drawings are only one of the components that form the legal contract document. Written descriptions of materials and systems to be used in the building, called *specifications,* are the other major component.

It wasn't always common practice to create a lot of drawings with multiple perspectives. The drawings for Independence Hall in Philadelphia, a building dating back to 1731, consist of two plans and an elevation on one sheet of *vellum* (fine-grained lambskin).

Okay, Now Do It Like I Drew It

Before construction begins, the working drawings are sent out for pricing estimates from builders. The pricing estimates serve as a good check as to whether the building is affordable for the client. If all the bids are too high, the architect can scale back the design to reduce construction costs. This is known as the *bidding phase* of a building project.

General contractors: Lots of cooks in the kitchen

After the bids are submitted, the owner (in consultation with the architect who may have worked with the builders before) selects a builder and draws up a contract with that person or firm that is separate from the contract with the architect. The builder, called a *general contractor,* hires subcontractors or individual trades, such as carpenters and metalworkers, to build specific parts of the building. This process is different from hiring a design/build firm, which is contracted to draw up the building and construct it for a set fee.

The two chief advantages of separately hiring an architect and a builder over a design/build firm are

- ✔ maintaining a system of checks and balances over the design and construction process
- ✔ obtaining competitive prices from a variety of builders

Design and building firms: A managed care plan

Design/build firms tend to keep costs down. They employ architects and builders who can consult with one another while a building design is being developed. This cost-consciousness approach, however, may not always result in the most creative design.

I did it my way

The late Frank Sinatra liked to do things his way — and a lot of architects do too, especially when their clients are paying big money to build their designs. While the structure is being built, most architects like to visit the construction site at regular intervals to make sure that the contractor is following their details as drawn. This review is usually part of the architect's contracted services, although some charge extra for it — especially when a client demands constant inspection of the progress.

Design revisions during construction are called *change orders.* They are often an expensive way to correct mistakes. To ease the building process, some owners hire a construction manager or client representative to act as a mediator between the architect and contractor.

The architecture of everyday items

Architects design more than just buildings. For centuries, they have created furniture, household items, and even clothing. The trend started in the 1700s when British architect Robert Adam designed chairs and tables to go with his ornate interiors. A century later, the Arts and Crafts movement spurred architects to coordinate every part of their buildings, inside and out. Frank Lloyd Wright took up the cause in his Chicago houses — among his furnishings were stained-glass windows and upright wooden chairs. He insisted on designing dresses for his wife so that she would blend in with his interiors.

This total look was also encouraged by the Bauhaus, the German arts school that revolutionized modern architecture (see Chapter 14).

The trend led Marcel Breuer to make bicycle-inspired furniture of tubular steel and Mies van der Rohe to create his famous Barcelona chair. Alvar Aalto gained fame for his sinuously curved glass vases and laminated birch stools. All these modern designs are still in production.

By the 1950s, plywood and plastic furniture by architects such as Charles and Ray Eames and Eero Saarinen was being mass-marketed to homeowners eager for the latest modern look. Contemporary architects have continued the tradition with everything from china to dog-houses. To the average consumer, Michael Graves is known more for his teakettles for Alessi and Target than for his buildings. His whistling Alessi teakettle is pictured here.

Photo courtesy of Michael Graves & Associates.

Chapter 6

A Simple Structure: How Buildings Stand Up

*E*very building requires a structure to stand up. This structure may be built of stone, wood, brick, concrete, steel, or a combination of materials, but its function is the same no matter how it is built. A structure must enclose space for a particular purpose while withstanding the pull of gravity and natural phenomena such as rain, wind, fire, and earthquakes. As you may have already guessed, straw and paper aren't popular options!

Columns, beams, arches, walls, and floors can be combined in myriad ways to make architecture stable and functional. But structures are limited in their capability to follow the laws of nature. They can be categorized into two basic types: *trabeated,* or post-and-lintel structures, and *arcuated,* or systems of curved elements. (Both types are discussed later in this chapter.)

Stonehenge and the Empire State Building, for example, are designed according to the same trabeated structural system — upright posts supporting horizontal elements called *lintels.* But while Stonehenge is built of huge rocks and manages simple loads, the Empire State Building is built with a more complicated system of steel (which is lighter) so that it can span greater distances and heights and resist greater forces.

May the Force Be with It: Carrying the Loads

All structures must resist a variety of weights and forces. The most basic weight is the weight of the structure itself — the walls, floors, ceilings, and roof — called a *dead load.* (No, a dead load isn't when someone in your apartment building leaves laundry in the washing machine for three hours after it's done. That's called a "problem load.") Impermanent loads on the structure generated by the movement of humans, animals, furniture, or equipment are called *live loads.* Taken together, these permanent and slowly changing weights on the building are called *static loads.*

Natural forces, such as gusts of wind, snowfalls, and earthquakes, are called *dynamic loads.* They are calculated according to the size, materials, and location of the building, taking into account the worst-case scenario. As you can probably imagine, one hopes that these types of loads don't get too dynamic.

Engineers can channel invisible forces too!

A successful structure works by channeling all of these loads to the ground. All of its elements must be properly sized and configured to channel the loads. (And you don't even need a psychic medium to help with all of this channeling stuff! How great is that?) Figuring out load transference can be difficult, especially when the building is large and complex. Architects often rely on engineers and computers to help them calculate solutions to complicated structural problems.

A beer, a hot dog, and some structural appreciation

You don't have to understand structural principles to appreciate architectural form. But an understanding of structural principles can make the experience of admiring a building even more enriching. You can't truly admire Gothic cathedrals until you comprehend the technical brilliance of their soaring arches and flying buttresses. Buildings such as sports arenas become even more awe-inspiring when you can discern the structural achievements of their huge spans and roofs. Now I'm not saying that you should waste those front-row seats to the hockey game by staring at the roof the whole time; heck you can do it during halftime!

Structural Forces: How a Building Gets Stressed

In many ways, a building's structure is like a human skeleton, and the building materials that cover it — stone panels, plaster, and so on — are like skin and clothes. The structure gets stressed when loads are placed upon it, and it strains under the pressure. No matter what its size, a structure will always choose the easiest route when channeling loads to the ground.

It's a tug-of-war every day: Tension and compression

A structure channels all loads through two simple actions: tension and compression. These loads are ultimately transferred to the ground. *Tension* refers to the forces that pull on the structure, and *compression* refers to the forces that push on the structure.

Each building material responds differently to tension and compression. Stone, brick, and concrete are stronger at handling compression — being pushed — than at handling tension. These materials are well suited for elements that support weight on top of them, such as a vertical post supporting a floor or ceiling above it. Steel and wood are tougher at resisting pulling, or tension, and are appropriate for structural elements such as beams that are placed horizontally — elements that have a tendency to sag. Wood generally works equally well in tension and compression. Reinforcing concrete with steel bars can help give a structure both the compressive strength of concrete and the tensile strength of steel.

Sometimes tension and compression are present in the same structural element. The presence of both tension and compression is called *bending*. When bending occurs, vertical loads are channeled in a horizontal direction. Wood and steel are examples of materials that perform well under bending stresses.

Statics: Seeking balance

All the elements of a structure seek a balance between the pressures of compression and tension. When this balance doesn't happen, a structure can become too stressed out, forcing it to buckle or break down. (Sort of like how people do when they have in-laws sleeping over for an extended length of time.)

Equilibrium between stresses in a building — or *stasis* — can be achieved by shaping and sizing materials into stable systems of elements. The analysis of forces acting upon building elements to achieve this balance is called *statics*.

The science of statics came about through trial and error. In the past, architects and builders would experiment with risky structures until, faced with failure, they would have to try something else. The daring brick dome of Hagia Sophia in Istanbul, one of the largest domes ever built (see Chapter 9), fell twice before it was finally able to stand freely.

Posts and Lintels: Trabeated Systems

The simplest type of structure is formed by balancing a lintel, or beam, between two posts or columns — a system referred to as *trabeated*. Since ancient times, posts and lintels have been used to construct wooden huts as well as huge stone monuments. The Greeks and Romans perfected the trabeated system in temples that were formed from carved stone columns and lintels holding up peaked roofs. By subtly changing the proportions and the details of the beams and posts, the Greeks and Romans revolutionized architecture with the classical orders (see Chapter 8). This type of structure definitely has history on its side. Hey, if it isn't broke, why fix it?

Post-and-lintel systems can be repeated to create a series of frames called *bays*. They can also be built on top of one another to create multistory buildings. The weight of the lintel is carried through the post to the ground. In most buildings, weight is transferred through the ground to an element called a *footing*.

A weighty issue: Footings and foundations

Like human feet, *footings* spread the load over a larger area than a foundation wall to reduce the pounds per square inch. They are typically constructed of stone or concrete. Footings may become so large that they touch each other, forming a single *foundation* mat.

The loads on the footings can be extremely heavy for a skyscraper — thousands of tons. Only solid soil can carry such loads. When this solid soil is buried deep below the ground, heavy, hollow steel cylinders called *caissons* are sunken into the earth and filled with concrete to support the weight. When the soil is sandy and weak or filled with rocks, long round poles called *piles* are driven into the ground to support the footings or the foundation mat. Sometimes the ground is so weak that the foundation mat has to be made hollow so that it can float within the liquid soil. This is called a *raft foundation*.

By itself, the post-and-lintel unit is not entirely sturdy. The weight of the lintel or beam pushes on the posts to create compression in each of them. At the same time, the beam wants to curve upward and bend. In doing so, the top of the beam shortens under compression, while the bottom pulls in tension. This bending action causes cracks to appear in beams made of low-tensile materials, such as concrete or stone. Steel rods are often set into concrete beams to help prevent cracks from forming.

Now it's an I-beam

In post-and-lintel units, the center of the beam doesn't change under the pressure of weight. Realizing this, a clever steelworker or engineer came up with the idea of moving the steel away from the center and placing it at the top and bottom to create an I-shaped beam. Just in case you'd like to impress someone at a party or pass yourself off as a junior architect, the tops of the I-beam are called *flanges,* and the center is called the *web.* This is the most efficient shape a beam can have when carrying vertical loads horizontally from one point to another. The efficient shape is why I-beams are used to construct high-rise buildings.

One way to stabilize a post-and-lintel structure is to brace it with diagonal supports called *trusses.* One of the world's most elegant examples of this type of construction is the Eiffel Tower in Paris. Nearly all of its pieces are formed from an open latticework of light iron trusses.

Your basic house that most folks live in

Most Americans are familiar with the post-and-lintel and truss structures used in their own homes. The typical house is built from wooden columns and beams — 2 x 4's, 2 x 6's, and the like — that are rigidly connected to create strong, wind-resistant frames. Floors increase this sturdiness with narrow wood braces called *joists* that are covered up in plywood. At the top of the house, a peaked roof helps to resist vertical loads of snow. It is constructed of simple triangular trusses. These trusses consist of inclined pieces of lumber, called *rafters* that are connected by horizontal pieces of lumber, called *purlins.* These roof trusses are placed parallel to each other along the top walls of the house. Planks of wood and roof tiles are nailed on top of the roof trusses.

Cantilevers: A balancing act

Post-and-lintel structures can withstand a lot of loads, but they can also be boxy and boring. And hey, who wants that? One way to transform them into more dynamic, open spaces is to extend a beam from one of the posts as you remove the other post from under the beam. This type of unencumbered beam is called a *cantilever.* It is most commonly used to support a balcony.

Modern architect Frank Lloyd Wright especially liked using cantilevers so that the roofs and terraces of his houses would appear to float in space. Bauhaus architect Marcel Breuer used one in the 1928 design of his Cesca chair.

The best way to understand a cantilever is to hold the end of a ruler out horizontally with your thumb and forefinger. If you push down on the free end, you'll notice that the ruler starts to bend down to create a slight curve. This bending indicates that the top is in tension and the lower part is in compression. To compensate for this tension and compression, the ruler-beam must be firmly anchored at its "root" with a plate or fastener.

Watch Those Curves: Arcuated Systems

Arcuated structures were a major advance over posts and lintels. These systems of curved elements allow more space to be enclosed with supports that are less massive. An *arcuated* structure is based on the *arch,* a curved support that spans an opening between upright posts or piers.

Little stone rainbows: Arches

Now, most people probably think about a popular fast-food chain when the talk turns to arches. However, if you really want to impress someone and sound as though you have a degree in something artistic, you have to do some name-dropping when it comes to arches. Arches are made from wedge-shaped stones known as *voussoirs* that are supported at their base by blocks called *imposts.* The earliest arches were built by stacking the voussoirs on a semicircular wooden framework. The stack of voussoirs was started from both ends and built up toward the top. When the largest wedge-shaped unit — a *keystone* — was placed on the top of the stack, the formwork was dismantled. Think of an arch as two weaknesses leaning against each other to make a strength (that's how fifteenth-century genius Leonardo da Vinci described the two halves).

Over time, arches were developed into many shapes to span doorways, windows, and entire rooms. Romanesque builders borrowed the rounded arches of ancient Rome (see Chapter 8): Gothic architects refined the curved top of the arch into a point, and Islamic designers (see Chapter 18) fashioned arches into horseshoe shapes. In the 1880s, American architect Henry Hobson Richardson made a wide, rounded arch part of his signature (see Chapter 11).

Every arch works basically the same way: It transfers loads downward and at an angle to its supports. This action causes an outward, lateral force called *thrust* that must be dissipated at the sides by weights or bracing mechanisms. If the thrust is not dissipated, the arch will collapse. Thrust can also be absorbed by side-by-side arches that are built in a row to create an arcade (see Chapter 9 for more on arches and arcades). The triangular-shaped area between two adjoining arches is referred to as a *spandrel* and is often decorated.

Vaults: Arches in 3-D

Okay, take out those funky 3-D glasses! Extending an arch in the third dimension forms a structure with a curved ceiling known as a *vault.* Rounded like half a barrel, this type of vault is called, logically, a *barrel vault.* Many of the great structures designed by the ancient Romans (see Chapter 8 for more of them) rely on the barrel vault, such as the Colosseum in Rome (it also has posts and lintels). Vaults can span larger spaces than simple arches.

Fly the friendly manmade skies: Domes

Another structure formed from arches is a half-spherical structure known as a *dome.* You can make a dome by rotating a series of arches 360 degrees around a vertical axis. The outward thrust is absorbed by a ring at the bottom and rings at various levels, called *parallels,* that prevent the arches from moving in or out under the load. Because a dome's arches, called *meridians,* are supported all the way to the top of the dome, they can be made much lighter than arches that are standing alone. A dome is a thin but strong structure that can span great distances.

As a spherical shape equal on all sides, a dome gives us a protective feeling of being under a manmade sky. Roman emperor Hadrian realized this when he built the first dome at the Pantheon, a temple to all the gods (see Chapter 8).

New Shapes for Modern Structures

During the Industrial Revolution, new technologies were developed that allowed frame structures to be more open and lightweight (see Chapters 12 and 13). Cast iron, wrought iron, and steel revolutionized spatial enclosures by allowing a building's weight to be distributed along interior columns and beams rather than through load-bearing exterior walls of stone or brick. This type of lightweight structural system allowed buildings to rise higher and higher. In the twentieth century, reinforced concrete and plastics pushed structures higher still.

Now they can soar: Getting hypar

For some modern architects, breaking out of the box meant using saddle surfaces — or a *hyperbolic paraboloid* ("hypar"), as those fancy architect folks call them. You can simulate this type of structure by pulling up on two opposite corners of a handkerchief and then pulling down on the remaining two corners. Now that was fun, wasn't it? While domes or barrel vaults have downward curvatures in all directions, a hypar has curvatures up in certain directions and down in others. This unique design gives it a soaring shape that resembles a butterfly or bird. In the 1950s and 60s, parabolic roofs became a popular way to provide buildings with organic, freeform shapes. A master of the hypar is Spanish-born architect Felix Candela, who built several innovative concrete structures in Mexico.

Thin shells that look like seashells by the seashore

Innovations in thin shells during the postwar era also led to more complex, sophisticated shapes. *Thin shells* are a type of form-resistant structure in which strength is obtained by shaping the material according to the loads that it must carry. Thin shells are thin enough to avoid bending (as in beams), but thick enough to support loads by compression or tension, or a combination of both. Although they can be constructed in a variety of materials, thin shells are best suited to reinforced concrete — a material capable of resisting both tension and compression.

One of most spectacular concrete shell structures is the Sydney Opera House (1957–1973) designed by Jorn Utzon. Made of concrete segments, its soaring, sail-like roofs are Australia's most famous architectural landmark.

Keepin' us in suspense: Suspension structures

Suspension structures, which are common structures for bridges, were another way of creating exciting architectural shapes. Following the example of the Brooklyn Bridge in New York and the Golden Gate Bridge in San Francisco, Finnish-born architect Eero Saarinen designed Dulles International Airport, outside Washington, D.C., with its roof suspended between concrete piers. Shaped like an upside-down arch, the roof is formed from steel cables that are prestressed by concrete and buttressed by the outward-leaning piers.

Tents: Under the big top

Some of the most impressive contemporary buildings have returned to the most basic of all structures — tents. Like nomads pulling skins over wooden poles, today's architects separate their tents into two components:

- ✔ A membrane of fabric that is stretched over steel cables
- ✔ Masts of steel and other materials that support the suspended cables and fabric

When pulled into place by the masts and cables, the fabric resists tension and can support a variety of loads. Tents are referred to as *tensile structures* and create interesting architectural forms because they resist loads by changing their shape.

Tents are now made of plastic fabrics that create a much stiffer structure than those of canvas and other natural fibers. Glass-reinforced fibers and self-cleaning Teflon coatings boost the fabrics' strength, fire-resistance, and insulating and reflective properties. Today, tents are used for canopies over airports and sports stadiums as well as for entire roofs. The largest tent in the world is the Millennium Dome in London, designed by British architect Richard Rogers to enclose 20 acres.

R. Buckminster Fuller: Structural visionary

Richard Buckminster Fuller (1895–1983), an engineer, theorist, and teacher, used basic structural principles to invent architecture of unconventional beauty. "Bucky," as he was known, began his career experimenting with industrial manufacturing techniques to produce designs that were ahead of their time. His Dymaxion House (1927) used tension cables to suspend the structure from a central mast, while his three-wheel, rear-engine Dymaxion car (1933) was aerodynamically streamlined. In 1940, Fuller patented a prefabricated one-piece bathroom molded from sheet steel. Ahead of their time, these inventions failed to win mass-market acceptance but are now respected for their ingenuity.

Fuller's most important achievement was the *geodesic dome,* a spherical enclosure made of triangular or octagonal metal frames. He also devised the *tensegrity dome* ("tension" plus "integrity"), which was made from tubular compression members joined by tensioned cables. Fuller's domes were used for radar systems and homes as well as for the gigantic U.S. Pavilion at Expo '67 in Montreal. Fuller, who claimed his domes were the most economical way of enclosing space, even proposed covering part of Manhattan Island with one of them. Now there's a thought . . .

Part III

Western Architecture: A Survey of the Most Important Structures

The 5th Wave By Rich Tennant

"I like the way the post-modern architecture is blended with the neo-Greek elements by the phrase 'Aerosmith Rules!' spray painted along the facade."

In this part . . .

From an indigenous hut to a postmodern skyscraper, architecture has continuously evolved over thousands of years. This part traces the major developments in Western architecture, identifying the greatest buildings and architects of each era.

It's by no means a complete history: It's intended to introduce you to the essential developments in architectural design and building technology. When you are more familiar with these basic artistic and structural movements, you are able to appreciate the ways that architects have revived — and rejected — various styles throughout the ages.

Chapter 7

Gimme Shelter: Prehistoric Structures and the Ancient World

Architecture originated as protection from the forces of nature. Yet no matter how humble their hut, people have always aspired to make their shelter more than merely practical. Even within the refuge of caves and cliffs, humans decorated their surroundings with paintings of animals and figures.

As nomads, early peoples built temporary dwellings of sticks and animal hides that were easily transported. Farming led to more permanent walled settlements to guard the crops. One of the earliest is the city of Jericho in Jordan, dating from about 8000 B.C. (see Chapter 19). Its citizens lived in stone houses with plaster floors, surrounded by high walls and towers, which are considered some of the world's first fortifications.

After people started sharing in community life, they began turning their attention to architecture that celebrated the spiritual and the sacred. Their tombs and temples imitated nature in gigantic forms resembling mountains and other landscape formations. What is astonishing is that these stone monuments and pyramids were all built without modern tools or machines — requiring a vast amount of labor, endurance, and time. But the effort was clearly worth it. Mysterious, abstract, and awesome, the architecture of the ancients still inspires us today.

From Tipis to Tombs: Prehistoric Architecture

People began building homes 15,000 years ago, during the Ice Age. These dwellings were designed in direct response to climate, local materials, and hunting patterns. Some of the earliest Ice Age structures, as archaeologists discovered in the Ukraine, were supported by mammoth bones and tusks and covered in mammoth hides. This skin-and-bone tradition continued to evolve over thousands of years. North American Indian and Mongolian tribes used a variation of this construction in covering sapling frames with bark, reeds, and animal skin. The Plains Indians eventually developed a portable version of the shelter called a *tipi,* shown in Figure 7-1. Poles were erected and covered in buffalo hides with entrance and smoke flaps. When it was time to move, the parts were packed up and pulled by dogs or horses.

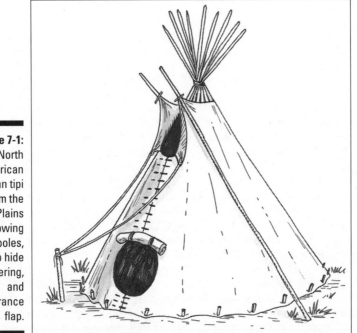

Figure 7-1:
North American Indian tipi from the Great Plains showing poles, buffalo hide covering, and entrance flap.

Ten thousand years ago, the Ice Age melted into the New Stone, or Neolithic, Age, when the Earth's climate warmed up. Hunters settled down to start farming communities and build houses of timber, stone, and mud with hearths for cooking and heating. As settlements became more permanent, new architecture was developed to represent communal and spiritual values. Sacred monuments, sanctuaries, and tombs of stone, made from rocks that were often hauled over long distances, were erected throughout Western Europe.

Some really big rocks: Stone megaliths

Ancient stone monuments are known as *megaliths* — *mega* meaning "big" and *lith* meaning "stone." They were erected throughout Western Europe starting around 5000 B.C. Most were not intended to enclose space but to mark a particular location and to be seen from a great distance. These megaliths have their own special terms, as follows:

- **Menhirs:** Single stones standing upright
- **Dolmens:** Several upright stones supporting horizontal stone slabs
- **Henges:** Circular ditches around which some megalithic monuments are arranged
- **Cromlech:** A circle of stones

Dolmens were made by piling huge boulders and blocks of stone on top of each other without using mortar. This construction system is the most basic of all structures and is called *trabeation*. It consists of vertical supports called *posts* that hold up horizontal elements called *lintels.* To understand this simple structure, imagine a very heavy house of cards (and go to Chapter 6 to find out more). During the Stone Age, Europeans arranged post-and-lintel structures into rows or rings to create some of the most enigmatic architecture ever built.

Why go to all the trouble of stacking huge rocks into such precise formations? No one knows for sure, but experts speculate that these rings and markers were used for religious rituals, seasonal celebrations, and scientific observation of the sun and stars.

Seeing circles: Stonehenge

The most famous of the surviving megalithic monuments is Stonehenge, on the Salisbury Plain in Wiltshire, England. Of the hundreds of stone circles built across the British Isles, Stonehenge is the most sophisticated in terms of its architecture.

The giant stones are not only set in a precise formation but follow a trabeated system of vertical posts and horizontal lintels (see preceding section). The top stones were attached to the pillars according to a method that carpenters still use today. Called *mortice-and-tenon,* this technique calls for carving the upright stones with a protruding part that fits into a slot in the lintel. Such exacting construction testifies to the advanced design and engineering skills of Stonehenge's makers.

How it all started

Beginning in about 3000 B.C., Stonehenge was built in several phases — it was remodeled in about 2100 B.C. to look like what we see today. The monument began as a large earthwork; a ditch or *henge* was dug into the chalky soil with tools probably made from deer antlers. Placed on the inside boundary of the circular ditch were pits used for the burial of human bodies. The pits are called *Aubrey Holes,* named for John Aubrey, who in 1663 surveyed Stonehenge for King Charles II.

The main monument at Stonehenge is formed by layers of upright stones arranged into circular and horseshoe patterns that enclose the center of the site. The innermost circle of stones was erected first. This structure consisted of about 60 *bluestones* (a blue-gray sandstone that is easily split into thin slabs), each weighing about 4 tons, which were transported almost 250 miles from the Preseli Mountains in southern Wales. (How they arrived at Stonehenge is still debated.)

The outermost circle was made of 30 sandstones that rose about 15 feet high; only about 17 of these stones now remain. Within this circle stood a grouping of larger sandstones arranged in a horseshoe shape, as shown in Figure 7-2. These stones were once part of five sandstone *trilithons* (Greek for "three stones"), a term meaning two pillars connected by a lintel.

Figure 7-2:
Stonehenge, Wiltshire, England, dating from about 3000 to 1500 B.C.

© Britain on View. Used with permission.

Many other stones also can be found on the Stonehenge site. One of the most intriguing is the Heel Stone. This large stone with a pointed top stands on a long avenue extending from the monument's open horseshoe.

How it may have been used

Although no one really knows why Stonehenge was built, some historians believe it was designed to celebrate the summer solstice, when the rising sun comes up exactly over the Heel Stone. Other experts speculate that the stone monument was used as a primitive computer for calculating lunar and solar eclipses, as a temple to the Sun, as a place for human sacrifice, or as a landing site for extraterrestrials.

Who the architects may have been

Stonehenge involved generations of skilled builders who lifted the huge stones into place with the help of wooden levers, platforms, and ropes. Over the centuries, theories about who actually did this heavy lifting have included the Greeks, Phoenicians, and Atlanteans (people described by Plato as building their cities in circles). In the 1600s, Stonehenge was linked to the Druids, an ancient Celtic priesthood, though many scholars claim that this religious practice did not take place in England at the time that the stone circles were built. Another legend is that Merlin, the magician from King Arthur's Court, reconstructed the monument on Salisbury Plain from a circle of giant stones in Ireland. These are just some of the myths that attempt to explain the talented architects behind this powerful monument.

Ancient Pyramids: Stairways to Heaven

From the ancient civilizations of the Near East to the native peoples of Central America, pyramid building has been a common architectural design for thousands of years.

What is so appealing about this tapering shape? Ancient rulers liked these artificial mountains for their great height (allowing them to commune with the gods) and commanding visual presence over flat river valleys. On a practical level, a pyramid concentrates most of its building on the lower half, so fewer stones have to be hauled to the top. The lower stories act as scaffolding for constructing the upper ones. Tomb and temple, straight-sided and stepped, pyramids assume a variety of functions and forms.

Stepping up nature: Mesopotamian ziggurats

Some of the oldest pyramids were built by the Sumerian civilization in what is now Iraq. Stepped structures, called *ziggurats,* were constructed with outside staircases and a temple or shrine at the top for worshipping the gods of nature. Clustered around the base of the ziggurat were artisan workshops, storehouses, and housing.

Ziggurats were built out of mud bricks made of dirt mixed with water and straw. The mud was poured into wooden molds and left to dry in the sun (or baked in kilns). Worn down by rain and sun, most of these mountainous buildings have disappeared or been reduced to shapeless piles of dried earth. Here are two famous examples of these early stepped pyramids:

- **Ziggurat of Urnammu at Ur:** A temple dedicated to the moon god, this structure was built by the Sumerian ruler, Urnammu, and his successors around 2125 B.C. Higher levels with terraces of diminishing size were added onto the original structure to give it the appearance of a wedding cake.

- **Tower of Babel:** As described in the Bible, this structure may have been built in Babylon (see the nearby sidebar "Babylonian wonders") around 600 B.C. by King Nebuchadnezzar II to "rival heaven." Greek historian Herodotus recorded that the ziggurat had seven tiers covered in colorful glazed tiles. The tower may have risen to a height of 300 feet and may have been used as a temple for worshipping Marduk, the god of the city of Babylon.

Building an afterlife: Egyptian pyramids

The ancient Egyptians built, for their rulers, more than 80 pyramids along the banks of the Nile near modern-day Cairo from 2700 to 1640 B.C. The pyramids were designed according to three forms:

- Step pyramid
- Bent pyramid
- Straight-sided pyramid (the most common type)

How they did it, sort of

Limestone for the pyramids was quarried on the east bank of the Nile, transported on boats, and then dragged from the river to the building site on wooden sleds with runners. No one knows exactly how the pyramids were built, but the heavy blocks were probably dragged up a straight or spiral ramp that grew as the pyramid rose in height. The exterior surfaces were covered with better quality stone and smoothed with copper chisels and stone hammers. The summit of the pyramid was often covered in gold.

Babylonian wonders

Babylon (from the word *Bab-ili,* meaning "Gate of God"), on the Euphrates River, was the center of the Mesopotamian empire. After Babylon was destroyed by several invasions, King Nebuchadnezzar II, who ruled from 605 to 563 B.C., rebuilt the city with ornate walls and structures. Among his most impressive accomplishments were the following:

✔ **Hanging Gardens of Babylon:** This royal palace was considered one of the Seven Wonders of the Ancient World. Its mud-brick walls were covered with glazed, colored tiles decorated with animal reliefs. Legend says that the sumptuous palace was terraced with lush gardens that were irrigated by water pumped from the Euphrates. (See the sidebar "Seven Wonders of the Ancient World" and the section "The pyramids of Giza," both later in this chapter, and Chapter 23 for more details on the Seven Wonders.)

✔ **Ishtar Gate:** This large, four-story portal dominated the processional avenue through the city. It was covered in glazed bricks, colorful tiles, and decorative figures of bulls and dragons. A reconstruction of the gate is exhibited in Berlin at the Pergamon Museum.

Reconstruction painting in oils by Maurice Bardin, 1937, after watercolor by Herbert Anger. Courtesy of the Oriental Institute of the University of Chicago.

Traveling to the sun: The spiritual significance

Egyptians believed that after death, pharaohs became gods and their souls traveled to the sky or sun. With their stepped or triangular sides, pyramids acted as staircases for this spiritual journey. The Egyptians also believed that the preservation of the body was essential to the immortality of the soul. They thought that if people needed the protection of buildings while alive, they also needed it after death. The pyramids protected the king's body and the goods that were to be taken to the next world. Some experts claim that the pyramids represented the rays of the sun that linked the reigning pharaoh to Ra, the sun god.

The pyramids were built on the west bank of the Nile by Egyptian laborers — not slaves. They were only too happy to work for the king, who fed and clothed them and promised to care for them in the afterlife. Some of the laborers were also given a funeral plot on the grounds of the pyramid that further guaranteed their afterlife.

Each pyramid was only part of a larger funerary complex arranged in a line that led from the banks of the Nile River. Along the riverfront was a temple (probably used to mummify the king), connected by a covered causeway to another temple (used for sacred rites) at the foot of the pyramid. Rectangular tombs for the king's family and courtiers, called *mastabas,* were built around the pharaoh's pyramid. The queens — pharaohs had many wives — had smaller pyramids of their own.

The pyramids of Giza

The majestic pyramids of Giza, near Cairo, have been a tourist attraction for thousands of years. When the Greek historian Herodotus visited them in the sixth century B.C., he gave them the names by which they are still known.

The largest pyramid is called the *Cheops pyramid* or *Great Pyramid.* It was built around 2550 B.C. for Khufu. The pyramid is surrounded by three small queen's pyramids and rows of small tombs. This awesome structure, shown in Figure 7-3, stands about 480 feet tall with a square base measuring 756 feet on a side. (The Great Pyramid is the only one of the Seven Wonders of the Ancient World still standing. See Chapter 23 and the nearby sidebar for more details.)

Figure 7-3:
Cheops, the Great Pyramid at Giza, Egypt, built around 2550 B.C.

Photo courtesy of GreatBuildings.com © Howard Davis.

HISTORICAL NOTE

Seven Wonders of the Ancient World

You can find out more about the Great Pyramid of Khufu in Chapter 23. Want the scoop on the other six Wonders?

✔ The Hanging Gardens of Babylon were laid out by King Nebuchadnezzar II around 600 B.C. (see the sidebar "Babylonian Wonders" earlier in this chapter); they may never have existed.

✔ The Temple of Artemis at Ephesus, a Greek temple in modern-day Turkey, was designed by architect Chersiphron and his son Metagenes around 550 B.C. The original temple burned down in 356 B.C. and was replaced by a second structure that also was devastated by fire.

✔ The Statue of Zeus stood in the Greek city of Olympia where the first Olympic Games were held. Sculptor Phidias (the same artist who worked on the Parthenon) created the 40-foot-high seated figure to stand inside a temple honoring the god. It was moved to Constantinople (now Istanbul) and destroyed by a fire in A.D. 462.

✔ The Mausoleum at Halicarnassus was built around 353 B.C. as a tomb for King Mausolus and queen Artemisia of the Persian Empire. Greek architects Satyrius and Pythius designed the marble structure with a pyramidal top. It was damaged by an earthquake in the fifteenth century and eventually pillaged for its sculpture.

✔ The Lighthouse of Alexandria was designed by Greek architect Sostratus around 270 B.C. and stood about 400 feet high in the harbor of Alexandria, Egypt. The last of the six wonders to disappear, the lighthouse — once the world's tallest structure — was destroyed by an earthquake in the fourteenth century.

✔ The Colossus of Rhodes, a giant bronze statue, is believed to have been sited to overlook the harbor of the Greek island of Rhodes. Created by the Greek sculptor Chares to honor the sun god Helios, the 120-foot-high figure was supported on the inside by stone blocks and iron bars, but it didn't survive a strong earthquake just 56 years after it was completed.

The second pyramid, 9 feet shorter than its neighbor, is named *Chephren,* which is Greek for *Khafre,* who was Khufu's son or younger brother. It was finished in about 2520 B.C. Next to it stands the *Great Sphinx,* an immense sculpture representing the head of Khafre on the body of a crouching lion.

Smaller still, at 218 feet high, is the third pyramid built by Khafre's successor, Mycerinus or Menkaura in 2490 B.C. To the south are three smaller pyramids, including one covered in granite that may have been the tomb of Menkaura's favorite wife, Queen Khamerernebty.

TECHNICAL STUFF

What's so remarkable about these structures is the precision of their construction. The bases from which they rise are absolutely level, and the joints between the stonework are extremely narrow. Originally, the pyramids were covered in smooth limestone, most of which has been pillaged over centuries for other buildings, except for a small area at the top of Cheops.

By 2000 B.C., the Great Pyramids were abandoned by Egyptian rulers after robbers continually looted their tombs. Pharaohs went on to build tombs and temples in the rocky cliffs and hillsides of the Valley of the Kings at Thebes, not far from Luxor. The temples were not places for communal worship but a meeting place between a god and his or her representative on Earth, the pharaoh. These buildings were not pyramidal in shape, but instead were tiered into the hillside with sloping walls. Inside, the temples were divided into halls, courtyards, and sanctuaries. In some of the halls, rows of heavy stone supports, carved and painted with plant-inspired decorations, created the effect of a forest. Two of the most famous temples are the Great Temple of Amun at Karnak (begun in 1530 B.C.) and the Temple of Luxor (begun in about 1400 B.C.).

Pyramids in the Americas

Hundreds of years after the Egyptians mummified their last pharaoh, the Incas of Peru, the Mayas of Central America, and the Aztecs of Mexico built their own pyramids. Construction of these immense sacred structures began in the region around 200 B.C. and continued for another 1,000 years. In the Americas, pyramids were mostly used as temples and were built of stone and adobe with steps and terraces rising to a flat top. Priests climbed the stairs to altars on platforms where they conducted sacred rites and sacrificed humans to the gods. A few pyramids were built over tombs.

Monumental in scale, pyramids were a prominent part of early Mesoamerican cities. Dominating the ancient city of Teotihuacan near Mexico City is the Pyramid of the Sun (A.D. 50). This pyramid, rising from a 712-foot square base to a height of 187 feet, was the largest of several temples built in this city, which flourished from 200 B.C. to A.D. 750 as a major religious center.

The first known architect

The first architect to be recorded in history was an Egyptian named Imhotep. Between 2700 and 2600 B.C., a king named Zoser (also called Djoser I and Neterikhet) hired Imhotep to design and build his tomb at the necropolis of Saqqara near the Egyptian city of Memphis. After he saw the design, Zoser decided to enlarge the structure into a pyramid of six steps. He then surrounded it with temples, tombs, and fake palaces commemorating his life. As the architect of this huge complex, Imhotep took the innovative step of translating structures that had been built of mud, wood, and reeds into stone. In doing so, he devised a complete system of columns and decorative details that predates the classical orders of the Greeks. The step pyramid at Saqqara is the oldest hewn stone monument in the world. In addition to practicing architecture, Imhotep was an astronomer, a magician, and a doctor, and the Egyptians eventually worshipped him as a god.

The Mayas of Central America built some of the most magnificent pyramids between A.D. 250 and 900. Although many of these stone monuments were constructed during medieval times, they followed ancient forms and traditions. Here are some striking examples:

- The Temple of the Magician in Mexico's Yucatan peninsula was part of a large Mayan city called Uxmal that flourished around A.D. 600–900. The pyramidal temple is one of several stone structures built in the architectural style known as Puuc ("low hill" in Mayan). Lower stories are rather plain, while upper sections are richly decorated with ornate carvings and mosaics. Mayas would often build a new temple over an existing one, and in this structure, five stages of construction have been found.

- The Temple of the Inscriptions at Palenque was dedicated to Mayan ruler Hanab Pakal, who has been called the "Mesoamerican Charlemagne." The 75-foot-high pyramidal temple was part of a city built from the sixth to the ninth centuries in the Mexican Chiapas highlands. The ruins of Palenque also include terraces, plazas, burial grounds, and a ball court — all with expressive stone carvings. In 1952, the tomb of Pakal was found in a crypt at the bottom of a staircase inside the pyramid.

- El Castillo (Spanish for "the castle"), a 98-foot-high pyramid, was built by the Itzas, a Mayan-speaking people, at Chichén Itzá (meaning "the mouth of the well of the Itzas") in Yucatan, Mexico, in the twelfth century. Stairways rise on all four sides of the pyramid to a temple dedicated to the plumed serpent god, Kukulcán, at the top. Serpent motifs decorate the staircase and other parts of the structure.

Mythology Comes to Life: The Aegean

For centuries, scholars believed that the legend of ancient Troy was just another tall tale made up by the blind Greek poet Homer. But a rich German businessman and amateur archaeologist, Heinrich Schliemann, proved that Troy really did exist. From 1870 to 1890, he excavated the area and discovered that the legendary city where the Greek army built their wooden horse was one of nine cities built on the islands around the Aegean Sea.

Don't get lost: Minoan palaces in Crete

The first city of the nine cities was built by the rich civilization that appeared on the Aegean island of Crete around 2000 B.C. It was a trading hub that flourished until between 1400 and 100 B.C., when it was obliterated by an earthquake or other natural disaster.

Architecture filled with sunlight, brightly colored walls, and sophisticated indoor plumbing supported the Cretan's laid-back, luxurious living style. One of the best preserved examples is the palace at Knossos, which was built by the island's legendary ruler, King Minos, around 1700–1400 B.C.

Covering about 5 acres, the building was arranged around courtyards and built of stucco-faced brick and stone walls. It had so many rooms that the Greeks thought it could be the labyrinth of the minotaur, the mythological creature who was half man, half bull. The royal apartments included bathrooms with ceramic tubs and toilets.

Fortifying the home: Mycenaean fortresses

After Crete fell, around 1400 B.C., a society of warriors called the Mycenaeans rose along the southeastern shores of Greece. They built fortresses rather than palaces — hilltop citadels enclosed by walls of immense stone blocks. The fortresses were so awe-inspiring that the later Greeks thought they might have been built by a race of one-eyed giants called *Cyclops* rather than by man.

One of most expressive structures to survive from the fort at Mycenae is a doorway carved with two lions flanking a column. It's known as the *Lion Gate,* and it dates from about 1250 B.C. The triangular shape of its decoration set over a post-and-lintel — or *trabeated* — structure foreshadows the classical tradition that developed in Greece and influenced all of Western architecture.

Chapter 8

Acropolis Now: Classical Greece and Rome

In This Chapter
▶ Greek architecture and the classical orders
▶ Etruscan architecture
▶ Roman structural inventions

Columns, capitals, and colonnades: These building elements, first developed in Egypt (see Chapter 7), became a highly refined style of architecture in ancient Greece and Rome.

The Greeks originated this orderly architecture for temples in the seventh century B.C. and continued perfecting it into several well-defined systems, They based the different proportions of these systems on mathematical ratios.

After the Romans conquered Greece, they copied the architecture of the earlier Greek civilization while coming up with their own design flourishes and technical achievements.

The architecture designed by the ancient Greeks and Romans came to be called *classical*. This classical architecture would be imitated for 2,500 years. "Classic" is Latin (the language of the Romans) for "elite" — it almost takes a superior being to identify every nuance of a classical building.

The Greeks: Pursuit of Perfection

For the Greeks, temples were not only places to worship the gods but also impressive symbols of their society and culture. They were built as focal points on the highest ground of every city in Greece and the conquered territories around the Mediterranean. Beneath the temples spread public meeting places, civic buildings, gymnasiums, stadiums, theaters, and housing (see Chapter 19).

Today, the remains of Greek cities can be found in Italy, Sicily, and Turkey. One of the reasons that they have lasted so long is that the Greeks built their temples, amphitheaters, and other major public buildings with limestone and marble. Blocks of stone were held in place by bronze or iron pins set into molten lead — a flexible system that could withstand earthquakes.

Following orders — classical, that is

Greek architecture followed a highly structured system of proportions that relates individual architectural components to the whole building. This system was developed according to three styles, or *orders*. Each order consists of an upright support called a *column* that extends from a base at the bottom to a shaft in the middle and a *capital* at the top — much like the feet, body, and head of the human figure. The capital was often a stylized representation of natural forms, such as animal horns or plant leaves. It, in turn, supports a horizontal element called the *entablature*, which is divided further into three different parts:

- ✔ The architrave (lowest part)
- ✔ The frieze (middle)
- ✔ The cornice (top)

These elements, in turn, were further elaborated with decorative moldings and ornamentation (see Figure 8-1). Each component of a classical order was sized and arranged according to an overall proportioning system based on the height and diameter of the columns.

The Greeks first constructed their orders with wood, and then switched to stone using the same forms. The ends of the wooden beams holding up the roof, for example, were translated into stone as a decorative element, called a *triglyph* ("three grooves"), in the entablature above the column capital.

The Greeks started out using only one order per building. But after a few hundred years, they got more creative and sometimes used one order for the exterior and another for the interior. The proportions of the orders were developed over a long period of time — they became lighter and more refined.

Some folks think that the orders are primarily a question of details, moldings, and characteristic capitals. However, in fact, the very concept of order and an overall relationship is really the most important thing here. Each of the orders is a proportional system or a range of proportions for the entire structure.

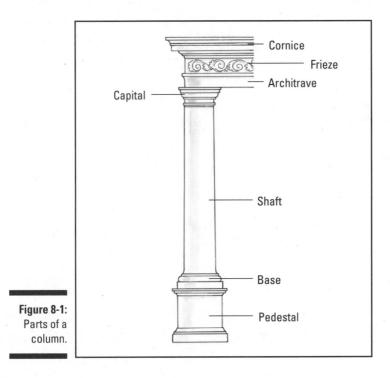

Cornice

Frieze

Architrave

Capital

Shaft

Base

Pedestal

Figure 8-1:
Parts of a
column.

Doric: Heavy simplicity

The oldest, simplest, and most massive of the three Greek orders is the *Doric*, which was applied to temples beginning in the seventh century B.C. As shown in Figure 8-2, columns are placed close together and are often without bases. Their shafts are sculpted with concave curves called *flutes*. The capitals are plain with a rounded section at the bottom, known as the *echinus*, and a square at the top, called the *abacus*. The entablature has a distinctive frieze decorated with vertical channels, or triglyphs. In between the triglyphs are spaces, called *metopes*, that were commonly sculpted with figures and ornamentation. The frieze is separated from the architrave by a narrow band called the *regula*. Together, these elements formed a rectangular structure surrounded by a double row of columns that conveyed a bold unity. The Doric order reached its pinnacle of perfection in the Parthenon.

Ionic: The Ionic Sea Scrolls?

The next order to be developed by the Greeks was the *Ionic* (see Figure 8-3). It is called Ionic because it developed in the Ionian islands in the sixth century B.C. Roman historian Vitruvius compared this delicate order to a female form, in contrast to the stockier "male" Doric order.

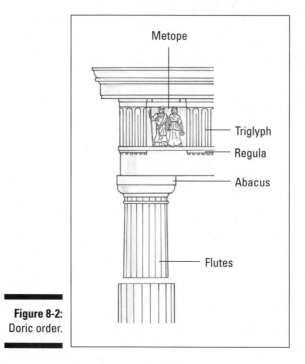

Metope

Triglyph

Regula

Abacus

Flutes

Figure 8-2:
Doric order.

The Ionic was used for smaller buildings and interiors. It's easy to recognize because of the two scrolls, called *volutes,* on its capital. The volutes may have been based on nautilus shells or animal horns.

Between the volutes is a curved section that is often carved with oval decorations known as *egg and dart.* Above the capital, the entablature is narrower than the Doric, with a frieze containing a continuous band of sculpture. One of the earliest and most striking examples of the Ionic order is the tiny Temple to Athena Nike at the entrance to the Athens Acropolis. It was designed and built by Callicrates from about 448–421 B.C.

Corinthian: Leafy but not as popular

The third order is the Corinthian, which wasn't used much by the Greeks. It is named after the city of Corinth, where sculptor Callimachus supposedly invented it by at the end of the fifth century B.C. after he spotted a goblet surrounded by leaves. As shown in Figure 8-4, the Corinthian is similar to the Ionic order in its base, column, and entablature, but its capital is far more ornate, carved with two tiers of curly acanthus leaves. The oldest known Corinthian column stands inside the fifth-century temple of Apollo Epicurius at Bassae.

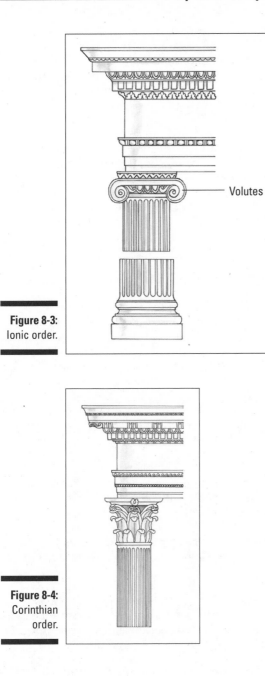

Volutes

Figure 8-3:
Ionic order.

Figure 8-4:
Corinthian
order.

Compensating for illusions: Straight or curved, who knew?

The Greeks continued to strive for perfection in the appearance of their buildings. To make their columns look straight, they bowed them slightly outward to compensate for the optical illusion that makes vertical lines look curved from a distance. They named this effect *entasis,* which means "to strain" in Greek.

Relationships between columns, windows, doorways, and other elements were constantly analyzed to find pleasing dimensions that were in harmony with nature and the human body. Symmetry and the unity of parts to the whole were important to Greek architecture, as these elements reflected the democratic city-state pioneered by the Greek civilization. (For more on symmetry, see Chapter 2.)

Inspiration on high: Greek temples

The most important buildings in Greek cities were temples. Because temples housed the gods that the Greeks worshipped, instead of the worshippers themselves, they were designed to impress people from the outside. Temples in 500 B.C. weren't bleached white like the ruins of the Acropolis in Athens. They were almost gaudy — vividly colored in red, blue, gold, purple, and green, and embellished with statuary and sculptural flourishes.

All temples were rectangular in shape and raised on a platform called a *stylobate.* Columns wrapped around the building perimeter and supported a triangular element, called a *pediment,* at the front and the back, and a pitched timber roof covered by terra-cotta or marble tiles.

The most important temples were grouped in a special precinct of the city. Each of the temples was dedicated to a different god or a different aspect of the same god, who might be honored with several temples in the same city.

In contrast to their symmetrical, well-ordered façades, the temples were informally arranged on a fortified hilltop known as an *acropolis,* which means "city-on-the-height" in Greek.

Although the individual structures on the acropolis were symmetrical in design, they were deliberately arranged asymmetrically. Buildings were often placed at odd angles to each other in order to take advantage of the topography and views, and to allow visitors to move freely around the site. The Erechtheion, built from 421–405 B.C. on the Athens Acropolis, for example, was built on two levels in response to the sloping hillside (see Figure 8-5). The irregular arrangement of the Greek acropolis stood in sharp contrast to earlier temple plans by Egyptian pharaohs.

Figure 8-5:
The Erechtheion on the Athens Acropolis, 421-405 B.C.

Photo courtesy of GreatBuildings.com © John A. Gascon.

The Parthenon

The temples on the Athens Acropolis date from the fifth century B.C., when Pericles ruled the city. The largest temple on this acropolis is the Parthenon, which was built from 447–438 B.C. in honor of Athena, the city's patron goddess.

Designed by architects Ictinus and Callicrates, the Parthenon is the supreme example of classical architecture. It combines the Doric order with elements of the Ionic order in the frieze around the innermost walls.

Surrounding the perimeter were 8 fluted columns on the two ends and 17 fluted columns on the sides. This arrangement, which was one of the Parthenon's great innovations, established a new proportional rule: twice the ends plus one. The architects used visual tricks to make the temple seem more imposing — the stylobate curves upward, the columns taper toward the top, the columns at the corners angle inwards and are thicker than the others, and the column flutes deepen toward the top.

A 43-foot-high gold and ivory statue of Athena, created by the sculptor Phidias, stood inside the Parthenon. Outside, statuary and reliefs, which were also created by Phidias, filled the pediment and architrave with scenes of Athena, the battles of Troy, and the annual processions from the city to the Acropolis.

Today, only a part of the Parthenon survives. In 1687, when it was being used to store gunpowder during the Venetian-Turkish war, a section was partially destroyed. Between 1801 and 1803, during the Turkish occupation of Greece, some of the sculptures were removed and sold to the British Museum.

A superb work of classicism, the Parthenon is still considered one of the most perfect structures ever built. The extraordinary, timeless beauty of its visual refinements has inspired generations of architects. For thousands of years, its design has been imitated in the construction of banks, custom houses, state capitols, and palaces. In 1897, a full-size replica of the Parthenon was created for the Tennessee centennial exposition in Nashville and then rebuilt in 1931 using concrete.

The Etruscans: Prelude to Rome

Ancient Greece eventually fell to Roman conquerors, who adapted the elegant architectural style invented by the earlier civilization for their own purposes. They also learned about Greek architecture from the *Etruscans,* the cultured people who came from Asia Minor to settle on the Italian peninsula (800–700 B.C.) until the Romans conquered them, too.

The Etruscans brought the Greek orders with them (see preceding section). They even invented an order of their own — a simplified version of the Doric order known as the *Tuscan,* which later became a favorite of the Romans. Tuscan columns have plain bases and capitals, and shafts without flutes.

Vitruvius and his how-to book

In the first century B.C., Marcus Vitruvius Pollio, a Roman architect and engineer for Emperor Augustus, wrote a textbook on how to make buildings that were both practical and beautiful. It was called *De Architectura* (On Architecture). The book was divided into ten chapters, with advice on everything from building materials and heating systems to acoustical design and rules of proportion. Much of our understanding of Etruscan architecture also comes from Vitruvius, who described Etruscan temples and other buildings in great detail.

Vitruvius urged Roman architects to design buildings based on the symmetry and proportions of the human body. He claimed that for architecture to be successful, it should embody three essentials — strength, utility, and aesthetics. While translating *De Architectura* in the seventeenth century, British writer Sir Henry Wotton changed the wording to "commodity, firmness, and delight." Vitruvius's book was wildly successful, and his advice was followed for two thousand years. The Roman's writings even inspired an American version of *De Architectura*, an encyclopedia of city plans published in 1922 and recently reissued.

They support an entablature with no decorations other than a few moldings. See Figure 8-6 to check out the Tuscan order.

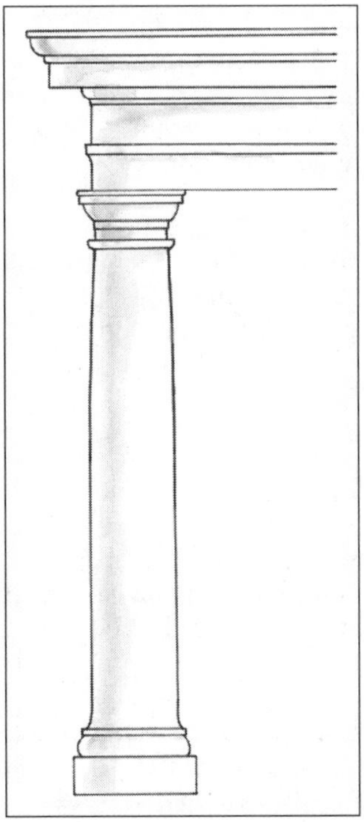

Figure 8-6:
Tuscan
order.

The Etruscans used their Tuscan orders to create wooden temples with pitched roofs that were richly decorated with terra-cotta tiles and sculptures. They also built underground tombs, which, like Egyptian pyramids, were filled with items for the afterlife. The tombs were built of large stone blocks, such as those of Mycenaean fortresses (see Chapter 7), and covered with a mound of earth above a circular wall. By grouping these tombs, the Etruscans built cities of the dead, called *necropolises,* that were separate from the regular cities.

Though the Etruscan civilization was wiped out to make way for Rome with a capital "R," much of its architecture was admired and copied by the Romans.

The Romans: Structural Revolution

From 753 B.C. to A.D. 476, Rome grew from a small town on the banks of the Tiber River into the capital of a vast empire stretching from northern England to northern Africa. Eventually, a fifth of the world's people would come under Roman control. They would experience grandeur on a new scale with public structures that were inspired by the Greek classical tradition.

The Romans based their architecture on the Doric, Ionic, and Corinthian orders of the Greeks. They also added the Tuscan order, which had been developed by the Etruscans, and the *Composite* order, which combines Ionic volutes with Corinthian acanthus leaves. The first example of the Composite order appears in the Arch of Titus in Rome (A.D. 82).

But the Romans didn't just imitate the Greeks: They advanced the classical style with new construction techniques that allowed them to build architecture of great size and complexity. The Romans' structural inventions — the arch, the vault, the dome, and concrete — were revolutionary, changing architecture forever.

Entering in style: The arch

Like the wheel, the masonry arch was one of civilization's great discoveries. It enabled architects to span great distances with small, wedge-shaped units of stone or brick, called *voussoirs,* that were in contrast to the huge pieces of stone required to construct the Parthenon.

Unlike a stone lintel (see Chapter 6), which is limited in its resistance to heavy loads, an arch has a lot of compressive strength — that is, it can support a lot of weight. It can hold up a wall while framing a window or doorway.

The Egyptians and Greeks experimented with the arch, but the Romans were the first to realize its full potential. They built variations on the curved structural support in brick and stone to create aqueducts, triumphal gateways, and buildings that enclosed vast interiors.

By extending an arch along its depth, the Romans created a *barrel vault.* By intersecting two barrel vaults, they invented a *cross* or *groin vault,* which opens a space in four directions. These vaults were used to create grand interiors for large buildings that combined cultural and recreational uses, such as the Baths of Caracalla. Built by the Emperor Caracalla, the bathing palace included swimming pools, a gymnasium, a library, and lecture halls.

Concrete: The first imitation stone

In erecting these vaulted structures, the Romans pioneered the use of a new material — *concrete.* In the third or second century B.C., they discovered that combining volcanic ash — called *pozzolana* — and lime with sand, water, and gravel creates a chemical reaction that bonds the materials tightly together. When dry, the mixture creates a rocklike material that is strong, cheap, and easy to use. And unlike real stone, concrete doesn't have to be quarried, cut, or transported. The Romans were able to mix it on the building site and cast it in a mold of virtually any shape.

Using concrete arches and vaults, the Romans created the first major public spaces of consequence: from theaters and temples to huge arenas for chariot races and gladiator fights. Their buildings weren't designed to be seen as independent, freestanding objects in the landscape (such as Greek temples or Egyptian pyramids) but as images within larger settings representing the power and majesty of the Roman Empire.

Take me out to the forum . . .

At the center of all Roman cities was a large open square called a *forum*. A descendent of the Greek *agora*, which was a marketplace or assembly place, this space started out as a marketplace and developed into an elaborate grouping of civic buildings. Its rectangular space, often organized around a central avenue, was much more ordered than its Greek counterpart. Dominated by a temple at one end, it was bordered by buildings that ranged from meeting halls to meat markets.

Rome had 17 forums at one time, with the oldest being the Forum Romanum, or "Roman Forum." Surrounded by the Palatine, Capitoline, and Esquiline hills, it was redesigned by successive emperors, including Julius Caesar. By the fourth century, the Forum Romanum had ten temples, three basilicas, four triumphal arches, and numerous monuments and ceremonial spaces.

Amphitheaters and circuses

Thrills, chills, and spills — the Romans were so fond of staging contests of daring and ruthlessness that they designed special buildings for them. Gladiator and animal fights were held in an arena called the *amphitheater*. It was yet another type of building adapted from the Greeks. Instead of terracing the seats into a hillside, the Romans tiered them within freestanding, oval buildings enclosed by walls of arches called *arcades*.

The Colosseum

The Colosseum was not the first amphitheater in Rome — temporary wooden ones had been erected in the forum — but it was the largest. It was a masterpiece of architecture and engineering. You can see it in Figure 8-7. It was begun by Emperor Vespasian in A.D. 70 and completed by Emperor Titus a decade later. Named after a colossal statue of Nero located nearby, the Colosseum could seat up to 50,000 spectators on three tiers of stone benches and a top gallery of wooden bleachers for women, children, and the lower classes. Its design, in turn, inspired smaller stone amphitheaters at Verona, Nimes, and Arles in southern France — and sports stadiums throughout the ages.

Figure 8-7:
Colosseum,
Rome, A.D.
70-80.

Photo courtesy of GreatBuildings.com © Kevin Matthews.

The Colosseum had concrete vaults resting on heavy limestone piers. It was one of the first buildings to use standardized parts — all the stairs are the same width, for example. The 160-foot-high walls were covered in stone and decorated according to the classical orders: Doric on the bottom, Ionic on the second story, and Corinthian on the third and fourth levels. The combination of orders on a single building was a Roman invention. The half-columns and entablatures framing the arches on the first three stories and the flattened columns, called *pilasters,* at the top were also Roman inventions.

The Colosseum was built over a labyrinth of tunnels, passageways, and rooms for the battling gladiators and wild animals. A system of pulleys and lifts allowed stage sets, combatants, and animals to be hoisted directly into the sand-covered, movable wooden floor of the arena. At the top of the building were *velarium,* canvas awnings, supported by a ring of wooden masts, used to shade the audience from the sun. Crowd control was also considered: People entered and exited the building through 76 different entrances. Each entrance had its own stairway to the seating.

Gladiator fights were banned in A.D. 404, but animal shows continued to be staged in the Colosseum until A.D. 523. After the fall of the Roman Empire, the Colosseum was used as a fortress, a bullfight arena, and a religious shrine. It became a tourist site in the late 1800s.

Circus Maximus

A special stadium was designed for chariot and horse races. The stadium, referred to as a *circus,* was a long, U-shaped building with stalls called *carceres* situated at the end where the chariots entered. The racecourse was divided down the center by a low wall, or *spina,* with columns to mark the turning point. Rome had a number of circuses, with the largest being the Circus Maximus. It measured about 2,000 feet long and 650 feet wide, with seating for 250,000 spectators.

Baths: Pampering in style

It's been said that the Romans took their bathing more seriously than their gods. You may agree with this saying after viewing the sumptuous establishments that were built for washing, as well as exercising, entertaining, and conducting business. Decorated in marbles and mosaics, the baths were organized with an elaborate sequence of rooms designed to ensure that the Romans were the cleanest of the ancients. From a changing room called the *apodyterium,* the bather entered a hot room, the *caldarium,* containing a hot bath. In the winter, he or she (men and women bathed at different times of the day) could enter a moderately heated room called the *tepidarium.* Furnaces that radiated hot air through hollow tiles and bricks in the walls and floors heated these spaces. In the summer, Romans cooled off in a room called the *frigidarium.* This room had a cold-water swimming pool. After a bath, bathers were rubbed with oil, which was thenscraped off with a tool known as a *strigil.*

The two largest bath houses — or *thermae* — in Rome were the Baths of Caracalla (A.D. 188–216) and Diocletian (A.D. 298–306). At 285,000 square feet, the Baths of Caracalla accommodated 1,600 bathers within vaulted interiors organized around a great central hall. The Baths of Diocletian were even larger. The main building held about 3,200 bathers and, like Caracalla, was surrounded by gardens and exercise rooms.

These grand spaces, even in ruins, would continue to inspire architects for thousands of years. In the sixteenth century, Michelangelo turned the vaulted frigidarium in the Baths of Diocletian into the church of Santa Maria degli Angeli. Centuries later, New York architect Charles McKim based his 1902 design for the Pennsylvania Railway Station in Manhattan on the Baths of Caracalla.

Temples in the round

Like the Greeks, the Romans built rectangular temples surrounded by columns to house their deities. The Romans, however, enclosed their structures with a room called a *cella* and added a flight of steps to one end. This type of construction often required the builders to attach the columns around the perimeter to the walls of the cella. A good example of this design is the Maison Carrée in Nîmes, France.

Temples were also built in circular form. The most famous is the Pantheon — Temple of all the Gods — in Rome. It is the greatest structure of Roman antiquity to have survived largely intact. Built by Hadrian between A.D. 118 and 128, it occupied the site of an earlier temple constructed by Agrippa.

The entrance to the Pantheon looked like the usual temple front, with a raised portico of columns and pediment. Behind it was something much more spectacular: an enormous circular room covered by a dome made of overlapping concrete rings. In the center was a hole, or *oculus,* 27 feet in diameter, which allowed sunlight to stream into the center of the room.

Basilicas: Meeting halls into churches

The *basilica* was one of the most important Roman building types. It was often a part of the forum, and it assumed many different functions — covered meeting place, courthouse, marketplace, and lecture hall, for example. A rectangular building with a peaked roof, the basilica was twice as long as it was wide. Inside, two or four rows of columns formed a central space with narrow aisles on the sides. The columns supported a roof constructed of wooden triangular braces called *trusses* — an alternative to the vault for spanning a large space.

It's no coincidence that the design of the basilica resembled a church — much of early Christian architecture is modeled on the Roman basilica.

The most famous basilica in Rome was the Basilica of Constantine, or Maxentius. Begun in A.D. 308 by Emperor Maxentius, its imposing structure of massive concrete piers, marble columns, and barrel vaults bordered the Roman Forum. Its ruins inspired Michelangelo in his designs for the Basilica of St. Peter's in Rome.

Chapter 9

Domes, Arches, and Vaults, Oh My: Byzantine and Medieval Architecture

● ●

In This Chapter

▶ Byzantine domes and other structures

▶ Medieval churches and castles

▶ Romanesque churches

▶ Gothic cathedrals

● ●

During the third century, the Roman Empire experienced a long economic and political decline. Its capital shifted eastward to Byzantium, which Roman emperor Constantine renamed Constantinople (now Istanbul, Turkey) after himself. As west met east, architectural innovations flourished in churches with interiors that promoted a sense of mystery. Middle Eastern decorative motifs and Roman basilicas were combined to create an original architectural style called *Byzantine* (even Constantine didn't change the name).

During the reign of emperor Justinian I (A.D. 527–565), Constantinople became a beacon of Christianity and a cultural center for all of Europe. Over the next 900 years, while barbaric tribes pillaged Europe, the city dazzled the world with its shimmering interiors of color and light.

Early Christian Churches

The innovations of Byzantine architecture grew out of the ideals of Christianity, which began as a secretive religion that was practiced in underground rooms and homes. In A.D. 313, the Roman emperor Constantine gave Christians the right to worship openly; they began building modest churches based on timber-roofed basilicas (see Chapter 8).

Emperor Constantine made Christianity the official religion of the Roman Empire in A.D. 325, prompting the building of new monumental churches (many in Rome) over the burial places of the saints to whom each church was dedicated. One of the most innovative churches was the first St. Peter's, which was torn down in 1505 to make way for the domed cathedral, also called St. Peter's, that now stands on the site.

The first St. Peter's introduced several new design elements to religious architecture. On the front of the church was an open-air porch called a *narthex,* where people could gather to hear the worship service. Inside, two aisles and a main worship area called a *nave* led to a vast transverse space at the end of the building, called a *transept,* that projected beyond the aisles to small chambers. This T-shaped arrangement focused attention on the *apse,* the semicircular space at the end of the church where the clergy sat. It foreshadowed the cross-shaped plans of Romanesque churches and Gothic cathedrals.

Aspiring to New Heights: Byzantine Churches

In A.D. 330, after Emperor Constantine moved the capital of the Roman Empire to Byzantium, a new style of mega-church emerged to entice worshippers with dazzling feats of engineering.

Where early Christian churches were laid out horizontally, leading to the apse at one end, Byzantine churches were focused inward on the middle. The idea was to celebrate God as the center of the universe. On one side of the church was the altar and clergy, on the opposite side was the entrance, and on the other two sides were spaces for the congregation.

Byzantine architects called attention to the center of the church by crowning it with a shallow dome. The Romans had previously used domes to impressive effect by positioning them over circular rooms so that the transition between the dome and its supports was seamless.

The challenge that Byzantine architects faced was how to place a dome over a square base — rather than above a round room, as in the Pantheon (see Chapter 8). This juxtaposition of different geometric forms required supports between the round base of the dome and the square walls. One solution was to support the dome with stacked arches, called a *squinch,* in the inner corners of the square walls.

But Byzantine architects came up with a better idea — one that was as innovative as the Roman arch and vault. Between the round base of the dome and the square walls, they inserted curved triangular panels known as *pendentives* (see Figure 9-1). These rounded supports blended into the dome elegantly to create a continuously curved surface.

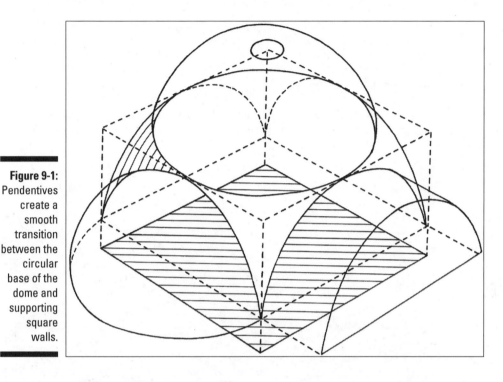

Figure 9-1:
Pendentives
create a
smooth
transition
between the
circular
base of the
dome and
supporting
square
walls.

This great structural achievement was made to appear magically ethereal inside Byzantine churches, which were deceptively plain on the outside. Glittering glass and gold mosaics covered the insides of the domes, colored marble was applied to the walls and floors, and intricately carved capitals (see Chapter 8) topped the columns. These richly decorated, luminous surfaces seem to dissolve the heavy structure and communicate the message of Christ as the "light of the world."

A new type of dome: Hagia Sophia

The most spectacular church built during the Byzantine Empire is the *Hagia Sophia* (Greek for "holy wisdom"). It was constructed by the emperor Justinian from A.D. 532–537 as the new cathedral of Constantinople. Instead of hiring local architects, the emperor employed two scientists, Anthemius of Tralles and his nephew Isidorus of Miletus, to design this huge edifice (see Figure 9-2).

The pair devised an ingenious structure that would set a precedent for domed architecture in Europe and Russia. Anthemius and Isidorus began the project by dividing the square-shaped church into three rectangles to create a wide central space and narrow aisles. In the middle of the church, they erected a square of stone piers to support a vast brick dome — its diameter only 8 feet less than that of St. Paul's Cathedral in London, which was built centuries later.

From the tops of the piers, Anthemius and Isidorus built four enormous brick arches. In the spaces between the corners of the arches and the dome above, they extended pendentives to form a circular base for the dome.

Instead of piercing the dome with a round opening, like the Pantheon, they set a row of small arched windows into its base and reinforced the dome with shallow ribs and buttresses. Smaller half domes were placed against the arches to help absorb the structural forces in the building.

Figure 9-2:
Hagia
Sophia,
Istanbul,
Turkey, A.D.
532-537.

Photo courtesy of GreatBuildings.com © Howard Davis.

Covered in mosaics, the dome appeared to float miraculously, without visible support, above the center of the church. Procopius, a historian who observed the construction, summed up the effect when he wrote that it looked like it was hanging from heaven by a chain.

The daring structure took only five years to complete, but its hasty construction may have made it unstable. The dome was destroyed during an earthquake in the sixth century — its replacement partially collapsed centuries later. In A.D. 1453, the Turks conquered Constantinople and turned Hagia Sophia into a mosque with four minarets.

Son of Sophia: Saint Mark's Cathedral, Venice

Anyone who's traveled to Venice has no doubt stood among flocks of pigeons to admire the domed cathedral at the edge of Piazza San Marco. The present church is the third on the site — it was begun in A.D. 1042. It incorporates many later additions.

Although it was built more than five centuries after Hagia Sophia, Saint Mark's Cathedral shares much in common with the earlier Byzantine church. A dome marks its center; the interior structure, sheathed in marbles and mosaics, shimmers with color and light. But in the Venetian church, space is clearly divided into discrete units — it doesn't flow from the center, as in Byzantine churches. Each end of the church has its own dome. This separation of a large building into fragmented units was a hallmark of medieval European architecture.

The Middle Ages: Not as Dark as You Think

From the completion of Hagia Sophia until the crowning of Charlemagne as Holy Roman Emperor in A.D. 800, few significant buildings — or at least, buildings that still exist — were constructed in Western Europe. Yet many Roman structures remained standing, reminding Dark Age "barbarians" of the great achievements of the classical world.

These antique relics provided inspiration for buildings completed during the ninth and tenth centuries. One of the best examples of a building influenced by Roman design is the Palatine Chapel (A.D. 796–804) built next to Charlemagne's palace in Aachen, Germany. It was designed by architect Odo of Metz, who copied the octagonal plan of St. Vitale, a sixth-century Byzantine-style church in Ravenna, Italy, that Charlemagne had seen on his way back from Rome. To span the spaces at the perimeter, Odo used barrel vaults like the ones in the Roman Colosseum. Ancient classical artifacts were also incorporated; the columns in between the upper gallery arches were recycled from antique imperial buildings in Italy.

To impress visitors, the chapel's entrance was placed below a huge curved niche that was located in between two towers. This type of monumental façade became a common feature of medieval cathedrals.

Early insurance policies: Medieval keeps and castles

Charlemagne attempted to bring order to Western Europe, but after his death in A.D. 814, the fighting among nomadic tribes continued for another two centuries. To protect their lives and their lands, kings and barons built castles and fortifications. At first, they dug a ditch around a hill and built a *stockade* — a defensive enclosure made of wooden posts — around the top to make the area harder to attack. This idea gave way to what are called the *motte-and-bailey castles* of the eleventh century. (See Figure 9-3.)

The *motte* was an earthen mound, encircled by a trench and stockade, with a wooden fortress at the top. Soon, stone towers called *keeps* began to replace wooden ones at the corners of the fortress. Situated below the motte was the *bailey,* a fenced-in courtyard to protect livestock. The Tower of London, built between A.D. 1087–1097, replaced a motte-and-bailey at the corner of an old Roman wall.

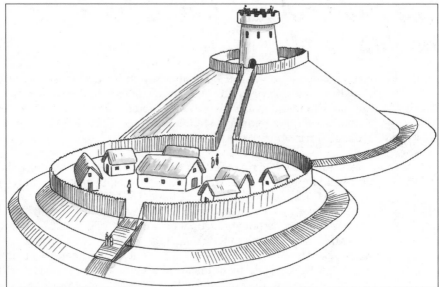

Figure 9-3:
A motte-
and-bailey
castle.

The fine line: Insurance or trap?

Eventually, castle fortifications were expanded to defend entire towns. Walls incorporating moats, towers, gates, and keeps were built to repel attacks from any angle. In the thirteenth century, Carcassonne in southern France was constructed with outer and inner stone walls to protect the castle, cathedral, and other buildings along the town's winding streets. The concept was also applied to guarding whole regions — much of the Great Wall of China, which stretches for 6,400 kilometers, was built during the Ming Dynasty, from the fourteenth through the seventeenth centuries, with towers and ramparts to prevent attacks from Mongol tribes (see Chapter 16).

Roman Glory Lives On: Romanesque Churches

Medieval architects did not think of their designs as part of a "middle age" between classical antiquity and the Renaissance. They believed their designs were a revival of Roman ideas. In fact, the next important developments in European architecture, starting around A.D. 1000, were called *Romanesque* — literally, "ancient Roman-like."

The force behind Romanesque architecture was a new religious fervor. It was expressed in mass pilgrimages to distant shrines and in the Crusades (an eleventh- through thirteenth-century military effort to recover the Holy Land from the Muslims). New churches were built on the pilgrimage routes to house relics and the growing numbers of worshippers and clergy who flocked to them.

The architects and builders of the pilgrimage churches gradually replaced T-shaped plans with cross-shaped plans formed by wings called *transepts* that extend beyond either side of the central space, or *nave*. These extended transepts and the *choir* (the space at the end of the nave behind the altar) are what changed the "T" into a "cross." Square, octagonal, or circular towers were placed over the crossing of the nave and transepts. On the sides of the church were covered walkways, called *ambulatories* or *cloisters* that linked the worship space to the smaller buildings of the adjacent monastery. To build these structures, Romanesque architects used Roman arches and vaults to support even larger spans.

Roman barrel and groin vaults held up the thick walls of the central nave and the lower aisles on either side of the nave (see Figure 9-4). The walls of the nave were divided into three parts:

- An *arcade,* or row of arches, on the ground floor screening the aisles on either side of the nave
- An upper story gallery, called a *triforium,* above the arcade
- A row of windows at the top, called a *clerestory*

Unlike early Christian and Byzantine buildings, which were fairly uniform in design, Romanesque churches differed according to the region where they were built. Architectural style was determined by individual monastic orders seeking to reflect their beliefs. Increasingly, larger churches called *cathedrals* were built as the seat of the bishop. Builders adapted the design of cathedrals to the needs of the local clergy as well as to the indigenous climate and available materials, creating regional variations on the Romanesque style.

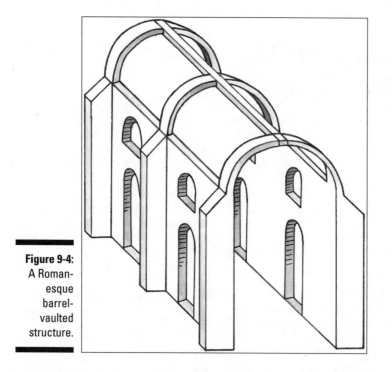

Figure 9-4:
A Romanesque barrel-vaulted structure.

It's not the size of the building that determines whether the structure is a cathedral. Technically, a cathedral is simply a structure that houses the *cathera,* which is the bishop's throne. Under this definition, cathedrals have been around since the creation of the first bishop in early Christianity.

Scaring them straight: Cathedral of Autun

In the Burgundy province of France, the Cathedral of Autun, begun in A.D. 1120, shows the influence of ancient Rome on the fluted pilasters and piers around its nave. The architects didn't have to go far to learn about Roman architecture; Autun was once a Roman city, and it still had remains of antique classical structures.

The column capitals and main façade of the church are embellished with realistic sculptures carved by the medieval artist Gislebertus. As in many Romanesque churches, the artwork is meant to teach the masses about Christian ethics — its scenes of heaven and hell are quite dramatic.

Lean on me: The Cathedral of Pisa

The Cathedral of Pisa, built from A.D. 1063 to 1092, exemplifies the exuberant decoration of Romanesque churches built in the Tuscan region of central Italy. Banded in red and white marble, it is covered with tiers of arcades and topped by a dome. Built next to it is a circular building used for baptisms, and the famous bell tower. Before it was finished in A.D. 1350, the tower began to lean as a result of an insufficient foundation. The builders tried to compensate by adding a bell chamber, set at a different angle, to the top of the tower. A new foundation was laid recently to stabilize the tilted tower.

Vaulting to new heights: Cathedral of Durham

English Romanesque architecture is more massive and austere when compared to the other variations of the Romanesque style. It is often called *Norman,* after William I of Normandy who came to power in A.D. 1066. Built in stone, English churches were the first to develop sophisticated vaulting.

One of the most technically innovative designs was the Cathedral of Durham, begun in A.D. 1093. Instead of incorporating the rounded barrel vaults and domes of churches in Italy and France, the cathedral was supported by a variation on the ancient Roman groin vault (Figure 9-5 shows a buttressed groin vault). In this variation, each bay of the nave was topped by four vaults that were divided by intersecting, pointed arches and strengthened by stone ribs. This type of structure is called a *ribbed vault*. See Figure 9-5.

The Super Church: Gothic Cathedrals

By A.D. 1200, Christianity had become a major force in the civilized world. Cathedrals were built in record numbers all over Europe. During the thirteenth and fourteenth centuries, their architecture became much larger and more magnificent to reflect an increasingly stable and affluent civilization. The goal was to build as high and as light as possible. This new type of structurally daring architecture came to be known as *Gothic*. (See the sidebar called "A barbaric style?")

France gives birth to the Gothic

From the mid-1100s to 1300, France witnessed a burst of building that ushered in the glories of Gothic architecture. The style, however, didn't originate in the cathedrals of Paris or Bourges but in the renovation of the church at Saint Denis, a town north of Paris.

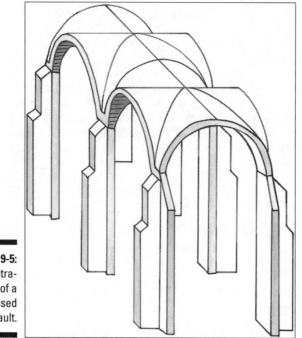

Figure 9-5:
An illustration of a buttressed groin vault.

Suger's Saint Denis

The mastermind behind this groundbreaking project was Abbot Suger, a friend of the French king and an architecture buff. He remodeled his church at Saint Denis (1135–1144) by replacing thick walls and small windows with slender supports and abundant glass that made the stone structure appear light, transcendent, and almost weightless.

Notre Dame's stone symphony

The light, transcendent, and weightless design elements (see preceding section) were then applied on a monumental scale to the Cathedral of Notre Dame in Paris, built from 1163 to 1250. Rising to a height of 110 feet, it was called "a vast symphony of stone" by French author Victor Hugo, who immortalized the Gothic monument in his novel, *The Hunchback of Notre Dame*. Tall stained glass windows, delicate arches, ribbed vaults, and a compact plan contributed to a feeling of spiritual uplift.

A phoenix rises from the ashes: Chartres Cathedral

The leap from Romanesque to Gothic continued in Chartres Cathedral outside Paris. The movement started when an existing church was destroyed by fire in 1194, leaving only the towers and west façade. Instead of restoring the cathedral to its original appearance, the architect rebuilt the cathedral in the latest Gothic style.

A barbaric style?

The delicate, daring architecture that emerged in Europe during the twelfth and thirteenth centuries wasn't always admired. In fact, Renaissance critics derided it as lacking classical lines, proportions, and restraint. They disparagingly referred to medieval architecture as "Gothic" after the Goths, the northern Teutonic tribesmen who had invaded ancient Rome and were considered to be uncultured barbarians.

Unfortunately, we don't know the name of this superb master, but he certainly was one of the more imaginative designers of the period. His bold ideas transformed the cathedral into a soaring space filled with light that displays all the elements of early Gothic architecture.

To follow the original Romanesque foundations, the new vaults had to cover a space far wider than usual. The architect solved this problem by erecting ribbed vaults on tall piers and bracing them on the exterior with flying buttresses (see "Harnessing the forces: Flying buttress" later in this chapter). This structure allowed the amount of stone on the walls to be reduced and the size and number of windows to be increased.

Clerestories, tall windows at the top of the walls, are divided into twin arch shapes, called *lancets,* and a multicolored rose window placed in the west front. The 176 windows are filled with brilliant blue and red stained glass, which was called flaming jewelry by Victorian art critic John Ruskin.

Deadlines? What deadlines?

Gothic cathedrals were certainly bigger, taller, and more fantastic than earlier Romanesque churches and classical temples. They were built to impress worshippers and rival clergy, as well as to symbolize the growing prosperity and civic pride of European cities.

Adorned with stained glass, sculpture, metalwork, and painting, a cathedral was an ambitious, complex undertaking that took decades to complete. The construction site was like a city, with housing and workshops for the scores of masons and artisans who collaborated on the project. The "master" of these workshops acted as architect, engineer, and builder all rolled into one.

Different regional flavors

Like the Romanesque style, Gothic architecture differed according to region. In the north, churches were higher, with steeply pitched roofs and large windows decorated with stained glass. Further south, where the sun was stronger, the roofs were flatter, windows and doors were smaller, and painted decoration was more common.

Underlying the regional variations of Gothic architecture was a common attitude toward structural virtuosity. Arches, vaults, and other structural elements were pushed to their limits to produce awe-inspiring, otherworldly effects. Like the Byzantine church of Hagia Sophia (see the section, "A new type of dome: Hagia Sophia" earlier in this chapter), the vaulted, decorated interior of a Gothic cathedral looked as though it had been created by a supernatural force or miracle. The following sections discuss some of the key elements of Gothic architecture and how they work.

The Arc de Versatility: Pointed arch

The main difference between Romanesque and Gothic architecture is the arch. Except for rare instances, such as the pointed arches of Durham Cathedral, Romanesque arches are rounded and can only be supported by piers arranged in a square bay. Gothic arches are pointed and can rise from rectangular, as well as square, bays. They follow the ideal curvature of an arch so that lines of force run exactly through the center. The design means that a pointed arch can be thinner than a round arch and varied in proportion of width to height. By changing the arch's dimensions, architects were able to create wider and taller structures.

A Norman export: Ribbed vault

Pointed arches led to a wide variety of vault designs. The earliest pointed arches were developed in England in the late eleventh century (see preceding section). They were divided into four compartments by diagonal stone ribs, called a *quadripartite vault.* By introducing extra ribs, called *tierceron,* the vaults could be divided into smaller sections. Connecting the main ribs with even smaller ribs allowed intricate geometric patterns to emerge. The most elaborate patterns were created by *fan vaults,* which became common to English cathedrals in the fifteenth and sixteenth centuries. These lacy networks of ribs had their own *bosses* — decorative medallions that covered the awkward intersection between ribs of different sizes.

Harnessing the forces: Flying buttress

As arches and vaults became higher, wider, and more complex, they required extra reinforcement to counter their outward and downward thrust on the walls. To avoid thickening the walls, Gothic masons designed stone reinforcements called *buttresses* to brace the arches and vaults. At first, the buttresses were simple stone piers. Then they grew larger and heavier, and became more richly ornamented with carved decorations that also played a structural role. *Pinnacles,* upright elements with spires, were added to the tops of the buttresses to exert pressure on the vaults and help counteract their outward thrust.

By the thirteenth century, the French had developed buttresses to transmit structural forces rather than resist them. Called *flying buttresses,* these powerful exterior arches transferred the thrust from the vaults inside the cathedral to the building foundations (see Figure 9-6). Flying buttresses led to thinner walls, larger windows, and higher vaults, as evident in the cathedrals of Amien, France, and Cologne, Germany.

Figure 9-6:
Wall section through cathedral showing flying buttress.

Roses, wheels, and spokes: Gothic tracery

Another important innovation during the Gothic period was the decorated window. This element became ever larger, making cathedrals of the fifteenth and sixteenth centuries seem more glass than stone. Gothic windows were divided by decorative patterns of stone called *tracery.* Many pieces of stained and painted glass depicting Biblical scenes were set within this stonework. Tracery was first applied in Romanesque churches to create circular wheel windows. The circular windows developed into rose windows during the Gothic period. Radiating spokes were replaced by an elaborate naturalistic tracery of glass petals and rosettes, and filled with brilliantly colored glass.

Early Gothic tracery that fills windows with large sections of stone is often referred to as *plate tracery*. Later designs of thin, branching stone sections are called *bar tracery*. In English cathedrals of the fifteenth and sixteenth centuries, tracery became more vertical and refined: It was called Perpendicular in contrast to the flowing lines of the earlier Decorative style.

Chapter 10

Beauty Meets Mathematics and Drama: From Renaissance to Rococo

During the remarkable period in Western civilization known as the Renaissance, human reason took its place alongside religious teachings. Architects no longer viewed themselves as servants of God. Instead, they viewed themselves as individuals capable of shaping buildings in harmony with nature and the human body.

Beginning in the fifteenth century, architects applied new theories — based in science and mathematics — to generate ideal proportions based on geometric shapes. These rational systems were combined with classical forms, copied from ancient Greece and Rome, to create dignified, orderly buildings.

In the seventeenth and eighteenth centuries, a new, more exuberant spirit overtook architecture. The regular, rational and restrained architecture of the Renaissance gave way to the swirling, opulent designs of the Baroque and Rococo. The theatricality of this architecture, however, had a practical purpose. It was meant to entice worshippers back to the Catholic church and symbolize the power of the monarchy.

The Renaissance: A Classical Revival with Some Mathematical Stuff

The Renaissance began in Florence, a prosperous city-state that fancied itself as the new Athens. In the early 1400s, Florentine civic pride was translated into buildings that represented humanistic ideals.

This interest in humanism grew from a new appreciation of the classical world of ancient Greece and Rome. So it's not surprising that the Renaissance originated in Italy — the center of the great Roman Empire — and spread westward to France and Germany, and then to England and Spain. During this period, buildings were based on simple geometric shapes — the square and circle — which were meant to symbolize ultimate perfection. The symmetrical forms were embellished with architectural features borrowed from antiquity.

Renaissance architects were not the first to borrow elements from ancient Greece and Rome, but they viewed their efforts as more authentic than earlier revivals. At the same time, they put their own spin on classical architecture by changing the sizes and proportions of the columns, arches, and ornamentation invented centuries earlier. These variations were based on mathematical relationships and the new science of perspective.

Compact and elegantly proportioned, Renaissance buildings stand in stark contrast to the extravagant engineering feats of Gothic cathedrals (described in Chapter 9). They are also much smaller. Visitors are often disappointed the first time they see Brunelleschi's Pazzi Chapel or Bramante's Roman Tempietto. The two chapels aren't nearly as impressive as a Gothic cathedral. But keep in mind that these human-scaled, symmetrical buildings are meant to represent human intellect as much as the power of God.

Engineering spatial harmony: Filippo Brunelleschi

Pioneering the new Renaissance style was Filippo Brunelleschi (1377–1446), a Florentine architect who started out as a painter, sculptor, and goldsmith. All the elements that define Renaissance architecture — symmetrical forms, proportions that relate one element to another, and the application of scientific perspective — first appeared in his work. In fact, many consider him the father of Renaissance architecture.

Brunelleschi had studied science and mathematics. In 1415, he discovered *linear perspective,* an illusion of three-dimensional space in which parallel lines meet at a vanishing point (see Chapter 5, Figure 5-4).

Brunelleschi's background in science and mathematics came in handy when devising an ingenious way to complete the dome over the Florence Cathedral. To reduce the weight, he drew on Roman construction techniques from a study of the Pantheon dome (see Chapter 8) to create a double shell of brick that tapers toward the top. Each course of brick supports the next, eliminating the need for scaffolding. Built over an octagonal drum, the pointed dome is buttressed from the inside by ribs and metal ties. It also gains strength from the herringbone pattern of its brickwork and the lantern at the top, which prevents the structure from spreading.

One of the earliest projects to show Brunelleschi's Renaissance inventions is the Foundling Hospital, which he designed with a classical façade. Soon after that project was underway, Brunelleschi designed a sacristy for the Romanesque church of San Lorenzo. The sacristy's mathematical ordering of space, emphasized by geometric patterns of dark-gray stone on light-colored walls, radically departed from the flowing interiors of Gothic churches. Brunelleschi also used this technique in the Pazzi Chapel, begun in about 1430, to call attention to its repeated barrel vaults and domes.

Nearly a century later, the ideas of Brunelleschi were further developed in Rome by architect Donato d'Agnolo Lazzari.

When size doesn't matter: Bramante's gift

Architect Donato d'Agnolo Lazzari (1444–1514), known as Bramante, was the foremost architect of the Italian High Renaissance. Born in Urbino, Bramante began his career in Milan and then moved to Rome in 1499 to spend the last 15 years of his life. Bramante's greatest achievement was to sculpt his symmetrical buildings with gutsy classical details; they created a dramatic play of light and shadow that made even the smallest buildings appear monumental. A good example is his Tempietto (1502), or "little temple," at Saint Peter in Montorio, Rome. Although it is tiny, this structure is one of the greatest buildings of the High Renaissance.

You can see the Tempietto in Figure 10-1. The round chapel was planned as the centerpiece of a circular courtyard, which was never built. The colonnade, strongly projecting moldings, and deeply recessed niches below its dome convey a weightiness that belies the building's diminutive size.

In 1506, Bramante was employed by Pope Julius II to design a new cathedral to replace the old basilica of St. Peter's. He proposed four identical façades topped by a huge dome. The construction was so slow that, in 1514, when Bramante died, only four piers at the crossing had been constructed. Michelangelo, who admired his plan, completed the basilica in a newer style.

Figure 10-1:
The
Tempietto,
San Pietro
in Montorio,
Rome, 1502,
by Donato
Bramante.

Photo courtesy of GreatBuildings.com © Donald Corner and Jenny Young.

For do-it-yourselfers: Treatises and pattern books

Where medieval craftsmen passed down their knowledge through on-the-job training, Renaissance architects and builders studied treatises and books of architectural drawings. These publications spread quickly throughout Europe, allowing architects in England or Spain to design in the latest style even though they had never seen a Renaissance or ancient classical building. Translated into many languages, the architecture books were based on ancient manuscripts that illustrated building plans, façades, and details. Renaissance architects used these drawings as inspiration for their own classical designs.

The most influential of the publications was a 10-volume treatise written by the Roman architect Vitruvius (see Chapter 8). It was discovered in 1414. The treatise soon led Renaissance architects to write and publish their own rule books.

Making it a profession: Alberti writes his own commandments

Vitruvius's treatise, the Ten Books of Architecture (see Chapter 8), served as the model for an important ten-volume text written by Genoa-born architect Leon Battista Alberti, who was also a brilliant theorist, historian, and scientist. Published in 1485, Alberti's book offered practical construction advice along with erudite observations on classical culture. It helped to promote architecture from an artisan's trade to a profession by calling for such rigorous intellectual requirements as mathematics, geometry, and philosophy.

Using his own stuff: Palladio turns houses into temples

Another popular pattern book was *The Four Books of Architecture,* published in 1570 by Venetian architect Andrea Palladio. In his treatise, Palladio included his own designs along with theories based on his study of antiquity. The book had a profound influence on architecture in England and other countries for more than two centuries. It inspired Thomas Jefferson's designs for his home, Monticello, and the University of Virginia.

Palladio wasn't just a theorist; trained as a stonemason, he enjoyed building many types of structures — palaces, churches, and public buildings. His greatest achievement was his design of a series of *villas* (large farmhouses), which were variations on a theme. Almost all these symmetrical structures were constructed between Venice and Vicenza in the 1550s and 1560s. Palladio organized each of his villas as a central building block flanked by side pavilions. He then changed the sizes and details of these elements according to location. One of his greatest designs is the Villa Rotonda (1566–1571), a grand hilltop home near Vicenza. Each side of its domed square block is faced with an identical porch and sculpture-topped pediment. By using these porticos, Palladio transformed the house into a classical temple.

Making it their own: The Renaissance in France and England

As the Renaissance spread throughout Europe, each region infused the classical language with its own national flavor. France was the first country to catch on to the style. In the sixteenth century, the French applied the style to palaces and castles called *chateaux*. One of the most important French Renaissance architects was Philibert de L'Orme, who studied in Italy and published an architectural treatise in 1569.

English architects adopted the Renaissance style much later (partly due to King Henry VIII's break with Rome and the Catholic Church — and applied it with a vengeance in the seventeenth century. Leading this revolution was a royal surveyor named Inigo Jones (1573–1652), who admired Palladio's teachings. He traveled to France and Italy to study ancient monuments firsthand, as well as the Renaissance buildings they had inspired. When he returned to England, Jones had developed his own style. His plainly dignified Queen's House in Greenwich, begun in 1616, and Banqueting Hall in Whitehall (1619–1622) mark a radical change from the half-timber, fussy decoration of earlier Jacobean and Elizabethan architecture in England.

Bridges to the Baroque: Mannerism

In sixteenth century Italy, architects broke away from the pure classicism of the Renaissance to develop a restless style known as *Mannerism*. Though once derided as artificial and even vulgar, this architecture is now recognized as an important transition between the Renaissance and Baroque styles. Pulsating with life, Mannerism is distinguished by exaggerated proportions and inventive combinations of elements that knowingly play with classical rules.

Breakin' the rules: Michelangelo Buonarroti

A genius ahead of his time, Michelangelo (1475–1564) was one of the first to rebel against Renaissance decorum. His unorthodox designs paved the way for Mannerism. Michelangelo began his career in Florence as a painter and sculptor and then took up architecture late in life — at age 70. His earlier artistic endeavors served him well — Michelangelo's buildings are much more forceful, expressive, and sculptural than the designs of Bramante and the earlier Renaissance architects. Instead of following classical rules, Michelangelo adjusted proportions and details to suit his purpose. When he couldn't find the right pediment, entablature, or ornament, he made up his own.

A rebel with a cause: Classicism gets turned on its head

Among Michelangelo's rule-breaking projects in Florence is the Laurentian Library designed in 1524 for Pope Clement VII, a member of the art-loving Medici family, for his vast collection of books. (See Figure 10-2.) When compared to the dignified classical buildings designed by Bramante and other Renaissance architects, Michelangelo's library design looks all wrong: The vestibule is excessively high and narrow, the stairs relentlessly flow downward, the niches around the huge staircase are blank, and the pediment above the door is broken. Michelangelo, of course, knew what he was doing. By using the classical language in a highly unusual way, he makes the visitor feel tense and uneasy, thereby heightening the physical and psychological experience of moving through space.

Running down a masterpiece: St. Peter's Cathedral of Rome

During the last 30 years of his life, Michelangelo worked on his masterpiece, St. Peter's Cathedral in Rome. He simplified Bramante's plan and increased the size of his crossing piers to create a vast interior that belies its size through graceful proportions. When Michelangelo died at age 89, the church was almost finished, apart from its dome and eastern wing. The dome was completed in 1590 by Giacomo della Porta and Domenico Fontana, and the unfinished eastern arm was added by Carlo Maderna in 1607–1612.

Figure 10-2: Laurentian Library in Florence, Italy, 1524, by Michelangelo.

Photo courtesy of GreatBuildings.com © Donald Corner and Jenny Young.

Here Come the Drama Kings: The Baroque

Where the Renaissance appealed to the intellect, the Baroque engaged the emotions through dramatic and illusionary effects. The Baroque ideal was to show that the individual was part of a greater social structure and that art and architecture could reach all levels of society. Buildings were no longer designed in isolation. They were to be carefully integrated into their urban surroundings.

Recognition of the Baroque style was an important development within Western history; however, this development is fairly recent. In the nineteenth century, works from the Baroque period were viewed as a strangely curved version of late Renaissance art and architecture. The word *baroque* is probably derived from the Portuguese *barroco,* meaning "an ill-formed or grotesque pearl" — it was first used as a derogatory term.

Emerging in Italy during the first years of the seventeenth century, Baroque architecture was based on a new way of thinking. It began with the reaffirmation of the Catholic Church after the Protestant-led Reformation. The underlying force of the movement, called the *Counter-Reformation,* was the reintroduction of spiritual values and the shared belief in something greater than the individual.

The Catholic Church brought people back into its fold by constructing religious buildings that awed, inspired, and converted their visitors. Architecture, paintings, and sculpture, often produced by the same artist, were integrated into all-encompassing designs to engage the emotions directly and provide concrete imagery of the spiritual world. Curved walls and ceilings, dramatic lighting effects, and sinuous ornamentation conveyed dynamic movement. These theatrical effects were very different from the art and architecture of the Renaissance, in which rational perspective and pure geometrical forms appealed to logic and reason.

The two great architects of the Italian Baroque were Gianlorenzo Bernini (1598–1680) and Francesco Borromini (1599–1667). Both were multitalented perfectionists who worked in Rome and kept the city going strong as the center of European art and architecture.

In the director's chair: Gianlorenzo Bernini

Gianlorenzo Bernini was to the Baroque what Michelangelo had been to the Renaissance. A painter, sculptor, architect, composer, and poet, this artistic giant enjoyed a long career and was revered by his contemporaries. His architecture, like his sculpture, was sensual, dynamic, and more exuberant than Michelangelo's. Like his predecessor, he worked on St. Peter's. Among his projects for the cathedral were a 95-foot-tall bronze-and-marble canopy, or *baldacchino,* over the burial site of the saint, and the Scalia Regia, a ceremonial staircase, between St. Peter's and the papal quarters, that makes the narrow flight of stairs seem longer and grander. Bernini's designs epitomize the opulence and illusionism of Baroque architecture.

Even more dramatic is Bernini's masterpiece in front of St. Peter's: a pair of vast curving colonnades that shape an elliptical space where crowds gather to receive the pope's blessing. The colonnades (1656–1667) were soon copied all over Europe, on both a large and small scale.

Before and after: Rome gets a makeover (no purchase necessary)

Around Rome, Bernini combined his skills in planning, architecture, and sculpture to create several fountains as prominent focal points within the city's most important public squares. His most famous is the Four Rivers Fountain in the Piazza Navona. The fountain's gigantic figures symbolize the four rivers of the world: the Danube in Europe, the Nile in Africa, the Ganges in Asia, and the Plata in the Americas.

At age 60, Bernini built what turned out to be a prototype for Baroque churches, Sant'Andrea al Quirinale (1658–1670). Like his grand colonnades, its interior was shaped into an oval, a more dynamic form than the static circle of the Renaissance.

The play's the thing: multi-disciplinary drama

Bernini's flair for the dramatic — he was also a stage designer and playwright — reached new heights with a chapel for Cardinal Federico Cornaro in the church of Saint Maria della Vittoria in Rome. Its centerpiece is Bernini's magnificent sculpture of the swooning saint, Theresa of Avila. She appears to be illuminated by heavenly rays that seem to emanate from the ceiling fresco but actually come from a window high above the altar. On the side walls, Bernini created an audience for this event by carving marble figures of the Cornaro family watching from balconies. By dispersing the dramatic action, Bernini links the various parts of his design — architecture, sculpture, and painting — into a forceful unity, where there are no clear distinctions between the different elements. The whole effect is like theater.

Turning stone into water: Francesco Borromini

Bernini's rival was Borromini, another genius who, when comparing personalities, was the opposite of Bernini. Where Bernini was effusive, charming, and happy, Borromini was introspective and morose, and he eventually committed suicide. This temperamental contrast is evident in their architecture. Borromini's structures reach further to challenge the concepts of classical architecture. Fluid, rhythmic, and often eccentric, his buildings are more intensely complex than Bernini's boldly simple, unified spaces.

Borromini's first major project was the church of San Carlo alle Quattro Fontane (1634–1682), which caused an immediate sensation in architectural circles. The church is not large, but it appears much bigger due to its pinched oval plan and undulating wall surfaces. Framed by columns and deep entablatures, the walls weave in and out as if formed from rubber rather than stone. This fluid movement marked a radical departure from the stable walls and static spaces of the Renaissance style. And unlike Bernini's spaces, its theatricality is created by architecture alone. Borromini designed the façade with exaggerated, undulating curves that were unparalleled in their freedom, but it wasn't completed until after his death.

Baroque palaces get nature into the act

From its beginnings in Italy, the Baroque spread throughout Europe to assume regional variations in all types of buildings. Its magnificent style of

Architectural models

Architectural models — the three-dimensional representation of buildings in miniature form — have been used for as long as permanent buildings have existed. The earliest known models were built in the ancient Near East, Egypt, and Greece. In the Middle Ages, they were used for studying and testing masonry vaults. By the sixteenth century, models had become standard tools for understanding a design and working out the details of construction.

Models became more prominent during the Renaissance, when the architect assumed a new role as both designer and construction manager.

The models were often constructed of wood, with elaborately carved details to impress prospective clients and win design competitions. Models served as valuable documents in recording construction systems, as well.

During the Baroque period, models became even more important as visual aids that were used to demonstrate the spatial complexity and dramatic lighting that came to characterize seventeenth- and eighteenth-century interiors. Many models could be taken apart to show the spectacular paintings, sculpture, and furnishings planned for the interiors of churches and royal buildings.

architecture served political goals by visibly demonstrating the powers of nation states. During the seventeenth century, Europe was constantly at war — only four years passed without a battle — and monarchs spent huge sums of money on architecture that reflected their military might. Arsenals, barracks, and military fortifications reflected ingenious solutions to the challenges of defense. Royal palaces and town halls achieved new heights of splendor and proclaimed the power of monarchies, states, and cities. These buildings gained even more prominence when they were integrated into a grand plan of radiating avenues and vistas.

Rulers went to extreme lengths to represent their power in grand palaces that entirely transformed vast tracts of countryside. The best-known example is the Palace of Versailles, outside Paris, which was built by King Louis XIV during the late seventeenth and early eighteenth centuries. The Palace of Versailles became a model for palaces all over Europe.

Versailles impressed visitors with its sumptuous interiors, such as the Hall of Mirrors, and its extensive gardens, which were laid out by Frenchman André Le Nôtre (1613-1700). Le Nôtre was one of the first great landscape architects. He had previously designed an extraordinary landscape at Vaux-le-Vicomte, a chateau built by the king's finance minister, Nicholas Fouquet. His terraces, pools, fountains, formal plantings, and vistas extended the Baroque design of the palace rooms into the landscape. Nature was shaped to symbolize the king's reign over France.

London blooms from the ashes: Christopher Wren

London was one of the European capitals that was greatly transformed by Baroque architecture. Following a devastating fire in 1666, plans were drawn up to rebuild the city. The architect responsible for this project was a young prodigy named Christopher Wren, who began his career in the sciences and then switched to architecture at age 30.

The new and improved (and Baroque!) St. Paul's Cathedral

Wren's major task was to replace London's heavily damaged Gothic cathedral of St. Paul's with an even more impressive church. The design reflects his encyclopedic knowledge of architecture: The façade recalls the Louvre in Paris, which Wren had visited on his only trip abroad; the clock towers and curved walls are inspired by Borromini's designs; and the huge dome and lantern reinterprets Bramante's Tempietto. (See Figure 10-3.)

Figure 10-3: St. Paul's Cathedral, London, England. 1675–1710, by Christopher Wren.

Photo courtesy of GreatBuildings.com © Howard Davis.

He built this city: Wren's other projects

In addition to St. Paul's, Wren designed 53 smaller churches in London, including St. Stephen Walbrook, in which the architect tried out ideas for his cathedral. Another Wren masterpiece is the Royal Hospital in Greenwich. The Royal Hospital incorporates colonnades and cupolas that are designed to be seen from a distance. The architect also enlarged Hampton Court Palace, which had been built in the Tudor style for King Henry VII. Throughout his long career, Wren remained true to his version of the Baroque, which was much more restrained than the curvaceous designs of his European contemporaries. Wren died in 1723 at age 91.

Early Funhouses: The Rococo

In France, Germany, Austria, and other areas of Central Europe, the Baroque evolved into a highly decorative style called the *Rococo.* This term was originally coined to describe a type of decoration invented during the eighteenth century. It comes from the French word *rocaille,* which describes the decoration of grottoes with irregular shells and stones. Rococo is most commonly associated with lightness, delicacy, and an emphasis of surface decoration over structure.

They're melting the walls!

Although Rococo building façades are plain and somber, interiors are covered in dazzling surfaces of white, gold, and pastel ornamentation. Daylight ripples across painted walls and ceilings to produce an effect of airiness and gaiety. Mirrors adorn the walls to magnify the sense of illusion. In Rococo buildings, it is often difficult to tell where real three-dimensional form stops and the painted surface begins.

Bavarian Rococo: Brothers Zimmermann

Rococo architecture reached its zenith in southern Germany during the eighteenth century. Churches were designed as symmetrical halls without long transepts to direct the viewer to theatrical effects near the altar.

An outstanding example of this style is Die Wies, a pilgrimage church in rural Bavaria built in 1746–1754 by Domenikus Zimmermann and his brother Johann Baptist. Its interior surfaces are so veiled in sculpture, paintings, and decorative effects that the structure almost disappears.

Let there be light: Johann Balthasar Neumann

Another important architect of the period was Johann Balthasar Neumann, who skillfully illuminated his interiors through hidden openings so that the walls of his buildings appeared to radiate light. Neumann used this technique in the church of Vierzehnheiligen (literally, "the 14 saints") and Archbishop's Palace in Wurzburg. In both buildings, round and oval spaces seem to merge and dissolve through a fantastic play of light and color.

Not the new kid in town anymore

The Rococo was short-lived. By 1750, architects in Europe had begun turning their backs on its frothy excesses. The Enlightenment ushered in a new era of clarity and reason. At the same time, architects began looking backward and reviving the styles of the past. (For more about revivals, see Chapter 11.)

Chapter 11

Revivals Everywhere: The Classical and Gothic Are New Again

. . . .

In This Chapter

▶ Classical revivals in Europe and America

▶ Romanticism and Gothic Revival

▶ Beaux-Arts eclecticism

. . . .

*B*efore the eighteenth century, building innovations developed from the church, the palace, and the fortress. The Industrial Revolution fundamentally changed this pattern of architecture from the late 1700s through the 1800s. Vast economic and social upheavals, stemming from mechanization and mass production, required new building types for industry, commerce, and transportation in the cities that were popping up across Europe and the United States.

The most progressive of these buildings were designed in the nineteenth century by engineers — not architects — out of new materials like cast iron, wrought iron, and steel. The bridges, factories, railway stations, exhibition halls, and markets that were erected heralded a new age of metal and glass. (These engineered marvels are discussed in Chapter 12.)

At the same time, architects responded to the Industrial Revolution by retreating to the past to revive historical styles. This look backward was nothing new — the Romanesque and the Renaissance recycled elements from classical antiquity. But in the nineteenth century, architects cast a far wider net in drawing from Classical, Gothic, Egyptian, Byzantine, Moorish, and even Chinese architecture to satisfy a variety of tastes, moods, and functions. Architects cloaked new types of buildings — hotels, department stores, courthouses, and museums, for example — in familiar garb, while introducing a few inventions of their own.

Rage Against the Baroque: Classical Revivals

Revivals of ancient Greek and Roman architecture dominated the eighteenth and early nineteenth centuries. This resurgence of classicism was a reaction against Baroque architecture, which was dismissed as "untruthful" because it was too ornamental and illusionistic. It was fueled by an increased knowledge of Roman, Greek, and Hellenistic architecture through exciting archaeological discoveries at Herculeneum, Pompeii, and Paestum. Widespread collecting of Roman and Greek artifacts and the recording of ancient monuments by architecturally savvy tourists on Grand Tours also contributed to this resurgence.

The classical revival corresponded with the rise of powerful nation states and the birth of new democracies. Its stately architectural imagery, derived from Roman republics and Greek city-states, was seen as being well suited to the ideals of democratic governments and the spirit of the Enlightenment. It gave birth to a whole new movement — *neoclassicism*.

Gentlemen architects: Palladian Revival

In the 1720s, a style of classical architecture based on the sixteenth-century designs of the Italian Renaissance architect Andrea Palladio was developed in England. The leader of this movement was Richard Boyle (1694–1753), the Earl of Burlington, who like many upper-crust gentlemen of the eighteenth century, also practiced architecture. Among his followers were architects Colen Campbell, whose book *Vitruvius Britannicus* illustrated examples of the Palladian Revival, and William Kent. The two architects designed country houses that were arranged similarly to Palladio's strung-out villas. Side pavilions were extended from a central block, but in a simpler, more geometric and austere way.

Stuck on you: The Adam style

In the mid-1700s, Scottish-born Robert Adam (1728–1792) changed the direction of neoclassicism by launching an ornamental style of interior design based on "authentic" Roman stucco patterns. Nearly every surface of his geometrically shaped rooms was embellished with delicate plaster garlands, medallions, and other antique-inspired decorations. (Some are reminiscent of the white-on-pastel look of Wedgwood plates.) The best examples of his intricate decor are found in Syon House — a Jacobean country house that Adam remodeled in the 1760s — near London.

. . . And architecture for all: Classical revivals in Colonial America

The Palladian Revival spread, through treatises and pattern books, to the American Colonies, where it was referred to as the *Georgian* style (after Britain's King George I and his descendents). (See Figure 11-1 for an example of the Georgian style.) Its architecture of spreading symmetrical wings became especially popular in plantation houses in the South. An excellent example of a Georgian-style plantation house is the Westover Plantation, near Williamsburg, Virginia, built by William Byrd from 1730 to 1734. Inspired by English Palladian Revival designs, the brick house is flanked by lower wings; the pediment over its doorway was copied from a pattern book. Its simple elegance epitomizes the Georgian style.

Another important influence on early American architecture was the classical work of Baroque English architect James Gibbs. His London church, St. Martin's-in-the-Field (1722–1726), with its steeple sitting atop a temple portico, was copied all over the Colonies.

Figure 11-1:
A Georgian-
style
window.

Even after the Revolutionary War, America followed English traditions in its architecture. Between 1780 and 1820, more refined, elegant details and proportions emerged in homes and other building designs. Called the *Federal Style,* it was an American version of the delicate, ornamental style developed by British architect Robert Adam, and it was applied mostly to interiors. (You can see this style in Figure 11-2.) The use of the circle and the ellipse was favored for room plans, staircases, windows, and doors. A pioneer of the Federal Style was Samuel McIntire, a woodcarver and builder who was based in Salem, Massachusetts.

Figure 11-2:
A doorway
designed
in the
Federal
style.

Our building fathers: Early American architects

Both builders and gentleman amateurs were responsible for designing the architecture of early America. Among the most accomplished self-taught Colonial designers was English-born Peter Harrison. A merchant and sea captain, Harrison brought back the latest books on architecture from his many trips abroad and used drawings published in these volumes as inspiration for his own neoclassical buildings in New England. His buildings include the Redwood Library (1748–1750) in Newport, Rhode Island; King's Chapel (1749–1754) in Boston, Massachusetts; and the country's oldest Jewish house of worship, the Touro Synagogue (1759–1763), which is also in Newport,

Rhode Island. Based on these sophisticated designs, many historians consider Harrison America's first architect.

Born in the U.S.A.: Charles Bulfinch

Some credit Boston-born Charles Bulfinch as the country's first professional architect, due to his skills as both a designer and a builder. Educated at Harvard, Bulfinch traveled through Europe for two years before establishing himself as Boston's leading architect in the late 1700s. He designed and supervised the construction of the Massachusetts State Capitol (1787–1798). In 1817, he departed Boston for Washington, D.C., where he worked on the U.S. Capitol.

Architectural sophistication knocks: Benjamin Latrobe

Bulfinch's predecessor at the Capitol was another accomplished architect, Benjamin Latrobe. An English engineer who had worked for several leading architects in London, Latrobe came to the United States in 1796 seeking new opportunities. He settled in Virginia and then moved to Philadelphia where he designed the Bank of Pennsylvania (1799), which was based on a Greek Ionic temple, and the city's waterworks. Even more original is Latrobe's Roman Catholic cathedral in Baltimore (1804–1818). Instead of turning to the popular Gibbs church model, Latrobe developed an impressive sequence of vaulted and domed spaces that were influenced by Byzantine architecture and the work of his English contemporary, John Soane (see "Ready for your closeup? John Soane," later in this chapter). Latrobe's designs represented a new sophistication in American architecture.

In 1803, President Thomas Jefferson appointed Latrobe surveyor of the nation's public buildings. One of his assigned duties was to complete the north and south wings of the Capitol. Latrobe embellished his columns with corn-cob and tobacco-leaf capitals to provide an American spin on the classical tradition. Some lunch and a smoke, anybody?

Inside the melting pot: They're comin' to America

Latrobe was only one of several foreign architects who emigrated to America and ended up designing some of the country's most important monuments. Frenchman Pierre Charles L'Enfant designed the nation's first government building, Federal Hall in New York, and the plan for its capital city, Washington, D.C.(see Chapter 19). William Thornton, a medical doctor who was born in the British Virgin Islands (formerly the West Indies) and educated in Scotland, won the design competition for the U.S. Capitol. Irishman James Hoban designed the White House.

Building democracy: Greek Revival

In the mid-eighteenth century, a new interest in ancient Greek architecture arose, as architects traveled and began documenting the Parthenon and other monuments in and around Athens.

Greek architecture had particular appeal to Americans searching for buildings that were expressive of the nation's democratic ideals. Architects began copying (from pattern books) the Doric orders of the Parthenon and other monuments, adding their own touches to the classical orders to make them more distinctly American. This style became known as *Greek Revival.* It was popular in all regions of the country from 1820 to 1860. It proved to be adaptable to all types of buildings, including houses, churches, civic buildings, and commercial structures.

German art historian Johann Joachim Winckelmann paved the way for this revival of Greek architecture with his persuasive arguments on the significance of Greek art in 1755. In 1758, Frenchman Julien-David LeRoy followed Winckelmann's writings on classical art with a book that contained detailed illustrations of Greek monuments. LeRoy's book was followed by *The Antiquities of Athens,* by English architects James Stuart and Nicholas Revett, which appeared in three separate parts in 1762, 1789, and 1795. (Even before his tour of Greece, Stuart had built a Greek temple on the grounds of a country estate near Birmingham, England.)

The three-part publication by Stuart and Revett soon popularized the Greek Revival style in Britain. From railroad terminals and post offices to the British Museum, Doric and Ionic colonnades began sprouting up across London in the early 1800s. Later in the century, Scottish architect Alexander "Greek" Thomson developed a highly original version of the Greek Revival style to transform Glasgow into the Athens of the North.

One of the earliest and most influential examples of American Greek Revival is the Second Bank of the United States in Philadelphia. Modeled after the Parthenon, it was designed in 1818 by William Strickland, a disciple of Latrobe. The design became the prototype for banks all over the country.

Back to basics: French neoclassicism

In France, a more intellectual, abstract version of the classical revival was hatched during the eighteenth century. It was based on the idea of simplifying architecture down to its essence, and it grew from the theories of a Jesuit abbot, Marc-Antoine Laugier. In his 1753 manifesto, *Essay on Architecture,* Laugier argued that the most basic and structurally direct architecture was neither Roman nor Greek but a primitive hut constructed of four tree trunks supporting a pitched roof of logs and branches. This search for a more elemental, rational, and crisp architecture was in sync with the Age of Reason's scientific discoveries and philosophical debate.

The desire to reform architecture led to a streamlined neoclassicism, first evidenced in the Church of Saint Genevieve in Paris, which was designed by Jacques-Germain Soufflot in 1756. The austere architecture of Soufflot's church united the structural lightness of Gothic cathedral construction with the simple lines of Greek architecture.

A Renaissance man in Colonial America: Thomas Jefferson

The first American to seek a new style of architecture appropriate to the new nation was Thomas Jefferson, who was inaugurated as the third president of the United States in 1801. Born in Shadwell, Virginia, in 1743, Jefferson attended the college of William and Mary but received no formal architectural training. Essentially self-taught, he assembled an impressive library of architecture books, including treatises by Andrea Palladio and other Europeans. In 1769, he experimented with ideas from these publications in the design of his house, Monticello, which took him 30 years to complete.

While serving as minister to France from 1784 to 1789, Jefferson studied France's architectural heritage. He gained insight into classical antiquity from site visits to Roman ruins, such as the Maison Carrée in Nîmes. His designs for the Virginia State Capitol (1785–1789) and the University of Virginia (1817–1822) were based on the architecture that he saw abroad. These groundbreaking projects reflect Jefferson's skillful ability to recast French, English, and Roman traditions according to American materials, needs, and ideals.

This unorthodox interpretation of classical forms became even bolder in the decade before the French Revolution. In the 1770s, architects Claude-Nicolas Ledoux and Étienne-Louis Boullée came up with the notion that building forms should directly communicate their function. A prison, for example, should not be disguised as a medieval fortress but be immediately recognizable as a place of confinement through grim, blank walls and slit windows.

Whether they were designing a saltworks or a library, Ledoux and Boullée preferred large, simple geometric shapes over fussy decoration. Their bold designs matched the revolutionary spirit of the times. While Ledoux was practical — he designed and built 50 toll booths at some of the entrances to Paris — Boullée was a dreamer known for his visionary drawings. One of Boullée's most compelling proposals was a giant, hollow sphere pierced by holes that was designed as a monument to the British scientist Isaac Newton.

Playing on Your Emotions: Romanticism

At the same time that classical architecture was on the upswing, architects began turning to other styles of the past to draw playful forms that addressed the emotions. This movement was called *Romanticism,* and it led to a loosening up of the rules that had long governed concepts of beauty. It allowed architects to tailor historical styles according to the particulars of building type and location.

Gothic Revival: Simply sublime

Part of Romanticism's goal was to achieve sublime beauty, an idea coined by English philosopher Edmund Burke in 1757. This effect was meant to strike terror from a safe distance, like watching a scary movie. To achieve it, architects began reviving the spooky, gloomy vaults and turrets of Gothic cathedrals and castles, which were seen as being full of sublime features.

One of the earliest Gothic Revival buildings was a rambling house owned by English critic and romance novelist Horace Walpole. The house, called Strawberry Hill, was expanded in the 1760s with an assortment of towers, turrets, and vaulted chambers. The quirky elements were added so that the structure would appear to have been built over centuries. Many details were accurately copied from medieval cathedrals.

Imitating Mother Nature: Random acts of beauty and the picturesque

Picturesque, a term first associated with seventeenth-century Italian landscape painting, was another important concept of the Romantic movement. It was a way of establishing a naturalistic feeling through irregular, asymmetrical compositions of building elements. This idea of informality, which is so familiar to us today, was radical at the time, because before the 1700s, only symmetrically ordered buildings were considered beautiful.

The earliest examples of the picturesque style were English landscapes surrounding Palladian Revival mansions that looked like they were designed by Mother Nature. Winding paths, clustered plantings, lakes, and rivers took the place of the Baroque's symmetrical promenades, formal rows of trees, and reflecting pools. Sprinkled within the landscape were small classical temples, or other buildings evocative of a distant time and place, known as *follies.*

A mover and a shaker: Lancelot "Capability" Brown

The master of the picturesque style was Lancelot "Capability" Brown (1716–1783), whose nickname came from his knack of doing almost anything to achieve a "natural" look; he made lakes from streams and moved entire hillsides. (Now that had to be an "earthshaking" project!) Many Europeans, including Russia's Catherine the Great, copied Brown's English landscapes. His landscapes were also models for American gardens and parks, including Central Park, designed by Frederick Law Olmsted, in the heart of Manhattan.

Retro rehash: John Nash flexes and bends

By the nineteenth century, architects had turned to the entire sweep of history as the source of picturesque designs. A virtuoso of this versatility was Englishman John Nash (1752–1835), who designed rustic, thatched-roof cottages, as well as classical townhouses. In 1815, he imaginatively combined Gothic, Chinese, and East Indian forms in the Royal Pavilion at Brighton on the south coast of England. Cast-iron onion domes and minarets added to its exotic appearance. Nash's most significant achievement was the transformation of parts of London into a picturesque garden city. For land owned by the Prince Regent, later crowned as King George IV, the architect drew up a plan in 1811 that called for a park encircled by grand townhouses. Much of this concept was realized as Regent Street and Regent's Park.

A beautiful compromise emerges: Romantic Classicism

Neoclassicism and romanticism — once considered opposites — overlapped during the early nineteenth century, as architects freely interpreted the classical orders to create banks, theaters, art museums, and other modern buildings.

Ready for your closeup? John Soane

Architect John Soane (1753–1837), a contemporary of Nash, was a master of Romantic Classicism. In 1788, Soane was appointed as the architect of the Bank of England, where he combined forms from classical and Byzantine architecture to create domed and vaulted spaces that were dramatically lit from the top and sides. (Sadly, his interiors were demolished in the 1930s. townhouses) Among his most imaginative projects are his own home in Lincoln's Inn Fields (now the Soane Museum) and the Art Gallery at Dulwich (1811–1814).

Of monuments and museums: Karl Friedrich Schinkel

The originality of Soane's buildings was echoed in the work of Prussian architect Karl Friedrich Schinkel (1781–1841). Schinkel, adept at working in various revival styles (Gothic and Renaissance, as well as Greek), composed the classical orders in a restrained yet monumental way to give new building types an assured presence. His Altes ("old") Museum (1824–1828) in Berlin, Germany, built to house the collections of King Friedrich Wilhelm III, is a masterpiece of Greek Revival architecture. Fronted by a majestic colonnade of tall Ionic columns, the two-story structure grouped galleries around a rotunda and set the standard for organizing museums. (See Figure 11-3.)

Figure 11-3:
Altes
Museum,
Berlin,
Germany,
1824-1828,
by Karl
Friedrich
Schinkel.

Photo courtesy of GreatBuildings.com © John A. Gascon.

Superior structures: Later Gothic Revival

During the first decades of the nineteenth century, Gothic Revival architecture was mostly limited to country houses and churches. From the 1840s through the 1880s, the Gothic style became more prevalent and followed medieval models more accurately. A spur to this revival was the rebuilding of the Houses of Parliament in London after a fire in 1834. The architects of the Houses of Parliament were Charles Barry and Augustus Welby Northmore Pugin, who argued that Gothic was superior to classical styles because of its religious and moral associations. In England, the Gothic Revival style became popular for town halls, museums, train stations, and other public buildings.

The Americans go Gothic

In the United States, architects such as Richard Upjohn, Andrew Jackson Downing, and Alexander Jackson Davis supported the Gothic Revival movement in the mid-1800s. (Check out Figure 11-4 for an example of the Gothic Revival style.) The style was translated into wooden houses and cottages and referred to as *Carpenter Gothic*. By the late nineteenth century, it was applied to college and university buildings and called *collegiate Gothic*.

It's all about the structure, baby

One of the most significant contributions to architecture made by the Gothic Revival was a renewed focus on structural systems. It came from French architect Eugène-Emmanuel Viollet-le-Duc (1814–1879). Viollet-le-Duc grew to appreciate Gothic structural principles through his overenthusiastic restorations of Notre-Dame in Paris, the walled city of Carcassonne, and other medieval structures. Modern architects, Viollet-le-Duc argued, should study the properties of materials such as iron and then use these materials to design as rationally and systematically as medieval architects did with their vaults and buttresses. This forward-looking idea would influence the technology-based architecture of the late-nineteenth and twentieth centuries (see Chapters 12 and 13).

Figure 11-4:
A Gothic Revival window.

Coming Full Circle: Beaux-Arts Eclecticism

In the nineteenth century, stylistic alternatives continued to increase as architects borrowed from the Renaissance and the Baroque, bringing revivalism full circle. This "re-revival" of classicism was epitomized in the Paris Opera House designed by Charles Garnier (1825–1898) as part of Baron Georges-Eugène Haussmann's modernization of Paris. In the 1850s, Haussmann, who had been appointed by Napoleon III, transformed the narrow streets of the medieval city with grand boulevards and avenues, apartments, and public buildings (for more on Haussmann, see Chapter 19). The glittering centerpiece of the new Paris was Garnier's opera house (1861–1875), a cultural "cathedral" that blended Renaissance and Baroque sources into an extravagantly eclectic confection. You can see the opera house in Figure 11-5.

Figure 11-5:
Garnier's
opera house
in Paris,
France.

Photo by Kevin Matthews © Kevin Matthews, 1998.

In designing the Paris Opera House, Garnier followed planning principles that he learned at the École des Beaux-Arts in Paris, which was established in 1819 by the French government. The school taught the classical orders, but more importantly, it also taught a way of organizing a building into a balanced hierarchy of spatial elements. This discipline was crucial at a time when architects were confronted with a bewildering choice of forms from the history of architecture.

The Beaux-Arts teaching method helped architects arrange their increasingly eclectic designs into a coherent whole. It created a design and planning system with a specialized vocabulary that is still used today:

- ✔ The student started with an *esquisse* or quick sketch.

- ✔ The sketch was developed into the basic scheme of the building, called a *parti* (from *prendre parti*, meaning "to take a stand").

- ✔ The parti was further elaborated into a *composition* showing the primary and secondary spaces within the building.

- ✔ When the design drawings were finished, they were placed into a *charette,* or cart, that was pushed through the studio. Charette has since come to mean an intensive design process that often requires all-night sessions.

For more on Beaux-Arts planning principles, see Chapter 5.

Beaux-Arts in America

By the late nineteenth century, the École des Beaux-Arts had become a training ground for architects all over the world. The first American to receive architectural training from the École was Richard Morris Hunt (1827–1895), one of the organizers of the American Institute of Architects. Hunt managed to work convincingly in almost every type of revival style — mostly for wealthy patrons. Among his structures in New York City (many have since been destroyed) are the original wing of the Metropolitan Museum of Art and the Statue of Liberty's stone pedestal.

His grand, luxurious mansions became synonymous with the *Gilded Age*. Among Hunt's best known works are two vacation homes completed for the Vanderbilts in 1895: the Breakers, an Italian Renaissance mansion built in Newport, and Biltmore in Ashville, North Carolina, which was modeled after a French chateau.

Making it simple

Another École-trained American architect was Charles Follen McKim, who set up a partnership with William Mead and Stanford White in 1879. Their New York firm, McKim, Mead, and White, applied the Beaux-Arts method to transform large, complicated projects, such as train stations and university campuses, into coherent, dignified, and monumental settings. Among their Renaissance Revival designs are the Villard Houses in New York (1882–1886) and the Boston Public Library (1887–1895).

From New World to City Beautiful

In 1893, McKim, Mead, and White, along with other leading American architects, designed buildings for a dazzling spectacle at the World's Columbian Exposition in Chicago. The fair, held to commemorate the 400th anniversary of the discovery of the New World in 1492 (the Chicago expo was held a year late), demonstrated the value of Beaux-Arts classical architecture and planning on a civic scale. White buildings, grand promenades, spacious plazas, and classical sculpture demonstrated what came to be called the *City Beautiful* approach to urban planning. The fair's principal planner, Daniel Burnham, went on to design similar schemes in Cleveland, Washington, D.C., and San Francisco (see Chapter 19).

Richardsonian Romanesque

The absorption of historic traditions led to more personalized forms of expression in the late nineteenth century, paving the way for the modern architecture of the twentieth century. One of the most gifted individualists of the period was Boston architect Henry Hobson Richardson. Richardson, called "the last great traditional architect," studied at Harvard and then at the École des Beaux-Arts in Paris until his income was cut off by the Civil War.

After returning to the United States, Richardson launched his own practice in New York and designed buildings that blended elements of Romanesque architecture. One of his earliest successes is Trinity Church (1872–1877) on Boston's Copley Square. The design was a powerful fusion of French and Spanish Romanesque with English Gothic Revival that established his national reputation. To convey his belief in the Romanesque Revival style, Richardson would often send his new clients a photograph of himself in a monk's habit. (This guy really understood the value of marketing.)

Unlike the fussy pastiches of his contemporaries, Richardson's Romanesque-influenced buildings were far bolder and more forceful in their interpretation of historical forms. Round-arched windows, solid walls of stone, and few ornamental details created what the architect called "quiet and massive" buildings. This philosophy is best illustrated in his Allegheny County Court House and Jail in Pittsburgh (1883–1888), shown in Figure 11-6, and his Marshall Field Wholesale Store in Chicago (1885–1887). The simple, muscular shapes of Richardson's architecture exerted an enormous influence on American architects of the next generation, including Frank Lloyd Wright.

Figure 11-6:
Allegheny County Court House and Jail, Pittsburgh, 1883-1888, by Henry Hobson Richardson.

Photo courtesy of Carnegie Library of Pittsburgh / Pittsburgh Photo Library.

**The Parthenon;
Athens, Greece;
447-438 BC;
by Ictinus and Callicrates**

Chartres Cathedral; Chartres, France; 1194-1220

St. Peter's Cathedral; Rome, Italy; 1506-1626; by Bramante, Michelangelo, della Porta, and others

Villa Rotonda; Vicenza, Italy; 1566-1571; by Andrea Palladio

Katsura Palace; Kyoto, Japan; 1616-1660

Soane House;
London, England;
1808-1809, 1812, 1823-1824;
by John Soane

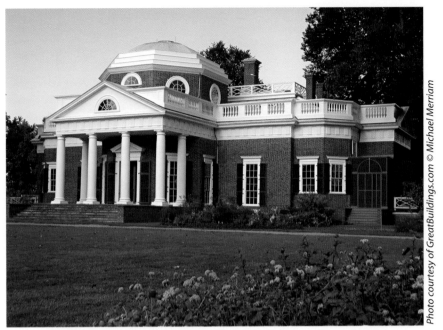

Monticello; Charlottesville, Virginia; 1769-1809; by Thomas Jefferson

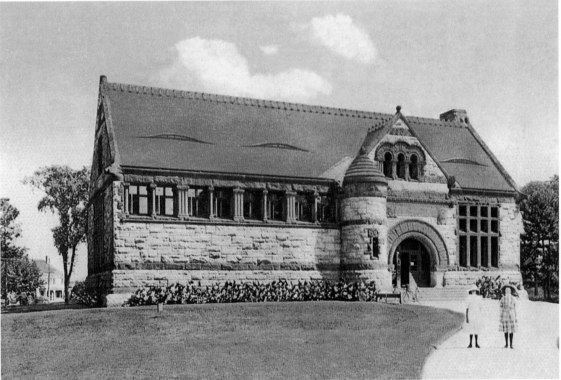

Crane Memorial Library; Quincy, Massachusetts; 1880-1882; by Henry Hobson Richardson

Secession Building; Vienna, Austria; 1897-1898; by Josef Maria Olbrich

Casa Milà; Barcelona, Spain; 1905-1910; by Antoní Gaudi

Schroeder House; Utrecht, The Netherlands; 1924; by Gerrit Rietveld

Fallingwater; Bear Run, Pennsylvania; 1934-1937; by Frank Lloyd Wright

Guggenheim Museum; Bilbao, Spain; 1992-1997; by Frank Gehry

Chapter 12

Here Comes the Industrial Age: Prefab Is Here to Stay

Advances in science, manufacturing, and engineering during the nineteenth century led to a greater variety of building materials and methods. Efficient production of cast iron, steel, and glass opened up new possibilities in architectural form and structure that would later lead to skyscrapers and other modern buildings.

As these new materials came into use, engineers challenged the role of the architect by designing new structures that pushed the limits of metal and glass. Architects, meanwhile, were slower to embrace the industrial materials and technologies that were deftly shaped by engineers. Debate ensued over the appropriateness of historical styles versus the invention of new forms in metal and glass. This quandary was solved in a variety of ways during the late nineteenth century, as architects shaped new buildings for the industrial age with both decorative and structural exuberance.

Mass Production Begins: Materials Get a Revamp

LINGO

Iron and carbon was mixed in blast furnaces to produce *cast iron,* a material that had been used in a limited way in the late 1700s to construct bridges. By the mid-1800s, the metal was produced in larger and cheaper quantities thanks to advances in smelting techniques. Building parts were prefabricated in factories and shipped to the work sites for easy, fast construction. Cast-iron windows, railings, columns, and even entire façades soon took the place of wood, stone, and other conventional materials.

They can get it for you wholesale!

In 1855, a process invented by Englishman Henry Bessemer led to the production of *steel*. Because steel has a lower carbon content and fewer impurities than cast iron, it can be molded into more durable structural elements. Beams and columns can be cut to the required length, shipped to the site, and bolted or welded together, thus reducing construction costs. Steel components, however, didn't become common until the 1890s.

Concrete also benefited from technical improvements. In the mid-1800s, concrete was mixed with Portland cement instead of lime to make it stronger, more durable, and fire-resistant. By the 1890s, concrete was being poured over steel rods (known as *rebar*) to protect the steel from rust and fire and create what's called *reinforced concrete*. This combination of steel and concrete has more tensile strength than plain concrete (see Chapter 6). Reinforced concrete was eventually molded to form beams, columns, walls, or vaults — elements of almost any shape.

Glass, formerly a handmade luxury, was another material that became widely used as new manufacturing processes made large, transparent sheets less costly. The panes of glass were held within cast-iron frames to create *ferrovitreous* — or iron-and-glass construction. Railroad sheds, greenhouses, and shopping arcades all took advantage of this technology.

Even traditional building materials such as brick and stone became less expensive and easier to handle, as they were efficiently transported in large quantities from brickyards and quarries. These materials were often combined with iron, steel, and glass.

Form follows material

Material innovations, in turn, led architects to explore new types of structures. Instead of having to use thick stone walls to support floors, ceilings, and roofs, architects could substitute lighter, smaller cast-iron-and-steel columns and beams to support the same loads. Walls no longer had to be massive with small windows; they could be filled with large panels of glass to allow daylight to stream into interiors.

Managing the Forces: Enter the Engineer

As buildings became larger and more complex, an in-depth understanding of the structural behavior of materials and forces was required. To meet this specialized need, a new type of professional emerged — the *engineer*. Unlike the architect, the engineer was not focused on visual effects but instead on building a strong, efficient structure. Nevertheless, many of the boldest and most beautiful designs that were created during the late 1800s emerged from feats of engineering.

Joseph Paxton: Petal to the metal

One of the most impressive structures of the mid-nineteenth century was a vast iron-and-glass pavilion masterminded by an English gardener, Joseph Paxton (1803–1865). After a series of jobs on large estates, Paxton went to work for the Duke of Devonshire at his country estate home of Chatsworth. Paxton built a dozen greenhouses at Chatsworth, including one in cast iron and glass with an elaborate heating system to protect the Victoria regia — a giant water lily imported from Africa. (Paxton also had a really green thumb!) According to the gardener-turned-architect, his structure's slender metal supports mirrored the stems of the lily.

The original Crystal Palace: A real dazzler

In 1850, Paxton won a design competition to create a huge exhibition hall at the first World's Fair in London. His scheme, a much larger version of his lily house, was built in only 9 months. The speedy construction was due to the exhibition hall's structure, which was made of cast-iron columns, girders, and beams that were prefabricated in a foundry and quickly erected on the site.

Paxton's Crystal Palace (see Figure 12-1) was six times larger than St. Paul's Cathedral and covered almost 1 million square feet. (No cracker-box proportions here, folks; we're talking the length of six football fields.) Like a cathedral, the vast greenhouse was divided into a tall nave and lower transepts and galleries. But there were few historical references in the Crystal Palace's glass-enclosed barrel vaults, roofs, and walls. Only the smallest details were decorated according to Victorian revivalist taste. By 1851 standards, the transparent building seemed futuristic. The insides of the halls were painted in bright red, blue, and yellow, and sunlight streamed through thousands of sheets of plate glass.

Figure 12-1: Crystal Palace, London, England, 1851-1852, by Joseph Paxton.

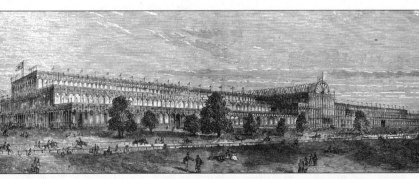

Photo by Delamotte © public domain by date. Photo courtesy of GreatBuildings.com.

The Palace, which was wildly popular, attracted 6 million visitors before it was dismantled in 1852. (Architects and critics, however, were less enthusiastic about the exhibition hall. They dismissed the prefab structure as a "glass monster" and "crystal humbug.") A slightly different version of the Palace was rebuilt in South London. A fire destroyed it in 1936.

Copycat! Other crystal palaces

Similar crystal palaces were subsequently constructed in New York (1853) and Munich, Germany (1854). Cast-iron-and-glass construction soon became popular for commercial and institutional buildings in Europe. Following are some examples of this style:

- An early cast-iron-and-glass building in Paris was the Halles Centrales (1853–1858), a meat and produce market. Victor Baltard designed the rows of sheds as part of Haussmann's transformation of the French capital (see Chapter 19). The building was demolished in 1971.

- Another impressive cast-iron-and-glass building in Paris was the department store called Bon Marché (literally "good buy"), created in 1876 by engineer Gustav Eiffel, the designer of the famous tower, and architect Louis-Charles Boileau. Its almost transparent interior, framed by skylights and glass walls, lured customers away from competing stores with similar merchandise.

- Iron and glass were also used to turn store-lined passageways into shopping arcades. The most famous example is the Galleria Vittorio Emanuele in Milan (1864–1878) by Gisueppe Mengoni, who fell from the roof and died a few days before the cross-shaped arcade opened in 1878. Its 640-foot-long main promenade links Milan's La Scala opera house on the north to the cathedral on the south. An iron-and-glass roof covers the 96-foot-high arcade, with a dome placed over the crossing of its two streets. Called *Il salotto di Milano* ("Milan's parlor"), the Galleria has been a popular gathering place for more than a century and home to some of Milan's finest stores.

Henri Labrouste: Early high-tech for the bookworms

Architects began to create light-filled modern spaces with cast iron at the same time that it was being used to construct markets and arcades. A pioneer of this tech-driven architecture was French engineer Henri Labrouste, who designed two significant libraries in Paris. The first was the Bibliothèque Ste. Geneviève (1842–1850), a rectangular stone library with large, arched windows. Inside, Labrouste topped the library's reading room with a barrel-vaulted tile ceiling supported by iron arches and columns. Recalling the architecture of a train station, the cast-iron structure symbolized the reader's journey into the world of knowledge. Pretty neat, huh?

Another Labrouste masterpiece was the reading room at the National Library (1858–1868). Cast iron was shaped into columns and arches to support nine top-lit metal domes. Book stacks were constructed of cast iron and glass to allow daylight to filter through the floors — a trick that the architect may have picked up from the engine rooms of steamships.

The Roebling brothers: The Brooklyn Bridge

Many advances in bridge construction were made during the 1800s. Experiments with roadbeds suspended from chains led to the development of stronger cables and the modern *suspension bridge*. The world's largest steel suspension bridge, built from 1869–1883, spanned the East River from Brooklyn to Manhattan. The engineers responsible for this remarkable achievement were John Augustus Roebling and his son Washington Roebling, who had previously collaborated on a smaller suspension bridge in Cincinnati, Ohio.

The design for the Brooklyn Bridge called for special devices and techniques to spin steel wire into four main cables and a web of diagonal stays. The cables were suspended from two stone towers with Gothic arches rising 300 feet above the water. The towers supported a roadway, with lanes for carriages and trains, and a broad promenade for pedestrians.

The bridge's mammoth structure had to be erected in deep, flowing water, calling for what engineers call *pneumatic caissons* — hollow, heavy wooden boxes driven into the riverbed. Men worked within the caissons' pressurized chambers to excavate rock and dirt from the river bottom. The bridge construction was extremely dangerous, causing many tragic accidents. Even the Roeblings were put in harm's way: John died as the result of an accident shortly after construction had started; Washington suffered a crippling attack of the bends and was confined to his apartment. But the engineer continued to direct the building of the bridge through his wife Emily, who supervised site construction. Since its completion in 1883, the Brooklyn Bridge has become a cultural symbol and an inspiration for painters, poets, and photographers.

James Bogardus: Cast iron for commerce

In the mid-1800s, cast-iron façades were more common in America than in Europe. The world's largest collection of nineteenth-century cast-iron buildings is still concentrated in a neighborhood of lower Manhattan known as *SoHo* (an acronym for "south of Houston Street"). With their large windows, slender columns, and decorative details, these loft buildings reflect the architectural sophistication that was possible with prefabricated metal.

The genius behind the spread of cast iron was New York entrepreneur James Bogardus, who claimed to have invented the cast-iron front in the 1840s. From his Manhattan factory (made of cast iron, of course!), Bogardus mass-produced prefabricated sections and shipped them to construction sites. He popularized his methods through a brochure, published in 1858, titled "Cast Iron Buildings: Their Construction and Advantages."

The prefabricated façades produced by Bogardus and others were mostly used for stores, offices, warehouses, and hotels. Cast-iron components were appealing to businesses because they were fire-resistant and inexpensive. Their prefabricated parts could be bolted together and easily replaced. Because cast-iron structures supported the weight of construction through columns rather than walls, they created open floor spaces and large windows that were particularly suitable for commercial uses. The cast-iron surfaces could also be painted and textured — with the addition of marble dust or sand — to imitate stone, at a much lower cost.

Bogardus's competitor was Daniel Badger, another innovative cast-iron manufacturer and designer in New York. Together, they had an international influence on cast-iron construction and the development of the early skyscraper (see Chapter 13). From 1850 through the 1880s, the fashion for cast iron had spread to such cities as Boston, Baltimore, and New Orleans, as well as to Europe and Australia. The metal façades were even shipped on wagon trains to the frontier towns of the Wild West.

Alexandre Gustav Eiffel: Tower of power

Experiments in iron construction reached a pinnacle in France with the construction of the Eiffel Tower (1885–1889). At 984 feet high, it was the tallest structure in the world until the completion of New York's Chrysler Building in 1930. Engineer Alexandre Gustav Eiffel designed the tower as the gateway to a world's fair that was held in Paris to mark the 100th anniversary of the French Revolution. It's shown in Figure 12-2.

Is it a bridge or is it a tower? You tell me . . .

Eiffel was an experienced bridge builder. When designing his tower, he applied some of the same engineering principles that were used in the building of bridges. He supported his tapering tower with four immense trusses of crisscrossing iron bars that rested on stone foundations. These tapering, curving piers rose from a 125-foot-square base and were connected at two levels by girders to create a structure of great stability. All the ironwork was prefabricated, including the punched holes for riveting.

Bon chic, bon genre (not!)

To the casual viewer, the tower looked unstable, provoking much controversy. Leading cultural figures protested its construction with a letter, calling the tower "monstrous" and a "menace to French history." Owners of buildings near the site filed a lawsuit against Eiffel, claiming that his structure was dangerous and could destroy their property. Even the French government refused to pay for the entire construction cost, hesitating over the soundness of its design. To complete his monument, Eiffel came up with the balance of the cost out of his own pocket. The tower was eventually accepted by the public and has since become a national symbol of France. Take that, you Parisian culture vultures!

Figure 12-2:
Eiffel Tower,
Paris,
France,
1885-1889,
by
Alexandre
Gustav
Eiffel.

Photo courtesy of GreatBuildings.com © Alene Stickles.

Another Eiffel creation: Statue of Liberty

Before engineer Gustav Eiffel embarked on the tower that would make him internationally famous, he designed the intricate framework inside the Statue of Liberty.

The statue, originally called Liberty Enlightening the World, was proposed by the French historian Edouard Laboulaye in 1865 to commemorate the alliance of France and the American colonies during the Revolutionary War.

Eiffel "builds a bridge" again!

French sculptor Frederic-Auguste Bartholdi designed the 152-foot-high statue in sheets of copper that were as thin as a penny. The copper, which was lighter than cast metal, was hammered inside wooden molds. This technique, called *repousse,* allowed the sculpture to be assembled from 350 pieces packed into 214 crates and shipped overseas. However, the statue's thin shell, enormous size, and irregular shape posed structural challenges that were solved by Eiffel's engineering. The copper panels were attached to iron bands that extended from a flexible metal skeleton anchored to a central core.

Standing tall and proud, finally . . .

The sponsors hoped that Lady Liberty would be completed in time for America's centennial celebration. But a lack of funds slowed progress on the huge statue and the 89-foot-high stone pedestal, designed by American architect Richard Morris Hunt, on which it was to stand. In 1876, her 30-foot arm was displayed in Philadelphia. Two years later, her head was exhibited in Paris. Finally, the whole statue was shipped to New York City, where the figure and pedestal were erected over an existing fort on Bedloe's Island (now called Liberty Island) to command the entrance to the harbor. Dedicated in 1886, the 305-foot-tall monument became a celebrated beacon of liberty and freedom for millions of immigrants. From 1983 to 1986, Lady Liberty received a badly needed face-lift (the exacting restoration also put the gilded shine back on her flame) in time to celebrate her 100th birthday.

Chapter 13

Flying High and Close to the Sun: Skyscrapers!

*B*efore the late 1800s, it was unusual to find a building higher than three or four stories. Taller structures were made possible as industrial materials, particularly steel, became cheaper and more widespread. The invention of the elevator and more sophisticated heating, plumbing, and electric lighting systems made the higher spaces as accessible and comfortable as the lower ones.

Early "skyscrapers" were not the towering, 50-story-plus structures of today. Most were only a dozen floors or so tall, and they were a peculiarly American invention. In the fast growing cities of Chicago and New York, real estate speculators quickly realized that constructing tall buildings would guarantee a faster rate of return on their investments. Skyscrapers provided offices and homes for more people while taking up the same amount of land. By the 1890s, the race for the highest tower had begun!

Buildings Go Up, the Sky Falls Down: The First Skyscrapers

Before the widespread use of steel, tall buildings were constructed of solid brick-and-stone walls that carried the weight of the building. The walls, which were constructed thicker in the lower stories, gradually became thinner toward the top of the buildings. This type of construction meant that the spaces inside the lower floors were smaller than those near the top because the thicker walls at the bottom took up more floor area.

To maximize space throughout the buildings, architects turned to steel to support the floors and walls. This type of construction first appeared in the Home Insurance Building in Chicago (1883–1885), which was designed by French-trained engineer William LeBaron Jenney. Although the building is only 10 stories high, it is considered the first skyscraper because of its innovative structure. (Until then, the term *skyscraper* was used to describe a high-standing horse, a hat, a tall man, or a fly ball in baseball, as in literally "scraping the sky" — at the very least, you have to love the mental picture it creates!)

For the first time, steel columns and beams carried the entire weight of the building. This type of structure is referred to as a *skeleton frame*. (No, it doesn't have anything to do with Halloween or how to make Halloween decorations stick to the walls better. Trust me, if I knew that one, I'd share it.) The skeleton frame allows for thinner walls and lots of windows. Instead of holding up the weight of the building, the exterior "skin," or "curtain walls," acts as a screen to keep out the weather.

Chicago's Steel Skeletons

Chicago got a jump on skyscraper design after a fire devastated much of the city in 1871. The stone-and-steel towers, which were more fireproof than earlier wooden structures, provided an efficient way to rebuild the city. These pioneering structures housed a greater number of offices and apartments than the smaller structures that had burned down, but they took up the same amount of available land. Over the next few decades, skyscrapers transformed the Windy City into a modern metropolis at the forefront of American architecture.

The architects of these new buildings were referred to as the *Chicago School* — even though all of them came from somewhere else. One of their favorite elements was a type of large horizontal window that came to be known as the *Chicago window*. It had a fixed pane in the center and narrower, movable sash windows on the sides. The following sections describe some of the most significant buildings created by the Chicago School.

The Rookery: Hangout for pigeons and politicians

The Rookery (1885–1888) was designed by two leading Chicago School architects, Daniel Burnham and John Wellborn Root. Its name comes from the temporary city hall that previously stood on the site at the corner of La Salle and Adams streets. It was nicknamed "the Rookery" after the pigeons and the politicians who roosted in the building. When Burnham and Root replaced the city hall building with their office high-rise, the name stuck.

From the outside, the Rookery looks fairly conventional: It was built of load-bearing granite and brick that was shaped into turrets and other historical details. But it takes advantage of such innovations as fireproof clay tile, plate glass, and the hydraulic passenger elevator. At the building's center, a court-yard lobby with a huge skylight is surrounded by surfaces of light-reflective glazed brick and terra cotta. Contemporary writers praised the Rookery as "the most modern of office buildings" and "a thing of light." In 1905, Frank Lloyd Wright renovated the ground-floor lobby in the courtyard with geometric ornaments and light fixtures. Many of these features, along with the original façades, were restored in 1992.

Old on the inside, modern on the outside: Monadnock Building

The 16-story Monadnock Building (1889–1891), also designed by Burnham and Root, was the last skyscraper in Chicago to be constructed with load-bearing walls of brick. To carry the upper floors, the walls at ground level were built six feet thick. Although the building is old-fashioned in its construction, the tapering tower is modern in its lack of exterior ornamentation. Rising inward and upward to an outwardly flaring cornice, it was once compared to an Egyptian column. In 1893, the building was expanded with a steel-framed addition.

Windows! We need windows!: The Reliance Building

The 14-story Reliance Building (1890–1895), designed by Charles B. Atwood of Daniel Burnham and Company, marked a new breakthrough in skyscraper design. (See Figure 13-1.) Its exterior walls are almost entirely composed of large Chicago windows. Between the windows, narrow bands of cream-colored terra cotta clearly correspond to the grid of the steel skeleton frame underneath. This light and airy architecture, which paved the way for today's glass-and-steel skyscrapers, was a radical departure from the heavier masonry buildings of the time. After decades of neglect, the Reliance Building was restored in 1999 and turned into a 122-room hotel.

Figure 13-1:
The
Reliance
Building in
Chicago,
Illinois,
1890-1895,
by Burnham
and Co.

Photo courtesy of GreatBuildings.com © Johnson Architectural Images.

Louis Sullivan: A visionary with a tall order . . .

The most visionary member of the Chicago School was Louis Sullivan. His ideas foreshadowed the modern architecture of the twentieth century. Born in Boston, Sullivan moved to Chicago in 1873 and briefly worked for William LeBaron Jenney, the father of the skyscraper. After studying in France, Sullivan returned to Chicago and eventually landed a job with engineer Dankmar Adler. In 1883, Sullivan and Adler became partners. The two men spent the next dozen years designing commercial buildings, theaters, and houses.

Form follows function: It's elementary, my friend

Sullivan's greatest contribution to the skyscraper was the organizing of its identical, stacked floors to express a strong visual identity. Instead of using historical imagery such as turrets or bell towers, the architect divided the exteriors of his tall buildings into three parts, like a classical column. The bottom stories containing the entrance were designed as the "base," the middle stories were given a vertical emphasis to resemble the shaft of the column, and the top floor was treated like an entablature with a cornice and a frieze filled with decorative ornament (just like those columns with different classical orders discussed in Chapter 8). Two stunning examples of this approach are the Wainwright Building in St. Louis (1890–1891), shown in Figure 13-2, and the Guaranty Building in Buffalo (1894–1895).

In 1896, Sullivan expressed his views in the essay, "The Tall Building Artistically Considered." The shape of the skyscraper, he maintained, should celebrate its soaring height. "Form ever follows function," he wrote. Over the next several decades, this phrase would become the mantra of modern architects everywhere.

Figure 13-2:
Wainwright
Building,
St. Louis,
Missouri,
1890-1891,
by Louis
Sullivan.

Photo courtesy of and © Jack Zehrt.

Keeping it real: Organic and inspired by nature

For Sullivan, ornamentation represented man's spiritual link to nature. It became a significant means for humanizing his imposing structures. His interlacing, geometric motifs were based on medieval Celtic designs and realistic plant forms that he often sketched from nature. The motifs were often created with the assistance of his chief designer George Grant Elmslie, who was born in Scotland and was familiar with Celtic art. Sullivan liked to call these swirling nature-inspired decorations *organic*.

A captivating example of Sullivan's decoration can be found in his last large commercial building, the Schlesinger and Meyer Store in Chicago. It was designed in two sections around the "world's busiest corner" at State and Madison streets. In 1904, a 12-story block was added to the original nine-story section (1899), and the building was renamed the Carson Pirie Scott Department Store. Sullivan simply divided the upper stories by a grid pattern of Chicago windows to reflect the supporting iron-and-steel framework underneath. He lavishly decorated the first- and second-floor windows and doors with cast-iron "organic" ornaments.

Prairie genius: Frank Lloyd Wright

Frank Lloyd Wright (1867–1959), who is considered by many to be an American genius, began his career working for Louis Sullivan. But instead of embracing Sullivan's ideas about tall buildings, Wright came to criticize the skyscraper as an abominable invention unsuited to Americans' desire for spaciousness. Only the landlord and the bank benefit from skyscrapers, he claimed in the 1930s. Buildings, Wright believed, should be spread out horizontally, instead of being thrown toward the sky.

Wright's interest in extending low structures into the landscape led him to create buildings of bold originality. His architecture managed to blend both Eastern and Western traditions and harmonize modern space with nature.

Born in Wisconsin, Wright studied engineering before moving to Chicago in 1887 to join the firm of Adler and Sullivan where he got his first inkling of modern architectural ideas. It wasn't long before Wright began applying these ideas to his own house projects outside the firm. When Sullivan found out about this moonlighting, the young architect was fired.

Wright opened his own practice in 1893 and built his own house and studio in Oak Park when he was only 22. In this Chicago suburb and nearby communities, Wright built dozens of homes with overhanging rooflines and flowing rooms. They were called *Prairie houses,* and their horizontal lines stretched out toward the expansive horizon. Some notable examples include the Ward Willits House (1902), Coonley House (1908), and the Robie House in Chicago (1909). Wright's early commissions also included an office building — the Larkin Company Administration Building (1902–1906, now demolished) in Buffalo, New York — and the Unity Church (1905–1908) in Oak Park. Both were blocky and inwardly focused; the innovative Larkin building centered on a four-story atrium.

In 1909, Wright left his wife and children to travel in Europe with Mamah Borthwick Cheney, the wife of a former client. Wright's work was featured in a book published in Germany in 1910–1911 that had an enormous influence on European avant-garde architects, especially the Dutch De Stijl group (see Chapter 14).

After returning to the United States, Wright and Cheney lived together at Taliesin (Welsh for "shining brow"), a home Wright had built in Wisconsin. Tragedy struck in 1914 when a servant murdered Cheney and six others, and set a fire that destroyed much of Taliesin. (Wright built a second Taliesin, but it, too, burned down.) Eventually the estate was rebuilt and turned into a school called the Taliesin Fellowship where apprentices came to live and learn under Wright. A winter location for the school, called Taliesin West, was eventually built outside Phoenix, Arizona.

Wright praised the virtues of an "organic" architecture rooted to the land-scape and animated by natural light. His highly personal work had a much more geometric quality than Sullivan's, but it was less austere than European modernism. Like many leading architects of his day, Wright designed furniture, stained glass windows, and other details of his buildings to create a harmonious whole.

The timber frames, screen walls, and open spaces of Japanese architecture also influenced Wright, who was an avid collector of Japanese prints. In 1905, the young architect made his first trip to Japan. He later returned to design and direct the construction of Tokyo's Imperial Hotel (1915–1922) (see Chapter 23).

Wright fell on hard times during the 1920s and early 1930s. Apart from a few houses in Los Angeles and his book, *An Autobiography,* published in 1932, he completed few projects. During the Depression, he drew up a visionary plan, meant to bring urban life to the country, that foreshadowed the postwar suburb. Called Broadacre City, the low-density settlement called for "small farms, small factories, small homes, . . . small schools," and an acre of land for each person.

Wright's fortunes changed when Pittsburgh department store owner Edgar J. Kaufmann approached him to design a home in the Pennsylvania country-side. The architect responded by cantilevering horizontal roofs and floors over a waterfall and calling his masterpiece *Fallingwater* (1934–1937).

Another Wright masterpiece of the 1930s is the Johnson Wax Company Administration Center (1936–1950) in Racine, Wisconsin. Encircled by stream-lined bands of brick, its most striking features were mushroom-shaped columns and windows made of stacked glass tubes.

In the years following World War II, Wright was in his 80s and still going strong. He received numerous commissions and created some of his boldest works: the Price Company tower, a slender skyscraper in Bartlesville, Oklahoma (1952–1956); the spiraling Guggenheim Museum (1943–1959); and his only government building, the Marin County Civic Center (1957–1962) outside of San Francisco.

Wright never retired; he died in 1959 at age 92.

A Skyscraper State of Mind: Rise of the New York Skyline

At the same time that Chicago was rebuilding its downtown commercial core after the fire, New York was building its first elevator buildings. They included the Equitable Life Assurance Building (1868–1870); the Western

Union Building (1872–1875), designed by architect George B. Post; and the Tribune Building (1873–1875), designed by Richard Morris Hunt, the Gilded Age architect who designed mansions for the Vanderbilts (see Chapter 11) and the Statue of Liberty's pedestal (see Chapter 12).

With their mansard roofs, arched windows, and other historical details, New York's 8- and 10-story masonry-supported structures were shorter and more conventional-looking than Chicago skyscrapers. But they were just as important to later skyscraper developments in their pioneering use of steam-powered elevators and sophisticated ventilation and electrical systems. The French Renaissance–inspired style of the early New York skyscrapers (called *Neo-Grec* by the Ecolé-des-Beaux-Arts-trained Hunt) also projected an image of wealth and prestige for commercial tenants.

The long arm of the law waves "hi" to the tall steel skeleton

In 1892, New York passed new laws allowing for steel skeleton construction. Soon tall buildings transformed New York's skyline with architecture far more fanciful than the flat-topped structures of Chicago. Like the earlier skyscrapers of the 1870s, the tall buildings were styled with historical elements such as Gothic tracery (see Chapter 9) and Renaissance arcades (see Chapter 10) and topped by spires, lanterns, and clock towers. Although criticized by twentieth-century modern architects as "historicist confections," these skyscrapers were as groundbreaking as those in Chicago. The following sections give a few examples of these buildings.

The Singer Building: Sewing it up

Taller than any Chicago skyscraper, the Singer Building (1906–1908) was designed by architect Ernest Flagg with French Baroque forms and ornamentation that he learned as a student at the Ecolé des Beaux-Arts in Paris. Flagg's brick-and-stone tower enlarged the sewing machine company's existing headquarters in lower Manhattan. The architect proposed a 35-story skyscraper, and the company decided to double it with a 612-foot tower. For a year, the Singer Building was the tallest in the world, until the Metropolitan Life Insurance Tower surpassed it in 1909. In 1968, the building was razed to make way for the U.S. Steel Building, which was renamed 1 Liberty Plaza.

Metropolitan Life Insurance Tower: Venice in Manhattan

Inspired by the bell tower in St. Mark's plaza in Venice, this slender, marble-sheathed tower was built (1907–1909) to advertise Metropolitan Life as the largest insurer in the world. Above its steeply pitched roof, the "light that never fails" glowed from its lantern to flash each hour and quarter-hour. The tower was designed by Napoleon LeBrun and Sons to rise 658 feet, but it ended up stretching to 700 feet.

In 1961, the building's balcony, moldings, and decorative details were stripped off in an attempt to modernize the building. Today, only the clock faces on the four sides of the tower remain from LeBrun's original façades.

Woolworth Building: Cathedral of Commerce for nickels and dimes

The slender, 792-foot Woolworth Building, completed by five-and-dime king Frank Woolworth in 1913, was the tallest office building in the world (only the Eiffel Tower was higher) until the opening of the Chrysler Building in 1930. Nicknamed the "Cathedral of Commerce," it was designed by architect Cass Gilbert in the Gothic Revival style (see Chapter 11) to soar high above New York's City Hall.

We're styling now: Optical illusion saves the day

The exterior of the Woolworth Building is covered in Gothic tracery (see Chapter 9) made from light-colored terra cotta with diagonal projections that catch light and cast shadows. Accenting these vertical elements are colored horizontal bands that express the steel skeleton underneath. To make the building appear uniform from a distance, the terra-cotta exterior cladding gradually becomes darker in color from the bottom of the building to the top. This change compensated for the increased intensity of daylight on the upper stories, which weren't shaded by surrounding buildings.

Is that Laurel and Hardy? No, it's Woolworth and Gilbert!

At the top of the building, the tower is decorated with flying buttresses (see Chapter 9), spires, gargoyles, and a copper roof that was originally covered in gold leaf. Gothic motifs are repeated inside the cross-shaped lobby. Among the marble sculptures in this vaulted space are caricatures of Woolworth counting his dimes, and Gilbert holding a model of his skyscraper.

Mr. Otis and his inventions

Elevators were in use as early as the 1830s, but it took Vermont-born inventor Elisha Graves Otis to make the power-operated lifts safe and comfortable. While using a hoist to lift heavy equipment, Otis came up with the idea of a catching device that would prevent the hoist from falling if the rope gave way. In 1854, he demonstrated his safety brake at the Crystal Palace in New York. After Otis went up in an open elevator, the hoisting cable was cut. The platform, caught by toothed guardrails on either side, stood in place — and the passenger elevator was born.

Three years later, the first commercial elevator was installed in a five-story building in New York City. By 1873, more than 2,000 elevators were moving up and down in buildings across the country. The rapid growth of taller buildings led to the development of the *hydraulic elevator,* which was widely manufactured in the 1880s. It was speedier, safer, and more compact than earlier steam elevators. In 1903, Otis introduced the gearless traction electric elevator, which helped lead to the construction of modern-day skyscrapers.

Just a few years earlier, Charles Seeberger had joined the Otis Elevator Company, bringing with him another invention that would modernize commercial buildings — the *escalator.* First shown at the Paris Exposition of 1900, this moving stairway was given its name by combining "elevator" with "scala," which is Latin for steps.

Forget the ribbon-cutting ceremony! We got the Prez!

The opening ceremonies in 1913 were equally as fantastic as the building. President Woodrow Wilson pressed a switch, from the White House, that lit up the skyscraper's interiors and façades.

More Recent Skyscapers

In 1916, New York passed a zoning law that influenced the shapes of its skyscrapers. Instead of rising as a single slab, the upper stories of the buildings were set back from their wider, lower stories to allow more sunlight and air to reach surrounding buildings and streets.

Sleek, geometric, and repetitive: Art Deco

By the 1920s and early 1930s, skyscrapers took on the modern flavor of the jazz age with zigzagging, futuristic ornamentation. This style was called *Art Deco,* a name that is based on the 1925 Paris Exposition Internationale des Arts Décoratifs et Industriels Modernes (International Exhibition of Modern Decorative and Industrial Arts) where the style was introduced. Based on sleek lines, streamlined geometric forms that repeat themselves, and industrial materials, Art Deco expressed the essence of mass production. (The best place to see Art Deco architecture is Miami's South Beach district, where hotels and apartment buildings convey the flamboyance and fun of this functional style.)

The most famous Art Deco skyscraper is the Chrysler Building in New York. Designed by architect William Van Alen, this jazzy tower is beloved for its quirky, zigzagged spire, metal gargoyles, and hood ornaments. Its design, along with the Empire State Building and other skyscraper landmarks, is discussed in Chapter 24.

The skyscraper, my friend, is blowing in the wind

By the 1950s, skyscrapers were sheathed in vast expanses of glass. They also stood much taller than the average 200-foot height of the prewar high-rises. These super towers confronted engineers with the new challenge of bracing structures against the wind. To solve this problem, steel columns and beams were clustered in skyscraper cores to create a stiff backbone. This core was used as an elevator shaft, and it allowed for unencumbered open spaces on each floor. In newer, taller skyscrapers, such as the Sears tower, engineers moved the primary structure from the core to the perimeter to create a hollow tube that is as strong and rigid as the core design but much less heavy. See Figure 13-3. For more examples of these wind-resistant skyscrapers, including the world's tallest building, see Chapter 24.

Figure 13-3: Illustrations of modern skyscrapers showing how a tube structure acts as a cantilever beam in resisting lateral forces (A at left); how tubes are bundled to form a modular structure (B at center); and how a tube forms an interior core (B at right).

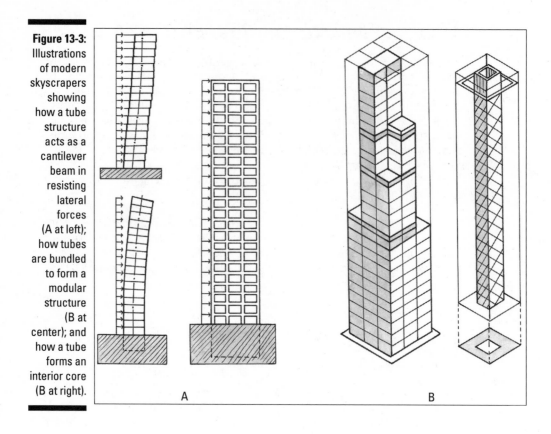

A   B

Chapter 14

Mother Nature versus the Machines: Modern Styles

*B*y the twentieth century, architects were ready to embrace new technology with new architecture. Instead of imitating past styles, architects looked to both nature and machines for inspiration. A rapidly transforming world was the motivator for this shift. Cities were mushrooming, nationalism was on the rise, religion was being questioned, and the role of women in society was shifting. Inventions such as the car, the telephone, and the electric light made urban living easier and more convenient than ever before.

Architecture reflected the sweeping changes in streamlined, spare buildings that conveyed a modern spirit. These creations were touted as more appropriate for a new century and morally superior to the fussiness of Victorian buildings. Through essays, manifestoes, books, drawings, models, and exhibitions, as well as buildings, architects proclaimed that their "purer," no-frills environments could actually improve society.

Far from being uniform, twentieth-century architecture was diverse, fragmented, and ever-changing. It reflected the revolutionary ideas of a world in constant upheaval. This was an epoch shaken by Einstein's theory of relativity, Freudian analysis, Cubist art, the Russian Revolution, and World War I.

Architects responded with buildings of increasing abstraction that were often compared to paintings and sculptures. The architects rejected the revival of historical styles and returned to the basics of architecture — structure, form, and proportion — to create a universal architectural language intended to express all the power and depth of ancient traditions.

All You Need Is Art: Arts and Crafts for Everyday People

The break with historicism wasn't abrupt. It grew slowly, spurred by a reaction against the ills of nineteenth-century industrialization. Squalid living conditions for workers and shoddy goods led reformers in the 1850s and 1860s to propose alternatives to modern manufacturing. Two leaders of this movement were British art critic John Ruskin (1819–1900) and designer William Morris (1834–1896). They looked to the arts and handicraft of the Middle Ages as a way of raising the quality of ordinary people's homes and household goods.

Putting his beliefs into practice, Morris established his own cooperative workshop based on the *medieval guild,* a close-knit association of artisans. This model would supposedly revolutionize workers' conditions and give them the initiative to reject machines and work like real craftsmen from the Middle Ages. In 1861, Morris set an example by starting a workshop for making fabrics, furniture, wallpaper, and stained glass.

The well-designed, well-made objects by Morris and his followers reflected the philosophy that fine arts, such as painting and sculpture, and handicrafts, such as furniture and fabrics, should be one and the same. Morris's goal was to create totally harmonious surroundings that were unified by a single aesthetic.

This idea of totally integrated environments had a tremendous influence on modern design and architecture in the twentieth century.

A Modern Style Takes Root: Art Nouveau and Its Architects

The British Arts and Crafts movement, started by William Morris, flowered into a more dynamic, sinuous style in the 1890s. This new style, named *Art Nouveau* ("the new art") after a Paris shop, was also based on the return to craftsmanship and the integration of art, design, and architecture. Inspired by nature, artists and architects developed stylized plant forms, whiplash curves, and geometric motifs to transform everything from jewelry and posters to furniture and entire buildings.

Art Nouveau took root throughout Europe and assumed variations in different countries from the 1890s until the outbreak of World War I in 1914.

In Germany, it was called *Jugendstil* (young style); in Spain, it was known as *Modernismo* (modernism); in Italy, it was named *Stile Floreale* (floral style), as well as *Stile Liberte* (liberty style) after the London department store, Liberty's, which sold arts-and-crafts-styled items. These names reflected the youthful, modern, and free spirit of Art Nouveau as a reaction against the historical, ponderous designs of the Victorian age.

Cast-iron wonderland: Victor Horta

The first full-blown example of Art Nouveau architecture was a townhouse in Brussels called the Hôtel Tassel (1892–1883). It was designed by Belgian architect Victor Horta (1861–1947), who believed that structural elements shouldn't be concealed but should instead double as decoration. Cast iron, which can be bent and still maintain its tensile strength, allowed Horta to meld structure and ornament into a single entity. In the stair hall of the Hôtel Tassel, plantlike tendrils spread from exposed cast-iron columns to the banisters, walls, and floors. Enough to make you think, "It's alive! It's alive, I tell ya!"

Horta was influenced by the writings of French architect Eugène Viollet-le-Duc, who, in the 1860s, argued for using machine-made materials to create "architectural forms adapted to our time."

In seeking new forms of expression, Horta turned to nature as a source of inspiration. He didn't imitate plants so much as capture their essence of growth and vitality to convey the spirit of the modern age. "I discard the flower and the leaf, but I keep the stalk," he said.

Budding flowers in the concrete jungle: Hector Guimard

Imagine walking up the steps from a gloomy subway station and seeing a plantlike structure that has flower-bud lamps glowing with electric light. That's the sight that greeted riders of the underground metropolitan railway in Paris. Designed by French architect Hector Guimard (1867–1942), the stemlike cast-iron gateways and pavilions for the Metro were completed to coincide with the World's Fair in 1900. Guimard's designs were so admired by the public that Art Nouveau in France was sometimes called the *Guimard Style* or *Style Metro*.

In his buildings, Guimard devoted as much energy to the interiors as to the exteriors. He coordinated every element, from window grilles and doors to lighting, furniture, and fireplaces. This approach was no doubt influenced by the British Arts and Crafts movement, which Guimard studied on a trip to England and Scotland in 1894. One of his most striking works was the Castel Henriette (1899), a castlelike house built on the outskirts of Paris. Named for its owner, Henriette Hefty, the house was used as a setting in the movie *What's New, Pussycat?* It was torn down in 1969.

Swirling fantasies: Antoni Gaudí

The quirky structures designed by Catalan architect Antoni Gaudí (1852–1926) in Barcelona, Spain, were more daring than the designs of Guimard. Combining Moorish and Gothic elements with naturalistic forms, their textured, undulating shapes recall waves, sea coral, and fish bones. Gaudí's dreamy, intensely personal style first emerged in a Barcelona park called Parc Guell (1900–1914). Benches embedded with tile fragments, underground grottoes, and flowing steps transformed the landscape into a fantasy world.

Gaudí used the same fluid lines to liberate his architecture from right angles and symmetrical shapes. One of his most dynamic buildings is a corner apartment block in downtown Barcelona called the Casa Milá (1905–1910). Encircled by deep, wavy ledges, its façades appear to be in constant motion. The swirling curves are also carried inside with the irregularly shaped rooms.

For Gaudí, such fantastic structures were perfectly logical. As he noted, there is no such thing as a straight line in nature.

Glasgow's gifted son: Charles Rennie Mackintosh

One of the most internationally recognized figures of the Art Nouveau movement was Scottish architect Charles Rennie Mackintosh. Mackintosh, who often worked with his wife, painter and designer Margaret MacDonald, created buildings and interiors that were more severe, linear, and abstract than the floral shapes that blossomed in Belgium and France. His collection of Japanese prints and books on Japanese architecture, as well as Celtic and Gaelic traditions, had a profound influence on his stark style.

Mackintosh first became known for a series of tea rooms in Glasgow. These light, airy spaces, furnished with chairs, tables, and wall decorations of his own design, were a complete departure from the dark, stuffy gentlemen's clubs and pubs of the period.

Those interiors were followed by Mackintosh's masterpiece, the Glasgow School of Art (1897–1909). Situated on a hilltop (like a modern castle), its façades of crisp, stone walls and huge windows looked far more abstract and modern than Art Nouveau buildings in Brussels and Paris.

Articles about the buildings and interiors designed by Mackintosh and MacDonald were published abroad, and the duo's work became much admired by turn-of-the-century artists and architects. In 1900, they were invited to exhibit their designs in Vienna, where architects were developing modern buildings in a similar spirit.

Mother Nature's Out the Door: More "isms" and Other Styles

Influenced by cubist and abstract art, architects working in Europe and Russia during the 1910s and 1920s proposed far more minimalist designs than the flowing tendrils of Art Nouveau.

Although their mini-movements didn't produce many buildings, they did generate important ideas that changed the course of modern architecture. The following sections describe the major players.

Down with ornamentation! Vienna Secessionism

In 1897, a group of Viennese artists and architects broke away from the official art establishment with the intention of putting art, design, and craft on an equal footing. Rejecting both stodgy academic design and the "decadence" of Art Nouveau, they called themselves the *Secessionists* and began stripping away moldings and other types of ornament. "New purposes must give birth to new methods of construction and by this reasoning to new forms," wrote Otto Wagner (1841–1918). Wagner's Post Office Savings Bank (1904–1906), with glass ceilings and floors, exemplified his belief.

The exhibitionist (of art, that is!): Josef Maria Olbrich

Another leader in the Secessionist movement was Josef Maria Olbrich (1867–1908), who designed an exhibition hall for the group to display its work. The hall's plain façades were painted with subdued decorations and topped by a large sphere of golden leaves. The interiors featured paintings by artist Gustav Klimt, another member of the Secessionist group.

It doesn't look like much, but the food is great: Josef Hoffmann

Another leader of the new architecture was Josef Hoffmann (1870–1956). Hoffmann was a founder of the Vienna Workshop, a British Arts and Crafts–style design studio. He was also a talented designer of furnishings and architecture. His most famous building is the Palais Stoclet (1905–1911), a luxurious mansion that was built in Brussels for Belgian financier Adolphe Stoclet and his wife Suzanne. Although the tower-topped house was spare on the outside, it was sumptuously decorated on the inside with Klimt murals, marble, and rich woods. The lavish home was truly a modern palace where the Stoclets could entertain the artistic elite of Europe.

Radical simplicity: Adolf Loos

Any decoration was too much for architect Adolf Loos (1870–1933), the most radical thinker of the Viennese group. He detested the ornament of Art Nouveau, preferring instead the simplicity and directness of machines and ordinary objects — railroad engines, bicycles, and men's suits. This no-nonsense attitude may have been influenced by Loos's three-year stay in the United States, where he came to admire the architecture of Louis Sullivan (see Chapter 13).

I gotta be me!

After returning to Vienna in 1896, Loos broke away from the Secessionists to design plain interiors and buildings. Among his most notable projects in Vienna are the tiny American Bar (1907) and Steiner House (1910), a concrete cube with a rounded roof and large plate-glass windows.

Un-tattoo you: Loos's writings

Loos's writings are far better known than his buildings. In 1908, he caused a sensation with his essay "Ornament and Crime," in which he compared decorated buildings to tattooed men. Although Loos found no fault in Papuan "savages" tattooing themselves, he claimed that "a modern man who tattoos himself is either a criminal or a degenerate." By logical extension, a modern building that was ornamented was also criminal. Loos concluded by noting "the evolution of culture marches with the elimination of ornament from useful objects." In other words, Loos believed that for a building to be truly modern, it must be totally free of decoration.

Heavy-metal muses: Italian Futurism

Enthusiasm for the machine age was taken to extremes in the early 1900s by a small group of Italian architects called the *Futurists*. "Just as the ancients drew their inspiration . . . from the natural world, so we . . . must find our inspiration in the new mechanical world," wrote architect Antonio Sant'Elia in a 1914 manifesto. New buildings should convey speed and movement by resembling locomotives, torpedo boats, and airplanes, not monuments of the past. A shopping center shaped like an airplane? Buildings with racing stripes? Well, maybe not. But the Futurists were ready to embrace speed, noise, pollution, cities, and movable parts.

Although the Futurists never built anything, Sant'Elia (1880–1916) produced striking drawings of boldly mechanistic skyscrapers, rail stations, elevated roadways, and the kind of futuristic cities that are portrayed in the film *Metropolis.* Sant'Elia died during World War I, but his ideas were taken up by leading architects in Germany, Russia, Holland, and France.

Crystalline visions: German Expressionism

During the early 1900s, avant-garde artists and architects often shared the same vision. One example of this shared vision is *Expressionism,* a European movement that was strongest in Germany following World War I. It generated jagged and dynamic forms in both painting and architecture.

One of the first architects to design in an expressionistic style was Bruno Taut (1880–1938). In 1914, Taut designed a faceted pavilion of glass, a material seen as symbolic of the modern age. Even more dramatically expressionistic was the renovation of the Berlin opera house (1919) by architect Hans Poelzig (1869–1948) into a fantastic, cavelike interior, ringed by icicle shapes hanging from the balconies.

Another key figure in the movement is Erich Mendelsohn (1887–1953). Mendelsohn was friends with Franz Marc, Wassily Kandinsky, and other artists from Munich who formed an informal group of expressionistic artists known as *Der Blaue Reiter* (Blue Rider).

In 1919, Mendelsohn opened an office in Berlin and began working on a research laboratory for studies relating to Einstein's theory of relativity. This led to his most famous building, the Einstein Tower in Potsdam (1920–1924). Its rounded, sculptural shapes and corner windows culminated in a telescope that was meant to reflect beams of light into a laboratory.

De Stijl: "The Style"

Abstract art also influenced early-twentieth-century architecture in the Netherlands. By 1907, painter Piet Mondrian had begun simplifying his landscapes into what would become his signature combinations of vertical and horizontal lines. Architects soon began translating these abstract shapes into three-dimensional designs that were free of traditional associations. The driving force behind this new Dutch abstraction was artist Theo van Doesburg, who started a magazine in 1917 called *De Stijl,* or "The Style." Doesburg also created a movement with the same name. Key participants of the De Stijl group were architects J.J. Oud and Gerrit Rietveld.

The anxiety of influence: Frank Lloyd Wright

The De Stijl architects' experiments were inspired by the work of American architect Frank Lloyd Wright (read more about Wright in Chapter 13), whose drawings were well known from a German book published in 1910 and 1911. Wright's influence was clear in the overhanging roofs and horizontal shapes of the De Stijl buildings. Another influence was the work of Dutch architect Hendrik Petrus Berlage (1856–1934), whose brick buildings, such as the Amsterdam stock exchange (1897–1904), marked a new boldness and simplicity. In 1908, the same year that Loos wrote his essay "Ornament and Crime," Berlage stated, "In architecture, decoration and ornament are quite inessential, while space-creation and the relationships of masses are its true essentials."

The whole kit 'n' caboodle

In De Stijl architecture, walls and floors were composed into vertical and horizontal planes that seemed to hover in space. Each architectural element of the asymmetrical buildings was painted a different color — red, white, and blue, plus yellow, black, and gray — to distinguish its function and location. Imagine a Mondrian painting in 3-D, and you get the picture.

The most famous building of the De Stijl school is a small house in Utrecht designed by architect Gerrit Rietveld (1888–1964). Located next to a row of brick houses, the bright building (1923–1924) stands out dramatically from its somber neighbors. Its flat walls and roof are precariously balanced like a house of cards on the corner site. Inside, Rietveld designed every element — from cabinets and movable walls to furniture and light fixtures — as a total work of art. The house was renovated and opened to the public in 1987.

The style-free style: Russian Constructivism

The Russian Revolution of 1917 offered the opportunity for architects in the Soviet Union to break free from the past and design buildings suited to new political ideals. Glass, steel, and concrete was used to build "constructivist" monuments and civic structures. Architectural "style" was not self-consciously applied. The style instead came from a building's materials and function.

And the contestants are . . .

Leading this revolution was Eliezer "El" Lissitzsky (1890–1941) and Kasimir Malevich (1878–1935), whose abstract artworks of dynamically arranged geometric shapes heavily influenced the design of propaganda posters, household items, and entire buildings — all produced by the new Communist regime.

Two important architects of the Constructivist movement were Alexander and Victor Vesnin. Like Lissitzsky, they composed buildings from contrasting shapes, each for a different function. One of their best-known designs is a competition entry for the Palace of Labor (1922–1923). It divides the structure into an oval-shaped auditorium and a rectangular office tower that are connected by a bridge and wires from radio antennae.

It smokes, it glows, it squeaks, it moves!

Like the Futurists, the Constructivists admired machines and designed their buildings with moving parts. The Vesnin brothers proposed a steel-framed skyscraper for the newspaper *Pravda* (1924) that incorporated revolving billboards, searchlights, and glass-enclosed elevators.

Even more kinetic was the Monument to the Third International (1919–1920) designed by architect Vladimir Tatlin. A cube, pyramid, and cylinder were to be built inside its spiraling metal armature — all to house the congressional halls of the state. Each of these buildings was designed to revolve at a different speed — completing a full rotation once a year, once a month, or once a day — depending on the institution. Talk about going in circles!

Economic difficulties under the newly formed Communist regime, however, prevented these visionary schemes from being constructed. One of the few Constructivists that was able to build was architect Konstantin Melnikov, who designed several workers' clubs and the Soviet pavilion at the 1925 International Exhibition of Modern Decorative and Industrial Arts, held in Paris (the same one that inspired the Art Deco style discussed in Chapter 13). Among his surviving projects is the Club Rusakov (1927–1928) in Moscow.

The Bauhaus

A school in Germany called the *Bauhaus* (*Bau* meaning "building" and *haus* meaning "house") was one of the greatest influences on modern architecture, even though it lasted only 14 years. Germany's leading architect, Walter Gropius (1883–1969), founded the Bauhaus in 1919. A grand duke had invited Gropius to set up the new arts school in Weimar. Gropius had made a name for himself by designing a shoe factory that was enclosed in walls of glass. At the Bauhaus, he put into practice his belief that art, design, and construction should be united — an idea dating back to Gothic cathedrals (see Chapter 9) and the British Arts and Crafts movement (see the section "A Modern Style Takes Root: Art Nouveau and Its Architects," earlier in this chapter). Every student in every discipline was required to take the same course in materials, form, and color. The school attracted artists and architects from all over Europe, including Wassily Kandinsky, Paul Klee, and Laszlo Moholy-Nagy.

The Bauhaus promoted the philosophy of "form follows function," a modernist credo coined by Chicago architect Louis Sullivan (see Chapter 13). Architecture was stripped down to ultra-modern shapes of concrete, glass, and steel that were austere and unadorned. The school's own building in Dessau, Germany, shown in Figure 14-1, is a perfect example. Gropius and his colleagues believed that architecture should have a social agenda, helping to house people displaced after World War I. Schemes for mass-produced, low-cost houses were designed and exhibited, influencing radical new housing projects built in Europe during the 1920s and '30s.

Figure 14-1:
Bauhaus
school,
Dessau,
Germany,
1925–1926,
by Walter
Gropius.

Photo courtesy of and © Corbis/Bettman.

Gropius moved the Bauhaus to Dessau in 1925 under political pressure. After moving, he designed and constructed a new building (1925–1926) for the school, with all the interiors created by staff and students. A rift in the school led to the resignation of Gropius and other faculty in 1928. Architect Hannes Meyer was appointed director. In 1930, architect Ludwig Mies van der Rohe replaced Meyer as director.

The rise of Nazism brought the school under political attack. In 1932, it was moved to Berlin. A year later, it was closed, and many of its faculty members fled Germany. Gropius, van der Rohe, and Moholy-Nagy relocated to the United States to head architecture and design schools and to introduce Bauhaus ideas of modern design to Americans.

Though criticized in recent decades — most notably by writer Tom Wolfe in his 1982 book, *From Bauhaus to Our House* — the teachings of the German school are still part of architecture and design programs around the world.

Modernism Gets Real: The International Style

The revolutionary architecture invented in Europe was introduced to America by a 1932 exhibition at New York's Museum of Modern Art. Called the *International Style,* this new type of architecture reflected the austere designs of the Bauhaus. Simple, functional, and unadorned, the International Style came to be associated with flat roofs, white walls, horizontal windows, and concrete and steel building materials. Much of this architectural vocabulary was developed by French architect Le Corbusier and German architect Mies van der Rohe in the 1920s and 1930s. The flowing spaces and stripped-down façades of their buildings had a profound influence on later generations of architects.

After World War II, the style was popularized in nearly every corner of the world. Today, some architects still follow the teachings of Le Corbusier and Mies van der Rohe. (Many of them simply refer to the two modernists as "Corbu" and "Mies.")

Machines for living: Le Corbusier

Swiss-born Charles Edouard Jeanneret (1887–1965), known as Le Corbusier, played a pivotal role in the development of twentieth-century modernism with his writings as well as his architecture.

Jeanneret's first major work was the Schwob house (1916) in his birthplace of La Chaux-de-Fonds. Though rather classical, the Schwob house had flat roofs and geometric shapes that hinted at a more abstract direction.

In 1917, the young architect settled in Paris and, with artist Amedee Ozenfant, began painting in a cubist-related style called Purism (see Chapter 15). Together the pair started a magazine called *L'Esprit Nouveau* ("The New Spirit"), which publicized their views on modern art and design. A collection of essays from the magazine was published in 1923 as a book, *Vers une architecture* (translated into English in 1927 as *Towards a New Architecture*). It turned out to be one of the most influential architecture books ever written. By then, Jeanneret had adopted a new name, Le Corbusier (a combination of his grandfather's name and a nickname "Corbeau," meaning "crow"), to signify his new identity as a visionary.

In his book, Le Corbusier argued that the modern age deserved a brand-new type of architecture based on both classical monuments and fast-moving machines. Illustrations included the Parthenon and St. Peter's in Rome, as well as ocean liners and airplanes. "The house is a machine for living," he wrote, meaning that residential architecture should be stripped down to its most essential functions.

In the late 1920s, Le Corbusier put his philosophy into practice with a series of white, cubic houses. The most famous of these is the Villa Savoye (1929–1931) near Paris. It reflects the architect's "Five Points of a New Architecture" that he felt were mandatory for modernism.

Le Corbusier's first requirement for a modern building was a new structural system of stilts, or *pilotis,* that lifted a building off the ground to allow people and traffic to pass underneath. With this support and a grid of columns above, the interior could be treated as what Le Corbusier called a "free plan" — rooms enclosed by non-load-bearing partitions. Because the exterior of the building didn't have to bear weight, it, too, could be "free" and treated as a thin curtain, with windows of any size. The architect preferred "long windows," glass strips running the full width of the façade, to let in the most light. On the roofs of his buildings, he recommended planting gardens to introduce nature into the city.

Le Corbusier's principles were applied to the design of entire cities. In such visionary schemes as La Ville Contemporaine (1922), the Plan Voisin de Paris (1925), and Villes Radieuses (1930–1936), Le Corbusier proposed highly ordered groupings of skyscrapers raised on *pilotis*. These dense plans were the opposite of Wright's Broadacre City (see Chapter 13). They were never realized, but Le Corbusier did go on to complete several high-rise structures. They include the Pavillon Suisse (1930–1931), a dormitory for Swiss students at the City University in Paris, and the Unite d'Habitation (1947–1953) in Marseilles, an apartment block with 23 different unit types.

In 1927, Le Corbusier entered the international competition for the Palace of the League of Nations. His design, even though it was rejected, became influential within architectural circles. The following year, he helped found the Congres International d'Architecture Moderne (International Congress of Modern Architects, commonly referred to as CIAM). This group of 24 architects, including Walter Gropius of the Bauhaus, aimed to advance the cause of modernism within the architecture profession. (The organization dissolved in 1956.)

After World War II, Le Corbusier struck out in a new direction. His white, boxy architecture gave way to more complex, sculptural shapes in concrete. Among his most striking works are the chapel at Ronchamp (1950–1955) and the monastery of La Tourette (1957–1959), both in France. During this period, Le Corbusier also designed his only building in the United States, the Carpenter Center for the Visual Arts at Harvard University (1961–1964). He was also among the architects selected to plan the United Nations headquarters in New York.

Le Corbusier's international reputation led to a commission from the Indian government to plan the city of Chandigarh, the capital of Punjab, and design its government center (1950–1970) and several other structures.

He died in 1965 while swimming in the Mediterranean.

Less is more: Ludwig Mies van der Rohe

Architect Ludwig Mies van der Rohe (1886–1969) enjoyed a 60-year career that was equally divided between Germany and the United States. He is best known for developing boxy, steel-and-glass architecture for nearly every purpose — from houses to skyscrapers.

Mies, as he came to be known, was an apprentice to his father, a stonemason, before leaving his hometown of Aachen for Berlin in 1905. After briefly serving in the German army, the young architect went to work for the Art Nouveau designer Bruno Paul. In 1906, at age 20, Mies received his first independent commission — a house for Alois Riehl (a professor of philosophy) and his wife Sofie. The Riehl House caught the attention of Germany's leading architect, Peter Behrens, who hired Mies two years later.

While working for Behrens, Mies grew to admire the early-nineteenth-century buildings in Berlin designed by the Prussian architect Karl Friedrich Schinkel (see Chapter 11). In 1912, Mies left Behrens's firm to establish his own office, where he designed a series of houses influenced by Schinkel's simplified classical style.

After World War I, Mies began studying the skyscraper. In the early 1920s, he drew up several innovative proposals for steel-framed towers sheathed entirely in glass. Although his designs were never built, the revolutionary high-rise projects drew critical praise and foreshadowed his towers of the late 1940s and 1950s. In 1921, he changed his name from Ludwig Mies to Ludwig Mies van der Rohe to signal a new chapter in his personal (he left his wife and family) and professional life.

Mies continued his spatial experiments during the mid-1920s in low-slung houses of brick, concrete, and glass. With fluid floor plans and strong connections between the inside and outside, these asymmetrical pavilions expressed ideas that Mies continued to explore throughout his career.

Among Mies's most famous buildings was the German Pavilion at the International Exhibition held in Barcelona, Spain, in 1929. The small building, now known as the Barcelona Pavilion, was used by the Weimar government as a ceremonial hall for receiving the Spanish king and queen and other dignitaries. It had a flat roof supported on chrome columns so that the pavilion's walls could be freely positioned (because they did not have to support the structure). Rather than divide the interior into a series of closed rooms, Mies created a continuously flowing sequence of spaces. Freestanding walls of luxurious marbles, onyx, and glass appeared to slide past each other, out from under the flat roof. Mies even created special furniture for the interiors, including his famous leather "Barcelona chair," which is still being produced today. Although it was eventually dismantled, the Barcelona Pavilion became highly influential in the development of modern architecture. In 1986, it was re-created on the original site.

Mies undertook many projects during the 1930s. But because of the sweeping economic and political changes that overtook Germany, few of his designs were built. The Bauhaus, where Mies was director and a teacher, was shut down in 1933 under pressure from the new Nazi government.

By 1937, Mies realized that he had few prospects under the increasingly oppressive Nazi regime. He decided to travel to the United States at the invitation of an advertising executive, Helen Resor, and her husband Stanley. They were eager to have Mies design their vacation home near Jackson Hole, Wyoming. After sailing to New York, Mies traveled to the West, via Chicago, to visit the site. As Mies was on his way back to Germany to settle things there, the couple decided to cancel the project. Despite the disappointing news, Mies decided to accept an offer to head the architecture department at the Armour Institute of Technology in Chicago. He moved permanently to the United States in 1938, a year before the Nazis invaded Poland.

After settling in Chicago, Mies was asked by the Armour Institute's president to design a new campus for the school, which was soon renamed the Illinois Institute of Technology. His master plan for IIT on Chicago's South Side marked a huge leap from his small European projects. Mies also designed many of the campus buildings. He used steel beams and columns to create an industrial image that was expressive of the institute's technological mission.

In the late 1940s, the architect continued to develop his steel-and-glass vocabulary. One of his most famous buildings from this era is a small weekend retreat outside Chicago that was designed for a doctor, Edith Farnsworth. A glass box framed by eight exterior steel columns, the Farnsworth House (1945–1951) is one of the most radically minimalist houses ever built. Its interior — a single room — is subdivided by partitions and is completely exposed to the outdoors.

Mies's design had an enormous influence on younger architects. One of the most famous examples is the Glass House (1949–1950) in New Canaan, Connecticut, which architect Philip Johnson built for himself.

Over the next decade, Mies realized his dream of erecting a glass skyscraper. The twin towers of the 860–880 Lake Shore Drive apartments (1948) were followed by similar high-rises in Chicago, Detroit, New York, Montreal, Toronto, and other cities. These structures were unique not only in their glass and metal detailing, but also in their siting. Placed on *plinths* — a kind of urban podium — they created ordered precincts that are distinct from busy city streets.

Designing women of the modern movement

The male architects who shaped the modern movement didn't do it alone. Several collaborated with female clients and colleagues, who also made important contributions to modernism in their own right. The accomplishments of these designing women have come to be appreciated only in recent times. Here are some of them:

✔ German designer Lilly Reich (1885–1947) trained under Austrian architect Josef Hoffmann, and began her career designing textiles and women's fashions. In the late 1920s and 1930s, she collaborated with Mies van der Rohe and developed furniture and interiors for many of his most important buildings. Reich also maintained her own office and taught interior design and weaving at the Bauhaus. She designed several ground-breaking displays of textiles, furniture, and building products, including a model house at a 1931 exhibition in Berlin.

✔ Charlotte Perriand (1903–1999) was a French designer trained at the École de L'Union des Arts Décoratifs in Paris who went onto to design cutting-edge furniture still being manufactured today. Perriand produced many interiors and furnishings for Le Corbusier ("Corbu"), including several in tubular steel that were previously attributed to Corbu. In the 1940s, Perriand created modern furnishings based on Asian traditions, and in the 1950s, she turned to modular designs.

✔ Another leading modernist was Irish-born designer Eileen Gray (1878–1976). After moving to Paris in 1902, Gray began producing furniture and screens using Japanese lacquer techniques. She opened her own gallery in 1922 to show her work. Several of her designs are still in production.

Gray also designed houses, including one in St. Tropez for architect Jean Badovici, a close friend and editor of *L'Architecture Vivant,* a highly regarded journal. Through Badovici, Gray met Le Corbusier and other important architects who shared her enthusiasm for the "spirit of a new age."

Enlightened female clients also played significant roles within the modern movement. Among those willing to finance and build risky architectural schemes was Truus Schroeder, a widow and mother of three. In 1923, she hired Dutchman Gerrit Rietveld to build his first piece of architecture — an unconventional house in Utrecht that became an icon of the De Stijl movement.

In California, heiress Aline Barnsdall (1882–1946), an arts patron and single mother, gave Frank Lloyd Wright a break in 1915 when she hired the architect to design a theater and artists' colony on top of a hill overlooking Los Angeles. Although Wright ended up only designing Barnsdall's residence, the Hollyhock House, the Mayan-inspired project marked a new phase in his work and led to other house commissions in Southern California.

The most elegant of Mies's towers is the Seagram Building (1954–1958), the headquarters that was built for whiskey distiller Joseph E. Seagram in midtown Manhattan (see Chapter 22).

In 1962, Mies's career came full circle when he was invited to design the New National Gallery (1962–1968) in Berlin, a museum that was to accommodate changing displays of contemporary art. Mies developed a glass-enclosed hall framed by a dramatically cantilevered roof resting on eight tapered columns. Although he returned to Berlin several times to see the gallery under construction, Mies was too sick to attend the opening in 1968. He died the next summer in Chicago.

Chapter 15

The Only Constant Is Change: From Modern Purism to Postmodern Pluralism

- -

In This Chapter

▶ Prelude to postmodernism

▶ Postmodernist architects

▶ Postmodernism here and abroad

▶ Modern revival

▶ Green architecture and other contemporary trends

- -

*B*y the mid-twentieth century, modernism had gone mainstream. Lean, spare architecture reflected the optimism and prosperity in the decades following World War II. In America, its acceptance was helped by European modern masters teaching at such universities as Harvard and the Illinois Institute of Technology (as well transforming their campus architecture). Architects such as Ludwig Mies van der Rohe, Walter Gropius, and Marcel Breuer (see Chapter 14) introduced a new generation to the abstract principles of the Bauhaus, while designing glass-and-steel buildings for corporate clients. By the 1960s, sleek, International Style design had become fashionable for nearly every type of building, from office high-rises to houses.

At the same time, a rebellion against modernism began stirring as architects — and the people who hired them — questioned the bland, sterile look of the boxy buildings that had begun sprouting from coast to coast. It was high time to reintroduce the decoration and the delight that had always been a part of architecture.

This anti-modern attitude toward architecture, influenced by the preservation movement (see Chapter 20), took hold in the 1970s and blossomed into what came to be called *postmodernism* during the 1980s. At its heart was a renewed appreciation for the rich traditions of architecture past. Instead of stripping buildings bare, architects began enlivening façades with color, pattern, and ornament. Even those architects who stuck with modernism loosened up their designs with playful planes and angles.

The origins of postmodernism and the pluralism that followed can be traced to the work of several architect rebels who began searching for a more human-sensitive modernism at mid-century.

Modernism Gets a Makeover by Late Modern Masters

While many mid-twentieth-century architects followed the International Style established by Mies van der Rohe and Le Corbusier in the 1920s and 1930s, others struck out in a new direction. These mavericks drew upon indigenous building traditions to soften modern's steel-and-glass palette with wood, stone, and brick. Their building designs were abstract, but they also responded to the climate and culture of their surroundings.

Several architects played a significant role in establishing this new direction. Their expressive modernism set the stage for a renewed interest in historical form and ornament.

Natural architect: Alvar Aalto

Finnish architect Alvar Aalto (1898–1976) was one of the first modernists to fuse technology with craft. He established his reputation in the 1920s and 1930s with such buildings as the Paimio Sanatorium (1929–1930) and Villa Mairea (1938–1941), and drew international acclaim for the Finnish Pavilion at the 1939 World's Fair in New York. Aalto's greatest skill was his ability to humanize modernism with curved walls and roofs and wood-finished interiors. Aalto was sensitive to the contours of the land and to a building's orientation to daylight. He always linked his buildings to their natural surroundings. "Nature, not the machine, should serve as the model for architecture," he said, a view that sharply contrasted with Le Corbusier's (see Chapter 14).

Aalto's first postwar commission was Baker Hall (1946–1949), a dormitory at the Massachusetts Institute of Technology. Its sinuously curved, textured brick walls broke away from the straight lines and slick surfaces of the International Style (see Chapter 14). That project was followed by several fan-shaped buildings, including a lecture theater for Helsinki University of Technology (1949–1966), a public library in Rovaniemi (1963–1968), and Finlandia Hall in Helsinki (1962–1971). As part of his projects, Aalto designed curvy glassware and furniture in laminated birch that is still being manufactured today.

Scandinavian eclectic: Eero Saarinen

Another prominent Finnish-born architect of the postwar decades was Eero Saarinen (1910–1961). His father, architect Eliel Saarinen (1873–1950), practiced in a romantic style and moved to the United States in 1923. Eero Saarinen grew up at Cranbrook Academy, outside Detroit, where his father taught.

In the 1950s and 1960s, Saarinen used advances in structural systems to create sculpturally expressive buildings. The most famous example is the soaring TWA passenger terminal (1956–1962) at New York's Kennedy Airport. Its winglike concrete shells celebrate the excitement of air travel. Following that structure was the vast, cable-suspended roof of Dulles International Airport (1963) outside Washington, D.C. No two Saarinen buildings are alike, however. His buildings followed a unique design direction according to the particulars of their site and purpose. Among the architect's more restrained designs are the John Deere office building in Moline, Illinois, and the CBS tower in New York, both completed in 1965 after his death.

Better late than never!: Louis Kahn

Another architect who humanized modern abstraction during the 1960s was Philadelphian Louis Kahn (1902–1974). A late bloomer — he received his first major building commission at age 52 — Kahn sought what he called the "immeasurable" in architecture. His work is often compared to ancient monuments, and it's easy to see why. Composed of circles, squares, and triangles, his designs were constructed of rough concrete and brick to convey a massive primal quality. (*Primal* meaning "imposing and godlike," not "Fred Flintstone.")

A great teacher, Kahn often lectured his students at the University of Pennsylvania and Yale on architectural fundamentals with aphorisms such as "design is but a single spark out of form." Architectural form, Kahn believed, should reflect a building's social purpose. "A plan is a society of rooms," he wrote. A library should be designed for "the person who picks up a book and goes to the light." One may wonder why Mr. Kahn didn't write a book of poetry, as well.

Let there be light!

Kahn's philosophy is reflected in such projects as the Phillips Exeter Academy (1969–1972) in Exeter, New Hampshire. With its sunlit atrium bordered by huge concrete circles, the building celebrates both the physical and the metaphorical implications of light through luminous spaces for reading and study.

Kahn often used a central communal space to convey the meaning of an institution. One of his most powerful works is the Salk Institute for Biological Sciences (1959–1965) in La Jolla, California. Laboratories are grouped into two blocks that frame a stark, paved courtyard. In the middle of the outdoor space, a channel of water runs down the center toward the Pacific Ocean.

The light-filled stage, with its view toward the sea and the horizon beyond, poetically symbolizes the institute's mission of researching the mysteries of nature.

Upstairs, downstairs: Served and servant spaces

Within his buildings, Kahn established a clear hierarchy of spaces. In the Richards Medical Research Building (1957–1965) at the University of Pennsylvania, he divided clustered towers into "served" spaces (laboratories and offices) and "servant" spaces (stairways, elevators, and utilities). This organization became his signature — it is an architectural principle that is still followed today.

Daylight continued to play an important role in Kahn's buildings. His mastery of natural illumination is best exemplified in the barrel-vaulted galleries of the Kimbell Art Museum (1966–1972) in Fort Worth, Texas. At the top of each vault, slots allow daylight to shine in, bounce off metal reflectors, and bathe the curved ceiling in radiance.

Building a bridge (pun intended!)

Although Kahn's work was controversial in its day, it is now revered by critics who consider him to be an important figure in the transition from modernism to postmodernism.

Lotsa Concrete, Folks: The New Brutalism Branch of Modernism

New Brutalism, or *Brutalism,* was inspired by the *béton brut* (raw concrete) used by Le Corbusier in his later buildings. The term was coined by British architects and critics during the 1950s. It was used to describe massive modern architecture built of reinforced concrete, with the concrete's rough, abrasive surfaces left exposed. Ouch!

The most famous American example of the New Brutalism style is the Art and Architecture Building at Yale University (1959–1963) designed by architect Paul Rudolph (1918–1997). The building, which is textured in ribbed concrete, is only seven stories tall but encompasses 36 levels. It became a sensation among architects still trying to figure out where to take modernism next. "It had some Le Corbusier, some Wright, a little Mies van der Rohe," said New

York architect and current Yale architecture school dean Robert A.M. Stern (he wrote the foreword to this book), "and it even addressed the Gothic of Yale." Rudolph's building, however, was highly unpopular with faculty and students. In 1969, it nearly burned down. (Legend has it that the students started the fire, but there was no proof.) In recent years, both the structure and its reputation have been resuscitated.

The Modernism Backlash: Postmodernism and the Past to the Rescue

By the 1970s, glass, steel, and concrete towers, once heralded as avant-garde, were being cheaply erected all over the world as symbols of corporate power and conformity. In cities, older neighborhoods were swept away by acres of identical, antiseptic buildings constructed in the name of urban renewal. A backlash against modernism, spurred by the historic preservation movement (see Chapter 20), slowly grew.

A small group of architects rejected the austerity of modernism and began reconnecting with the past. They developed what came to be called *postmodernism,* also known informally as "Po-Mo." Their designs juxtaposed historic details, ornament, color, and texture in playful combinations. The fun was back!

Robert Venturi, grandfather of postmodernism: Less is a bore

Leading the challenge to orthodox modernism was Philadelphia architect Robert Venturi (1925–) who became the most influential architectural theorist of the late twentieth century. His 1966 book, *Complexity and Contradiction in Architecture,* shook up the architectural establishment. Instead of following modernism's puritanical logic, Venturi suggested that architects should embrace ambiguity, decoration, and "messy vitality" in their buildings. "Less is a bore," he retorted to the Miesian credo of "less is more."

Venturi, who was a student of Louis Kahn and had worked for Eero Saarinen, argued for a more expansive view of architecture. He suggested the great monuments of the Renaissance and Baroque had as much to teach architects as modern buildings by Aalto and Le Corbusier. His vision was an architecture of "both-and" rather than "either-or." Venturi's critique led to the development of the postmodernist movement in the 1970s and a more pluralistic attitude toward architecture that still prevails today.

Venturi also put his theories into practice. Among his groundbreaking buildings are the Guild House (1960–1963), a retirement home in Philadelphia with a huge arch and a TV antenna, and a house for his mother in Chestnut Hill (1962–1964) that dared to have a pitched roof. You can see this house in Figure 15-1.

Figure 15-1:
The house Venturi designed in 1962 for his mother in Chestnut Hill.

Photo by Rollin R. LaFrance. Courtesy of Venturi, Scott Brown and Associates, Inc.

In 1972, Venturi collaborated with his partner and wife, Denise Scott Brown (1931–), and his associate, Steven Izenour (1940–2001), on another influential book, *Learning from Las Vegas.* (No, not *Leaving Las Vegas, Learning from Las Vegas.* So don't expect to see Nicholas Cage anywhere!) It analyzed the form and meaning of the commercial strip, from casinos and gas stations to signs and billboards. Venturi and his co-authors contended that architects should emulate such "ugly, ordinary" environments much in the way that pop artists borrow everyday imagery from commercial products and cartoons. "Main Street is almost all right," they asserted. Buildings should be designed as "decorated sheds," simple enclosures with attached decorations, rather than as "ducks" where the structure itself becomes the decoration.

In the 1980s and 1990s, Venturi and Scott Brown designed many university buildings and campus plans, as well as fabrics and furniture. The vivid patterns and colors, and the startling juxtapositions of architectural elements in the building designs convey the architects' playful wit and sharp intelligence. Their most prestigious project is the Sainsbury Wing at the National Gallery in London (1985–1991).

Other postmodernist players: Historical eclecticism and revivalism

Inspired by Venturi's writings, other architects began reviving past styles in a looser, more personal, and exaggerated way during the 1970s and 1980s.

Leading postmodernists, such as Robert A.M. Stern and Charles Moore, pumped up classical elements like columns, keystones, and arches. Philip Johnson, once an advocate for the International Style, became one of postmodernism's biggest promoters. He caused a furor when he shaped a New York skyscraper for AT&T (1978–1984) into a Chippendale chest of drawers (see Chapter 23 for more on this unusual skyscraper).

Neo-neoclassicism: A revival one more time

Postmodernism also led some architects to embrace history quite literally and design in a super-accurate neoclassical style. Their buildings are so faithful to the past that you'd swear they were built in the eighteenth century (except for the bathrooms and air-conditioning). No playful pediments or oversized keystones for them! Among the leaders of this neo-neoclassicism are Allan Greenberg in the United States and Quinlan Terry in the United Kingdom.

Po-Mo goes abroad to foreign shores

Po-Mo (postmodernism) was largely an American phenomenon, although foreign architects also embraced its hybrid, ironic style.

- ✔ Italian Aldo Rossi practiced a toned-down version by distilling classical and vernacular architecture down to their essence. His stripped-down buildings have a haunting quality that recalls the surreal cityscapes of Italian painter Giorgio de Chirico.

- ✔ Spanish-born architect Ricardo Bofill applied giant classical orders to the design of public housing in France. His apartment blocks in Marne-la-Vallee outside Paris (1978–1983) were modeled on Roman amphitheaters and the Colosseum, but were constructed of precast concrete and glass.

- ✔ Austrian architect Hans Hollein combined metaphorical references and exquisite details to join the Old World with the New. His travel agency in Vienna (1976–1978), planted with gold palm trees and eroded columns, expressed fantasy and illusion.

Po-Mo goes to Buckingham Palace

Aiding and abetting the return to the past was Britain's Prince Charles, an architecture buff who publicly criticized modern design starting in 1984. He wrote down many of his ideas in a book called *A Vision of Britain* (the book was accompanied by a television show of the same name). In 1992, he even started a school in London devoted to classical architecture and design. You go, Charlie!

Rebels with a cause: Postmodern titans

In every artistic movement, some people always stand out as the most influential. Among the most skillful postmodernists were architects who started out as modernists and then began juicing up their abstract designs with diverse references to history.

High-tech meets Po-Mo: James Stirling

British architect James Stirling (1926–1992), who used to be a proponent of New Brutalism and high tech, began quoting history in the late 1970s. Unlike many postmodernists, he sculpted his buildings to convey solidity rather than paper-thin decor. And Stirling's architecture does look heavy and solid — the big bad wolf couldn't blow any of this stuff down! Too bad for the three little pigs. Anyway, Stirling's masterpiece is the Neue Staatsgalerie (1977–1984) in Stuttgart, Germany, a striped stone building of diverse elements. Wavy windows framed in bright green metal and ramps with electric blue and fuchsia handrails look high tech. A rotunda encircled by statuary is inspired by the neoclassical work of Karl Friedrich Schinkel (see chapter 11). Other postmodern projects by Stirling designed in collaboration with partner Michael Wilford include the Arthur M. Sackler Museum at Harvard (1979–1984), the Clore Gallery for the Tate Gallery in London (1980–1987), and the performing arts center at Cornell University in Ithaca, New York (1982–1986).

The child within us all: Michael Graves

Michael Graves (1934–) first became famous as a member of the New York Five (see the following section "The New York Five: Keeping the modernist faith"), designing house additions in a *neoCorbusian* style. At the end of 1970s, he began incorporating decorative, historical references within his abstract designs. His Portland Public Services Building (1979–1982) in Portland, Oregon, was one of the first full-blown examples of postmodernism. Check out Figure 15-2 to see it. Its bright façades, filled with decorative motifs, infuriated the architectural establishment. Similar controversy swirled around his proposed addition to the Whitney Museum of American Art (1985), which was criticized for cannibalizing Marcel Breuer's original 1966 building. (Graves's addition was never built.)

Graves, a skilled sketcher and painter, renders his collage-like buildings in earthy colors derived from nature. His architecture often has a childlike, cartoonish quality, shown to exaggerated effect in his buildings for Disney. Graves was at his most playful in designing the Dolphin and Swan hotels (1989) for Disney World in Orlando, Florida, and the Team Disney building (1990) in Burbank, California — it has columns shaped like the Seven Dwarfs. Among his urban projects are the Humana Building (1985) in Louisville, Kentucky, and Denver Public Library (1995). Graves is also well known for his designs of furniture and household items, including a teakettle with a bird-whistle spout for Alessi (turn to Chapter 5 for a photo) and kitchenware for Target.

Figure 15-2:
The Portland Building, Portland, Oregon; 1979-1982, by Michael Graves.

Photo by Proto Acme Photo. Courtesy of Michael Graves & Associates.

East meets West: Arata Isozaki

A student of the leading Japanese Metabolist Kenzo Tange (see Chapter 16), Arata Isozaki (1931–) began his career designing boldly geometric buildings such as the Gunma Prefectural Museum (1971–1974). In the late 1970s, he introduced Western classical elements, such as barrel vaults and archways, into his work. This openness to Western traditions was innovative in Japan, where even modern architects clung to Eastern traditions.

One of the few Japanese architects to build in the United States, Isozaki is responsible for the Museum of Contemporary Art in downtown Los Angeles (1981–1986) and the Team Disney Building in Orlando, Florida (1989–1990).

Modernism with a Postmodernist Twist

The postmodernism thing didn't appeal to everyone. Some architects continued to hold on to their faith in modernism. They criticized postmodernism's historical motifs as silly and superficial while continuing to produce abstract, boxy buildings without ornamentation. In reality, these hold-outs were just as interested in architectural history as their postmodern colleagues. They looked to the early modern architecture of Le Corbusier and Russian Constructivists for inspiration, instead of the more ornate buildings of classical architects. Some of these neomodernists (Michael Graves, for example) even went so far as to change stripes and go Po-Mo. Others jazzed up Bauhaus purity with colorful angles and sculptural forms that were as provocative as any postmodernist design.

The New York Five: Keeping the modernist faith

Leading the modern revival was a group called the *New York Five,* which consisted of the following:

- Peter Eisenman
- Michael Graves
- Charles Gwathmey
- John Hejduk
- Richard Meier

The members of the New York Five were fascinated by the 1920s designs of Le Corbusier. They produced elegant, planar houses in the 1960s and 1970s before taking off in different directions. The five were nicknamed the "whites" for their light-colored abstractions, which were in contrast to the "grays" (gray referred to their buildings' stylistic ambiguity and weathered shingles) of the Venturi camp. Although they claimed to be in opposition, the two sides shared a common interest in the imagery of architecture rather than in architecture's social ramifications.

Of the five, the architect who has kept the modernist flame burning the longest is Richard Meier (1934–). His sleek, white buildings display a consistency and commitment to modern abstraction, making no attempt to blend into their surroundings. Many of Meier's most striking works have been built abroad: the Museum of Decorative Arts in Frankfurt, Germany (1981–1985); the Canal Plus Television headquarters in Paris (1988–1991); the City Hall and Central Library in The Hague (1986–1995); and the Barcelona Museum of Contemporary Art (1987–1996). More recently, he has laid down his modern law in two striking federal courthouses; one is in Islip, New York, and the other in Phoenix.

Meier's most ambitious project is the Getty Museum (1984–1997), a cultural acropolis of six buildings situated high above a Los Angeles freeway. The $1 billion, 110-acre hilltop complex of galleries and offices is a departure from the architect's signature white panels because it uses sand-colored stone.

High tech: Inhabitable machines

Another mutation of modern architecture in the 1970s and 1980s used the technology of building in a highly expressive way. The style, dubbed *high tech,* was pioneered by British architects Richard Rogers and Norman Foster and Italian architect Renzo Piano. They took Le Corbusier's motto — "a house is a machine for living in" — literally by designing buildings that look like huge pieces of equipment. One of the first high-tech buildings is the contemporary arts center in Paris known as the Centre Pompidou (1971–1977), which was designed by Piano and Rogers. It's in Figure 15-3. By placing the innards of the building — structure, ductwork, pipes, and escalators — on the exterior, the architects allowed for open, flexible interiors.

Rogers goes inside out

Rogers (1933–) is known for draping pipes and ducts all over his façades for a picturesque effect. His masterpiece is the Lloyd's of London tower (1978–1986), a Gothic-like structure of stainless-steel-clad service towers topped by a glass barrel vault reminiscent of Paxton's Crystal Palace (see Chapter 12). Another Rogers blockbuster is the controversial Millennium Dome in London. Spanning 80,000 square meters, it is the largest fabric-covered structure in the world.

Figure 15-3: The Centre Pompidou, Paris, France; 1971-1977, by Rogers and Piano.

Photo courtesy of GreatBuildings.com © Howard Davis.

Foster keeps it clean

Foster (1935–) almost never exposes mechanical ducts on the outside of his buildings. He prefers a slick, clean skin of metal and glass that is articulated by structure, as is exemplified in his Hong Kong and Shanghai Banks (see Chapter 24). Among his recent projects are terminals for Stansted Airport near London (1991) and the Chek Lap Kok Airport in Hong Kong (1998), and the renovation of the Reichstag in Berlin (see Chapter 20).

Piano lightens up

Since his early success with Rogers, Piano (1937–) has flourished on his own with offices in Paris and Genoa. He has moved away from the high-tech exuberance of the Centre Pompidou to a quieter, lighter architecture (for more about Piano, see Chapter 21). His love of engineering is still apparent in projects such as the Menil Collection (1982–1986). A roof of concrete "leaves" illuminates the galleries of this subdued Houston museum.

Deconstructivism: Violated perfection

In 1988, New York's Museum of Modern Art held an exhibition to examine another architectural trend. Called *Deconstructivist Architecture,* the exhibit showed how architects in Europe and the United States were using bent, angled, and exploded forms to represent the uncertainty of our times.

The designs drew upon the dynamic geometries of Russian Constructivism (see Chapter 14) and the literary theories of French philosophers such as Jacques Derrida, who holds that there is no fixed truth but only multiple interpretations. Deconstructivist architects speak of *violated perfection,* that is, overturning long-held traditions of stability and symmetry in architecture with unbalanced discontinuous designs. Modernist in orientation, their buildings are composed of leaning walls and sharply projecting roofs poised to fly off into space.

Deconstructivist architects include Peter Eisenman, Frank Gehry, Zaha Hadid, Coop Himmelblau (Viennese architects Wolf Prix and Helmut Swiczinksy), Daniel Libeskind, and Bernard Tschumi. Among the most interesting Deconstructivist buildings are Eisenman's Aronoff Center for Design and Art at the University of Cincinnati (1996); Libeskind's Jewish Museum in Berlin; Hadid's Vitra Fire Station (1993) in Weil-am-Rhein, Germany; and Tschumi's Parc de La Vilette (1989) in Paris. Gehry's Guggenheim Museum in Bilbao, Spain (1997), is now considered a masterpiece. (For more on Gehry, Hadid, and Libeskind, see Chapter 21.)

New Directions for a New Millennium

In recent years, architects have dumped Po-Mo's gimmicky historicism and Deconstructivism's crooked chaos for leaner, plainer forms. Pluralism still reigns in the search for new ways to express the complexities of contemporary life. The following sections describe a few directions that have emerged.

Another revival! Sensuous minimalism

Younger architects are reviving modernism and giving it a new kick with sensuous materials and subtle details. They draw upon elements of nature — light, water, and earth — to create haunting, poetic effects. (For more details about some of these architects, turn to Chapter 21 in The Parts of Ten.)

- **New York architect Steven Holl:** His contemporary art museums in Helsinki and Seattle interact with light and water.

- **Swiss architects Jacques Herzog and Pierre de Meuron:** They designed the Dominus Winery in Yountville, California, with wire-cage walls filled with rocks.

- **French architect Jean Nouvel:** The walls of his Arab Institute and Cartier Foundation in Paris play with daylight to create special effects.).

- **New York architects Tod Williams and Billie Tsien:** This husband-and-wife teamcreates special hand-crafted, tactile elements for each project, as in the new Museum of American Folk Art in New York City.

Drafting tables be gone: Digital design

Computers are changing the way buildings are designed and experienced. Drawings and documents that used to take hours to draft are now easily completed and coordinated through *computer-aided design* (CAD) programs. Sophisticated 3-D modeling software, first developed by the aerospace industry, has made irregular surfaces and complex curves easier to conceive and build.

Get down and get sculptural with the digital revolution!

Architects are taking advantage of digital advances to design complex buildings that were impossible to construct only a few years ago. Leading this revolution is Los Angeles architect Frank Gehry (1929–) whose artistic architecture has grown ever more sculptural over the past decade (see Chapter 21). Using sophisticated software known as *Catia,* Gehry can provide engineers and builders with the exact dimensions of whatever curvy forms he dreams up.

Never a dull (or dumb) moment

Innovations in electronic media are also being incorporated into buildings themselves. "Smart" buildings are wired to coordinate heating, cooling, security, and other building systems at the touch of a button. Video screens, electronic signs, and audio systems are turning walls into kinetic surfaces that pulse with images, text, and sound.

Taking care of Mother Earth: Green architecture

The energy crisis during the 1970s led to buildings with solar heating panels and other conservation devices. In the 1990s, environmental sensitivity returned with a more holistic approach to building. Instead of plugging in a few products, architects now consider land use, transportation issues, energy efficiency, indoor ecology, and waste reduction when designing buildings. This approach, called *green* or *sustainable design,* is gaining ground within the architecture profession.

A building may be "green" and respond to the growing environmental problems of our planet in many ways. The following sections show you a few examples.

Using materials for healthier buildings

Many of the products used to build a home or workplace may be toxic and contribute to what is called *sick building syndrome.* They may emit unhealthy gases and substances into the air for years after construction. Green architects cure sick buildings — or avoid them in the first place — by using nonhazardous materials, natural ventilation, and other environmental tonics.

In addition to their healthy content, green building materials are often chosen for their low *embodied energy* — the energy used to extract, manufacture, and ship them. These materials may be constructed of recycled materials or reused from other buildings. Those that deplete natural resources, such as wood components made from forests of old-growth timber, are avoided. Green architects prefer durable products over cheaper ones because they last longer and contribute less to solid waste problems.

Gaining energy efficiency through systems and siting

Green architects save energy in a variety of ways. A few of the biggies are

- ✔ Recycling existing buildings instead of constructing new ones on pristine open space.

- ✔ Reducing the size of a building — small is certainly better if you're going green.

- ✔ Lowering energy consumption within the structure itself. They accomplish this through a variety of elements: solar heating, insulated walls, energy-efficient windows, natural ventilation, energy-efficient appliances, and lighting. Water from sinks, showers, or clothes washers (called *graywater*) is often recycled to irrigate lawns and landscaping.

But even the most energy-efficient, state-of-the-art passive solar house becomes a big environmental burden if its owners have to get in a car each morning and commute dozens of miles to work. Over the past decade, architects and planners have developed new, more environmentally sound communities aimed at stemming suburban sprawl. Houses are clustered close together within walking distance of shopping and offices, and access to public transportation. This approach is called *New Urbanism* and *Smart Growth* (see Chapter 19).

Greening the architectural form

Style isn't important to green architects, but shape and size matter so that buildings respect vegetation and climate patterns, as well as protect wetlands. Amenities such as recycling facilities and indoor gardens may be incorporated into the design of a green building. Room layouts often accommodate new lifestyles and telecommuting. The architecture often aesthetically reflects local or regional building traditions — adobe in the Southwest United States, or wood shingles in New England.

Some architects pick out just one aspect of green design — recycled building materials, for example — and hold that up as their environmental banner. But to be truly green means considering the total environmental impact of the building. Energy performance, for example, can sometimes be improved by simply adjusting a building's orientation, while using a floor tile made of recycled materials may increase cost significantly for relatively little gain. Compromise is the name of the green game.

Part IV

Eastern Architecture: A Survey of the Most Important Structures

The 5th Wave   By Rich Tennant

"Here, Judy—take a few steps back to really admire the intricate design and construction of this building."

In this part . . .

This part explains the development of architecture in Asia and the Middle East and the methods of construction used to achieve it. It examines the exchange of design concepts and building technologies among different countries, including cross-cultural currents between East and West.

Journey through China, Japan, India, and the Islamic world and savor the striking architecture built in these exotic lands. Monumental temples, sculptural mosques, and richly decorated palaces testify to the strong architectural traditions that have changed little over centuries.

Chapter 16

China and Japan: Traditions in Wood

*I*solated from the rest of the world, China developed and maintained its own strong tradition of wooden architecture. The tradition slowly evolved from the Han Dynasty (206 B.C.–A.D. 220) to the nineteenth century as it followed the same building methods. This architectural continuity directly contrasted with the enormous stylistic changes of Western architecture over the same period.

Chinese buildings shift architectural attention away from the walls to the roof. The overhanging, protective roofs of Chinese architecture developed in response to the hot sun and frequent rains and soon became the main focus of building design. Walls of typical Chinese buildings — and Japanese buildings — are not solid, permanent enclosures of stone and brick (as they are in Western architecture). Instead, they're constructed of modular, wooden supports and panels that form a more flexible system.

The most important Chinese buildings — palaces and temples — were constructed of timber. Brick and stone, on the other hand, were reserved mostly for pagodas, tombs, bridges, and fortifications.

In the sixth and seventh centuries, China's wooden architecture spread through Korea to Japan, where it formed the basis of a simpler style. By medieval times, Japanese architecture had developed its own identity with Zen-inspired refinements that eventually had an enormous influence on modern architecture in Europe and the United States.

Chinese Architecture: The Basics

While each period of Western architecture is identified according to different styles, Chinese architecture is best described in terms of design principles that have remained constant over centuries.

The ting's the thing

The organization of space is simple and straightforward: It's based on a standard rectangular room called the *jian*. The jian may be expanded or repeated to form a building or a group of buildings. When extended horizontally — but not necessarily to form a rectangle — it becomes a hall, or *ting*.

Another important feature of classical Chinese architecture is the way buildings are arranged. Instead of being concentrated in one area, as is common in the West, they are dispersed around courtyards, and the entire grouping is organized around a central pathway or axis. The largest and most important structure is typically placed at the northernmost part of the site. Surrounding structures and courtyards gradually increase in size as they get closer to the main building.

Feng Shui: Going with the flow

Most buildings in China, except for those in special circumstances, face south or southeast to take advantage of prevailing winds and sunshine. This concept of orientation developed into an art called *feng shui* (meaning "wind water") that is aimed at arranging architectural elements so that they are in harmony with nature. Masters of feng shui determine everything from where doors and windows should face to the placement of bathrooms and mirrors. The goal is to promote the optimal flow of positive energy *(ch'i)* within the building.

Instructions for a song

During the Song Dynasty (960–1279), wooden architecture became more elegant as construction methods were refined and standardized. In 1103, architect Li Jie (also known as Li Ming Zhong) published *Methods of Design and Architecture,* the first Chinese building manual.

The 34-volume book provided technical information on materials and craftsmanship. The book also outlined a system of modular proportions for wooden construction that became popular for buildings all over China.

Feng shui is still practiced in China, forcing contemporary architects working in Chinese cities such as Hong Kong to learn tough lessons about its importance. When Chinese-American architect I.M. Pei designed the Bank of China tower, he first ignored the art of feng shui only to confront widespread opposition to the pointy angles and height of his building. (He eventually consulted a feng shui master.) In recent decades, this Chinese art of placement has become popular in the West, especially for the home.

Raising the roof

Chinese architects have sought to achieve a unity of structure and decoration in their timber structures. Historically, wooden beams and columns framing walls and roofs were connected with elaborate joinery called *duogong* (see Figure 16-1). These brackets are akin to the column capitals of classical Western architecture because they serve as both structure and ornamentation.

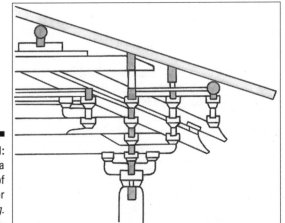

Figure 16-1: Detail of a Chinese roof bracket, or *duogong.*

Another distinguishing feature of Chinese architecture is a broad, spreading roof that is often covered in colored ceramic tiles. Roofs can be categorized into four basic types that are tied to a building's purpose:

- ✔ **Hip roof:** This type of roof crowns the most important buildings. It has an inward curve and upturned corners.

- ✔ **Half-hip roof:** This roof type is called the *xie shan,* and it covers secondary buildings. The xie shan has low overhangs and decorative gables.

- ✔ **Conical roof:** This type of roof is called a *cuan jian.* It tops pavilions and tall buildings.

- ✔ **Gabled roofs:** These simple roofs are used on houses.

Temples and fortifications

The tall Buddhist temples known as *pagodas* are a distinctive form of Chinese architecture. Pagodas may have been derived from the ancient Eastern Indian shrine known as a stupa (see Chapter 17). These towers were considered the most important part of a temple complex, serving as a beacon for guiding pilgrims to the site. Pagodas vary in style according to the period and region in which they were built. Early examples from the Tang Dynasty (618–907) were square brick towers stacked with projecting eaves. Later pagodas include stucco-covered structures shaped like jars, and tiered wooden towers with upward-curving eaves.

Fogong Pagoda

One of the most outstanding examples of pagoda architecture is the Fogong Temple Pagoda in Yingxian. Dating from 1056, this octagonal-shaped structure occupies the center of a temple complex. Its 220-foot-high tower is built entirely out of wood. Two rings of columns support floor beams and upturned eaves, and verandahs on the lowest floor strengthen the structure. Graceful in its outline, the pagoda underscores the sophisticated wooden construction of Chinese architecture.

Temple of Heaven

Temple compounds include worship halls that have sometimes taken the place of the pagoda as the major building within the enclosure. One of the most striking examples of the worship hall is the Temple of Heaven in Beijing. Part of a vast religious complex covering nearly 700 acres, the circular wooden prayer hall was built in the early 1400s by the emperors of the Ming and Qing dynasties. It is raised on concentric, round terraces to represent the circle of heaven, and it is surrounded by rectangular courtyards symbolizing the earth. Three blue tiled roofs radiate out from wooden walls colorfully decorated in bright red, yellow, and green. Two concentric rings of 12 pillars each, all made from tree trunks, and four large central columns support the roofs. Within the hall's vast space, emperors prayed for a good harvest under a colorful, coffered ceiling supported by blue and green brackets and beams.

The Great Wall

Built as a protective barrier against enemy raids, The Great Wall, China's most famous structure, was masterminded by Qin Shih Huana Ti, the first emperor of the Qin Dynasty, in about 210 B.C. The Great Wall, nearly 10,000 miles long, was built over many centuries. The first section of the wall was built of dry-laid stone; in other stretches, earth was compacted, layer-by-layer. By the time the wall reached the Gobi Desert, builders resorted to laying a bed of reeds and twigs at the bottom of a wooden frame and then filling it with a mixture of water and fine gravel. When the mixture dried, the frame was removed, leaving a slab of earth strengthened by the sticks (a method similar to the steel rods used to reinforce concrete). During the fifteenth and sixteenth centuries, the wall was refaced in stone. Massive blocks form a winding wall that averages from 15 to 30 feet high and from 15 to 25 feet wide, with watchtowers at frequent intervals.

Palaces: Walled cities

Unlike European monarchs who conducted their courtly activities under one roof, Chinese rulers built palaces consisting of a large group of buildings, each housing a different function. These mini-cities included temples, reception halls, residences, and service buildings.

Forbidden City

The most impressive and best preserved of the imperial palaces is Beijing's Forbidden City — home to 24 emperors over the past 500 years. It gets its name from the fact that only the members of the imperial household and their visitors were allowed into the walled complex (for most people, that meant the palace was forbidden territory).

Built from 1406 to 1420 by emperor Zhu Di, the great halls of this complex are arranged on either side of a five-mile-long axis. The halls are grouped around courtyards and raised on stone platforms surrounded by marble balustrades. Wooden walls are painted in bright shades of red, yellow, green, and blue and topped by curving tiled roofs decorated with dragons. At the center of the city is the Hall of Supreme Harmony, a ceremonial building with an ornately carved interior and throne.

Summer Palace

On a hilly, 140-acre site to the northwest of Beijing, emperors created another palace in the early 1700s. This palace, used as a summer retreat from the Forbidden City, was a place for watching sporting events and celebrating important occasions. The wooden buildings of the palace are less formal than their urban counterparts; they're nestled into the landscape to harmonize with nature. Causeways and small bridges over lakes and creeks connect pavilions, courtyards, and gardens.

Potala Palace

The imposing Potala Palace was built in Lhasa, Tibet, in the late 1600s for the fifth Dalai Lama, the spiritual leader of the Tibetans. Rising from a high ridge, the Potala Palace has served as a home, the seat of the Tibetan government, a school for religious training, and a pilgrimage destination. Its massive structure is divided into two parts: a central red palace, containing tombs and chapels; and a white palace housing living quarters, dining halls, and offices. The architecture looks as if it has grown from the hillside, with clifflike stone-and-stucco walls supporting wooden structures with colorful balconies and tiled roofs. Although parts of this historic structure have been restored, it's in urgent need of repairs.

HISTORICAL NOTE

Chinoiserie taste in the West

The exotic art and architecture of Asia have long inspired Western imitations. Chinese silks and blue-and-white porcelains were reproduced in Italy and France as early as the Renaissance. After China lifted a ban on foreign trade in 1684, a huge craze for Chinese motifs, or *chinoiserie,* sprung up in the late seventeenth and eighteenth centuries. The demand for chinoiserie was expressed in Dutch ceramics, French embroideries, and imitation lacquered, or "japanned," English furniture. In European palaces, whole rooms were decorated with chinoiserie paintings and furnishings as part of the playful Rococo style. Chinese-inspired buildings also became popular. A Chinese pavilion was erected at Versailles outside Paris, and a pagoda-like structure was built at the Nymphenburg castle in Germany. Chinoiserie buildings became the focus of picturesque English gardens in the 1700s. British architect William Chambers, who had traveled in China, completed a 10-story pagoda at Kew Gardens outside London following the publication of his book, *Designs of Chinese Buildings* (1757). The craze also reached the American Colonies, where Thomas Jefferson used what he called a "Chinese railing" around the terraces and roofs of his Virginia home, Monticello.

Japanese Architecture: Chinese Refinements

Japanese architecture is a combination of indigenous and imported styles. It is built on timber traditions — even more so than Chinese architecture. Japanese architecture does not use stone in a substantial way: Stone is mainly used to build foundations and miniature pagodas. Nearly all traditional Japanese structures are made of wood with paper screens, plaster and clay (for walls), straw matting (on floors), and wood planks or tile (for roofs). This construction gives Japanese architecture simpler, more delicate lines when compared to Chinese architecture. Japanese architecture's gracefulness is underscored by asymmetrical, informal groupings of buildings; this is in contrast with the more formal, axial arrangements of Chinese buildings.

Indigenous originals: Shinto shrines

The best way to understand native Japanese architecture before the introduction of Buddhism and its Chinese influence is to look at a group of temporary shrines devoted to Japan's native religion, *shinto*. Intended for brief visits by the gods, these shrines were destroyed and rebuilt every 20 years. One of the best surviving examples of these shrines is the Shinto Imperial Shrine at Ise, dedicated to the sun goddess. It shows how these timber structures have been designed for thousands of years. Resembling a storehouse (worshippers filled the shrine with crops as offerings), the main wooden shrine is raised on piers. Its pitched roof is thatched, and boards at either end project upward to form a forked roof ornament *(chigi)*. The temple compound is entered through a large, freestanding timber gateway, or *torii*.

Buddhist temples

After Buddhism was introduced in Japan from China — via Korea — in the middle of the sixth century, the Japanese began building temple complexes in the Chinese style. The Horyuji Temple outside Nara (the capital of Japan from 710–784) is the oldest of these temple complexes; it was constructed in the seventh century. Like its Chinese counterparts, the temple consists of a grouping rather than the single structure that was common with Shinto shrines. Its meeting hall, image hall, covered corridor, inner gate, and five-story pagoda are the world's oldest surviving wooden structures. As a reliquary, the pagoda was the central structure of the Buddhist compound. But it gradually relinquished its primary position as the *kondo* (the building that houses Buddhist images) gained importance as a prayer hall. By the eighth century, the pagoda was more symbolic than functional.

In Japanese, the meeting hall is the *kodo,* the image hall is the *kondo,* the covered corridor is the *kairo,* and the inner gate is the *chumon.*

Architecture of Zen

In the thirteenth and fourteenth centuries, the Zen sect of Buddhism led to another architectural style in Japan. Zen temples were well-ordered compounds of buildings symmetrically arranged around a central axis. This regimentation reflected the religious discipline required of Zen Buddhism, which was practiced by monks, intellectuals, and warriors.

Within the temple compound, the architecture of the buildings was heavily influenced by Chinese traditions. Hip roofs were shaped with upturned corners and elaborate brackets. But Japanese carpenters built these structures using local methods, such as covering the roofs with wood shingles instead of ceramic tiles. They also introduced an innovative type of double roof that allowed the interior roof structure to be set at a different angle than the pitched roof of the exterior. This system made it possible to build wider spaces without having a steep drop in the angle of the roof.

The Golden Pavilion is one of the most striking Zen-style buildings. Ashikaga Yoshimitsu, a powerful military commander (or *shogun*), built the three-story pavilion in 1397 as his personal retreat. Located on a Kyoto estate at the edge of a pond, the pavilion has wide eaves, removable walls, and an open interior — elements that represent the lightness achieved by Japanese architecture during this period. Nearly every surface of the small building is covered in gold leaf. The reflection of this splendor in the adjacent pond forms an impressive sight. The present structure is an accurate reconstruction of the original pavilion that burned down in 1951 — in a fire set by a crazy monk, so the story goes.

Going the way of tea

Zen Buddhism favors utmost simplicity and an appreciation of things in their unadorned natural state. Beauty is seen in a stone, a tree, and even raked gravel. This sensibility flowered during the Muromachi era (1338–1573), which produced much of what is considered the essence of the Japanese aesthetic. Cultural developments such as ink painting, Noh theater (stylized drama using mime, dance, and masks), and rock gardens blossomed during this period.

One of the most influential of these cultural developments was the *tea ceremony,* an upper-class entertainment, adopted from Zen monasteries and still practiced today, that calls for preparing and drinking a special kind of green tea according to a strict set of rules. The tea ceremony has spawned special buildings, called *chashitsu,* with few decorations and furnishings to distract attention. This spiritual retreat is isolated within an ornamental garden, called a *roji,* with a gate and waiting area where guests meet the host, who then ushers them into the teahouse. The garden represents nature in miniature, which guests can contemplate from inside the house.

Two of the most celebrated garden teahouses are in Kyoto: the Silver Pavilion (1489) and the Katsura Teahouse, which was built as part of the Katsura Villa (see Chapter 22). Inside the teahouses, paper screens slide back to enlarge the rooms and let in sunlight. These elegant structures have made an enormous impression on modern architects, including Frank Lloyd Wright, who first traveled to Japan in 1905 (see Chapter 13).

Japanese castles

While the medieval period in Japan spawned such cultural refinements as the tea ceremony, this period was marked by battles and political instability as the island nation struggled to attain power. Between the twelfth and nineteenth centuries, Japan was dominated by *shoguns* (military commanders), who established law and order through loyal warriors called *samurai.* The shoguns built large fortresses to protect the countryside and to impress their enemies. The height of this castle-building era — the late sixteenth century —

produced dazzling hilltop structures with multi-story keeps, or *donjons,* colorful walls, and curvy roofs — a far cry from the severe stone castles of Europe.

The most striking of the dozen donjons that have survived is Himeji Castle (constructed from 1601–1614) in Himeji City. It is nicknamed "the White Heron" for its swooping roofs and white plastered timber walls. Located on two hills, the complex consists of a main donjon connected to three secondary donjons by hallways and passages that form an inner courtyard. In the southeast corner of the court is an area called *harakiri-maru,* where a samurai would commit suicide.

Japanese homes: Sized for the mat

During the Muromachi period (1338–1573), a new type of residential architecture called *Shoin* (meaning "writing hall") emerged in Japan. The style was adapted from Zen monasteries, and it featured many of the elements now associated with Japanese houses — straw mats on the floors, a decorative alcove, staggered shelves, and paper screens reinforced with a wooden lattice. In the early 1600s, this type of design was documented in manuals that encouraged builders to follow modular proportions to achieve architectural harmony. An important component of this proportioning system was the rectangular straw mat on the floor, called *tatami* (about 1×2 yards in size). For centuries, the area of a room has been determined according to the number of mats it contains.

Specifically, the decorative alcove is a *tokonoma,* the staggered shelves are *chigaidama,* and the paper-covered wooden lattice is a *shoji.* The modular proportions that builders follow are known as *kiwarijutsu.* The books featuring the modular designs are called *kiwarisho.*

Japanese Baroque: The Shrine at Nikko

Not all Japanese architecture is minimalist. During the Edo period in the seventeenth century, an opulent style emerged that was similar to both Chinese Buddhist temples and the Western Baroque in its sumptuous decoration and sense of movement (see Chapter 10). This style first emerged in the Shinto shrines built for shogun Tokugawa Ieyasu and his grandson Iemitsu in the area of Nikko during the mid-1600s. Layer upon layer of brightly painted ornate carvings, including dragons and lions, decorate the shrines and gateways. The structures are arranged on the hilly site so that each building pops into view at a different point to surprise the visitor. The splendor at Nikko was soon imitated in shrines around the country.

Rising son: Kenzo Tange and the new style

Japan's rapid economic expansion during the decades after World War II led to new architecture that combined the island nation's traditions with the latest Western design. A leader of this movement was architect Kenzo Tange (1913–). Influenced by Le Corbusier, who designed the National Museum of Western Art in Tokyo (1955–1959), Tange began his career by designing the dignified Hiroshima Peace Center (1949–1955).

Tange has remained a force within contemporary Japanese architecture for 50 years. His buildings skillfully blend modern technology with references to traditional Japanese architecture — a good example is his Yamanashi Communications Center in Kofu (1964–1967). With its floors held up by huge cylindrical service towers, this massive structure recalls both a twentieth-century machine and a samurai castle. Tange's other monumental master-pieces include the National Gymnasium for the Tokyo Olympics (1961–1964), with its sculptural tensile roof, and the Tokyo City Hall (1991). Tange's only building in the United States is an addition to the Minneapolis Art Museum (1975).

During his long career, Tange has been a leading theoretician of architecture and an inspiring teacher; Fumihiko Maki and Arata Isozaki (see Chapter 15) are among the well-known architects who studied under him.

Chapter 17

More Than the Taj Mahal: Architecture in India

....

In This Chapter

▶ Looking at ancient architecture in India

▶ Discovering Asian Indian architecture and its influence in southeastern Asia

▶ Exploring the Mughal style of architecture

▶ Recognizing Western architecture's influence on India

▶ Introducing contemporary architects working in India

....

Most people associate architecture in India with the Taj Mahal. But this subcontinent is far richer in architecture than a single famous landmark would suggest. For centuries, different religions and foreign cultural influences have been absorbed and transformed by Asian Indian architects and builders into a wide variety of styles.

The earliest permanent buildings in India were stone shrines and temples constructed by Buddhists in the third century B.C. Before the Buddhists built in stone, religious structures were made of mud, timber, and bamboo. By the seventh and eighth centuries A.D., Buddhism had declined and Hinduism had become India's leading religion. In building temples in southern India, Hindus developed a more ornate style of architecture. Stone structures, elaborately carved as if made of wood, rose in pyramidal tiers. This architecture spread southward as Hindus left India to colonize areas of Southeast Asia.

From the twelfth century to the middle of the eighteenth century, religious and political power shifted to Muslims who came from central Asia, Persia (Iran), and Afghanistan and settled in northern India. They erected ornate mosques, palaces, and tombs following Islamic traditions and set a new architectural style. Europeans also founded colonies in India during this time, beginning with Portuguese traders on the west coast. In the early 1600s, Britain established a presence that would last more than 300 years and eventually dominate the entire subcontinent. In cities such as Calcutta, Bombay, and Delhi, British and colonial architects designed new civic architecture in the eclectic revivalism of the Victorian era. After India's independence from

Britain in 1947, a new generation of architects emerged to meld indigenous traditions with the latest modern architectural styles.

Early Temples and Shrines

All surviving examples of ancient Asian Indian architecture are temples and religious buildings constructed of stone. Huge structures shaped like earth mounds and mountains achieve a nature-inspired majesty associated with the pyramids of ancient Egypt and the Americas (see Chapter 7). The structures, decorated with sculptures and reliefs of plants, animals, gods, and people, were designed to be appreciated from the outside; their exteriors have grown increasingly more lavish over the centuries. Some of these shrines have no interior spaces, while others have dark, cavernous rooms decorated with statuary.

Great Stupa at Sanchi

One of the oldest and most impressive Buddhist shrines or *stupas*, the Great Stupa at Sanchi was built in central India as part of a monastery. The Mauryan Emperor Ashoka built it between 273 and 236 B.C. (what survives today, however, was altered by the British). The main structure consists of a large brick dome raised on a circular platform. It is encircled by carved stone railings and four gates, or *toranas,* which symbolize the four corners of the universe. On the top of the dome is a platform with an umbrella-like mast rising from the center. (Legend has it that Buddha determined the shape of the stupa when he placed his begging bowl onto a cloth and crowned the top with a stick.)

Modeled on earlier religious structures built of timber, the stupa shows how builders literally copied carpenters' designs in stone. The posts and beams of its gates would later be emulated in China and Korea and become the temple gateways called *torii* in Japan. See Chapter 16 for more about this.

Cave temples at Ellora

Another type of early Asian Indian religious architecture was the cave temple. These sanctuaries housing statues of deities were built by digging out the rock of the mountainside and carving it into richly decorated structures. The most architecturally significant examples of this temple type are the 34 temples built in Ellora on an important trade route through western India. Their concurrent construction and use by Hindus, Buddhists, and Jains testifies to the religious tolerance of ancient India.

Built from the sixth to eighth centuries, the Ellora temples represent several architectural styles. The Buddhists built the oldest shrines with rooms sculpted with figures of gods and ornate ceilings supported by faceted and fluted pillars. One of the most impressive Hindu structures is the 98-foot-high Kailasa temple, which took more than a century to build. Hewn of a single rock, its massive exterior is intricately carved with niches, pilasters, and images of deities and other figures.

Shore Temple in Mamallapuram

Buddhism eventually declined in India, giving way to Hinduism as the leading religion. One of the oldest freestanding Hindu temples is the Shore Temple, built of granite blocks in the eighth century. Its name comes from its location on the shore of the Indian Ocean in Mamallapuram, also called Mahabalipuram, at the southernmost tip of India. This seaport was established by the Pallavas, who ruled over much of South India from the first century B.C. to the eighth century A.D. The area features some of the greatest architectural and sculptural achievements in India.

In addition to the Shore Temple, the group of monuments in Mamallapuram includes *rathas* (temples in the form of chariots), *mandapas* (cave sanctuaries), and giant reliefs.

The Shore Temple consists of three shrines within a walled compound (legend has it that there were originally seven and four were washed into the sea). The tallest shrine is a five-story, stepped pyramid, or *sikhara,* that is heavily encrusted with relief carvings. In Hinduism, everything is considered divine, from gods to living creatures to inanimate objects. This interrelationship is reflected in the temple's layers of decorative figures — animals, kings, and gods — that rise toward the heavens. In Hindu temples, sculpture, not structure, reigns supreme.

India's Influence on Southeast Asia

As trade grew between India and Southeast Asia, the Buddhist and Hindu architecture of the stupa and the sikhara spread southward. Rulers in Indonesia, Cambodia, and Burma sought ways to localize Asian Indian traditions by relating them to the beliefs held by their peoples. In doing so, they succeeded in building some of the most extraordinary religious structures in the world. With the decline of these early civilizations, however, many of the architectural marvels fell into ruins, only to be rediscovered and preserved in the nineteenth and twentieth centuries.

Javanese Pyramid of Borobudur

Built on the island of Java, the intriguing Buddhist monument called Borobudur was probably constructed under the ruling Sailendra dynasty between 760 and 830. It incorporates three of the most significant symbols of Asian Indian design — the holy mountain, the visual representation of the universe, and the stupa, a type of Buddhist shrine (see the preceding section, "Great Stupa at Sanchi").

Shaped like a flattened hill, Borobudur is designed as a stepped pyramid rising to five levels that diminish in size as they go up. It rests on a 403-foot-wide base that may be shaped to represent a *mandala,* the geometric symbol of the universe. On the sides of the first four levels are terraces decorated with sculptures that trace Buddhist legends and scenes of Javanese life. Staircases lead from the middle of these galleries to three concentric rings of 72 bell-shaped shrines at the top; each houses an image of a seated Buddha. The shrines surround a 52-foot-high empty stupa in the center. Inside the galleries, more than 1,200 sculpted panels tell stories from the life of Buddha. Borobudur, after all, means "Temple of the Countless Buddhas."

No one knows the exact meaning of *Borobudur,* but many believe it may represent the path to higher spirituality and eternal truth. After climbing 3 miles to the summit of this man-made mountain, pilgrims were encouraged to grasp the meaning of Buddha's teachings through both a visual and physical experience.

For centuries, the site lay buried under layers of volcanic ash and rain forest until it was cleared in the early 1800s. In 1975, a major restoration was undertaken to clean and preserve the monument using state-of-the-art techniques to battle microorganisms eating away at the stone. The restoration cost $25 million and took 8 years to complete.

Avalanche! Cambodia's Angkor Wat

Southeast Asia's supreme architectural achievement is Angkor Wat, located about 200 miles to the northwest of Cambodia's capital, Phnom Penh. This vast, mysterious complex — 5,000 feet long and 4,500 feet wide — is the largest temple in the city of Angkor, which was once the thriving center of the Khmer civilization. Suryavarman, king of the Khmer empire, began Angkor Wat in the twelfth century to honor the Hindu god Vishnu (kings were considered the gods' representatives) and serve as the king's tomb after he died. The buildings are arranged around courtyards and rise on a series of platforms that are set behind colonnaded walls. Five towers, symbolizing the mythical mountain of Meru, top the central temple to create a distinctive silhouette. The entire complex is surrounded by a 2.25-mile-long moat and entered from a causeway with balustrades shaped like giant serpents. Talk about a dramatic entrance!

Walls and roofs are constructed from sandstone blocks piled on top of one another without mortar. They rely on weight and gravity to keep them in place. Unlike Roman and medieval European architects, the Khmers used no rounded arches or vaults to cover a space. Instead, stones were stacked to reach inward as far as possible and touch at the top. This structure, called a *corbelled arch,* was far less stable than rounded arches or vaults and often collapsed. See the real thing in Figure 17-1.

In the early 1400s, Angkor was plundered by the Thais and abandoned by the Khmer. For centuries, the city was considered "lost" in the jungle until it was rediscovered in 1858 by French explorer Henri Mouhot, who brought Angkor Wat to international attention. A restoration project was launched in 1908. But it was left unfinished and subsequent restoration attempts were disrupted by warfare and political upheavals in Cambodia. In recent years, international efforts to save Angkor Wat have led to the preservation of portions of the monument.

Figure 17-1: Angkor Wat, Angkor, Cambodia, twelfth century.

Photo courtesy of and © Karen Su/China Span.

The Islamic Golden Age, Mughal Style

Muslim conquests introduced India to the exotic architecture of the Islamic world (see Chapter 18) as early as the eighth century. But the dome and the arch didn't flourish in India until the mid-sixteenth century, when Afghan chieftain Babur marched into the country and defeated the sultan of Delhi. In establishing Mughal rule, Babur and his successors ushered in a golden age of Islamic architecture in northern India and what is now Pakistan. They built tombs, palaces, forts, and mosques in a style, known as Indo-Islamic or Mughal, that blended traditions from India and Islam. Ruler and architectural patron Shah Jahan played an important role in the development of the Mughal style. In the 1600s, he built such celebrated monuments as the Red Fort in Delhi and the Taj Mahal in Agra. These buildings followed Islamic traditions more closely than earlier Mughal architecture.

The Taj forerunner: Humayun's tomb in Delhi

The oldest of the great Mughal monuments is a mausoleum built in Delhi for Babur's son, Humayun. It was commissioned in the early 1560s by Humayun's widow and may have been designed by architect Mirak Mirza Ghiyas, who had worked for Babur.

In contrast to earlier Hindu temples, this Islamic-influenced structure is simple in its lack of sculpture. Yet it conveys a dramatic presence through the design of its setting, bold architectural forms, and colorful materials. Placed within a formal water garden divided by channels and fountains, the tomb is flanked by four octagonal towers, and the entire building is raised on a huge plinth. Its red sandstone exteriors are decorated in white and black marble and punctuated by arched windows, doorways, and colonnades. A bulbous, white marble dome, encircled by domed canopies and minaretlike spires, rises over the center. The commanding architecture of Humayun's tomb is a forerunner of the Taj Mahal.

King of the hill: Fatehpur Sikri

In 1568, Humayun's son Akbar built a hilltop town about 25 miles west of Agra in Sikri, where a mystic had predicted the birth of his son, Prince Salim. The walled town, renamed Fatehpur Sikri to celebrate the Mughal conquest of

Gujarat (a coastal area of northwestern India and the early center of Muslim culture), served as a seat of government for 16 years. (The eventual abandonment of the city may have been caused by a water shortage.)

Among the buildings of Fatehpur Sikri (1568–1580) is a monumental gateway, a palace complex, and a mosque that demonstrate the type of urban planning carried out during the Mughal Empire. One of its most unique structures is a hall called a *diwan-i-khas* that was used for private audiences with the ruler. The sandstone hall, which is divided by projecting moldings called *chajja,* gives the impression from the outside of having two stories. But, inside, there is only one room centered on a huge pillar with ornate, radiating brackets that once supported a throne. The architecture exemplifies the blend of Hindu and Islamic forms that marked the early Mughal style.

The Taj Mahal: A love story

A national emblem of India, the Taj Mahal in Agra (1632–1653) is the most renowned example of Mughal architecture. Shah Jahan built it as a tomb for his wife, Mumtaz Mahal (meaning "Chosen One of the Palace"), who died in 1631 after giving birth to her fourteenth child. Saddened by her death, Shah Jahan resolved to immortalize their love in a white marble mausoleum surrounded by gardens.

The Taj Mahal ("Crown Palace") follows many of the design precedents set by Humayun's tomb in Delhi (see the previous section, "The Taj forerunner: Humayun's tomb in Delhi"). Like the earlier monument, it is placed on a *chahar bagh,* a platform at the end of a walled garden divided by canals. Framed by four minarets at each corner of the platform, the marble building is sculpted with arched recesses and towers surrounding a 187-foot-high dome. Its white marble façades are decorated with floral motifs and a type of inlay called *pietra dura* to create a delicate effect. Inside the octagonal space under the dome, carved marble screens set with precious stones enclose the royal tombs of Mumtaz Mahal and Shah Jahan. See Figure 17-2 to experience this thing of beauty.

Some experts, however, don't believe the Taj Mahal was built in the seventeenth century as a mausoleum. One historian claims the structure was constructed in the twelfth century as a Hindu temple and later renovated by Shah Jahan into a royal family tomb.

Figure 17-2:
The Taj
Mahal.

Spoils of the British Empire: West Meets East

Western-influenced architecture reached its peak in India after the British assumed control of the country in 1858. Grand civic buildings, universities, museums, and railway stations were built in cities all over the country to support the imperial regime. Mughal and Hindu touches were mixed with English Victorian Gothic and classical revival styles (see Chapter 11) to produce highly eclectic architecture.

India's own White House and Edwin Lutyens in New Delhi

Leading English architects Edwin Lutyens and Herbert Baker created the greatest architecture under British rule. Their grand classical buildings established a new national identity for India in response to Britain's decision in 1911 to move the country's capital from Calcutta to Delhi. Lutyens and Baker were put in charge of designing a new government precinct within Delhi called New Delhi.

Building this new center of government, however, wasn't easy. The plan, scheduled to take only 3 years, actually took 20 years to complete due to bureaucratic squabbles. (Ironically, India became independent almost as soon as the new capital was finished.) Lutyens and Baker became involved in their own squabble over whether their buildings should reflect the architecture of India; they eventually stopped speaking to each other.

Lutyens was well known for designing English country homes and gardens. With these projects, he blended classical and Arts and Crafts traditions (see Chapter 14 for more on the British Arts and Crafts movement) into a highly individualistic style. Arriving in Delhi in 1912, he greeted the indigenous architecture of India with disdain, claiming in a letter to his wife that there was no great design tradition in the country.

Yet Lutyens managed to blend elements of European and Asian Indian architecture into the Viceroy's House (1913–1929), one of the most extraordinary buildings of the twentieth century. Massive and imposing, its 630-foot-long exterior (longer than Versailles) looks as though it was carved from a single block of sandstone. Gigantic classical colonnades and a marble dome are combined with abstracted elements from Mughal and Buddhist architecture. The elements include an overhanging molding projecting 8 feet from the façade; rooftop turrets called *chattris* (despite Lutyens's dismissal of them as "stupid useless things"); and a railing, derived from the Great Stupa at Sanchi (see the earlier section, "Great Stupa of Sanchi") around the base of the large dome.

The Viceroy's House stands on a broad boulevard that works its way through a massive war memorial arch, which was also designed by Lutyens. It now serves as the residence of India's president.

Le Corbusier in Chandigarh

India's independence in 1947 and the establishment of the Pakistan republic a year later prompted the building of new government centers in modern architectural styles. In 1951, French architect Le Corbusier drew a plan for Chandigarh, the new capital of the Punjab, based on his ideal city of light, greenery, and open spaces (see chapter 19 on urban design). His monumental civic buildings — the Secretariat (1952–1956), the High Court (1952–1956), and the Assembly (1955–1960) — connect modern and ancient traditions. Sculpted of raw concrete, their imposing, abstract forms incorporate overhanging roofs, shady colonnades, and sun screens. Le Corbusier collaborated on the designs for Chandigarh with his partner and cousin, Pierre Jeanneret, and British architects Jane Drew and Maxwell Fry. For more on the architecture of Le Corbusier, see Chapter 14.

Louis Kahn in Bangladesh

Le Corbusier's Chandigarh was followed by another modern government complex, the National Assembly Building in Dacca, East Pakistan (now

Bangladesh), designed by Philadelphia architect Louis Kahn (see Chapter 15) in the 1960s. Kahn's National Assembly Building looks like a group of huge building blocks and is even more abstract than Le Corbusier's buildings at Chandigarh. It is made up of boxes and cylinders constructed of concrete and strips of marble. Large triangular, square, and circular openings are cut into the façades. Powerfully monumental, the sprawling complex expresses the primal quality of ancient religious architecture in India.

Kahn spent the last 12 years of his life on the Dacca project at the same time that he was designing the Indian Institute of Management (1962–1974), a government-run business school in Ahmedabad. When Bangladesh declared its independence in 1971, construction of Kahn's Dacca building was halted, but the architect kept working away on his designs. The government of Bangladesh hired him back the next year, but the project was not finished until 1983, 9 years after Kahn died.

Contemporary Architecture in India

Architects practicing in the years after India declared its independence looked to the modernism of Le Corbusier and Kahn as a source of inspiration for their own work. Since the 1970s, many architects have emerged from the shadow of these foreign masters to create architecture sensitive to India's climate and culture. Two outstanding Asian Indian architects working today are Balkrishna Doshi, who practices in Ahmedabad, and Bombay-based Charles Correa. Both combine ancient forms and symbols with new shapes and materials.

Doshi, keeping local traditions alive

Doshi (1927–), who worked for Le Corbusier in France and India, is best known for adapting bold modern forms to Asian Indian traditions. Among his buildings are the Ghandi Labor Institute and his own office complex in Ahmedabad.

Correa, low-cost housing pioneer

Charles Correa (1930–) studied architecture in the United States before returning to India to start his own practice in 1958. His work covers a wide spectrum, from a memorial to Mahatma Gandhi to pioneering work on urban issues and low-cost housing in the Third World.

LINGO

"Archi-speak" of India

Understanding the diverse buildings of India requires learning how to speak its architectural language or "archi-speak." Some exotic foreign terms are sure to spark some interest the next time you find yourself at a cocktail party discussing architecture! Here are few terms to get you started:

- **chahar bagh:** four-part garden
- **chajja:** overhanging cornice
- **chattri:** small, umbrella-shaped turrets
- **diwan-i-am:** hall for public audiences
- **diwan-i-khas:** hall for private audiences
- **gopura:** temple gatehouse
- **jali:** patterned screen

- **kapota:** eavelike cornice
- **lenya:** cave temple
- **mandala:** mystical, geometric diagram of the universe
- **mulaprasada:** main temple block containing a shrine
- **prakara:** walled enclosure around a temple compound
- **shikhara:** pyramid-shaped structure or spire on a Hindu temple
- **torana:** ceremonial gateway
- **vastu:** residence

Chapter 18

The Islamic World

In This Chapter

▶ Considering early Islamic mosques

▶ Introducing mosques of the Middle East and North Africa

▶ Discovering the architectural style of the Moors

*W*hen the first Arabian Muslims set off from their desert homeland to convert others to their faith, they had no architecture. They quickly discovered, however, that the monumental structures built by the ancient Mesopotamian, Syrian, Persian, Byzantine, and Roman civilizations could be adapted to their rituals, symbolizing the powerful message of their faith. Less than a century after the Prophet Muhammad's death in 632, Muslims had established a new architecture that was instantly identified as Islamic. Like Western architects, the Muslims constructed their religious structures from columns, arches, vaults, and domes to enclose large interior spaces. But these elements were shaped differently to create a unique style that lasted hundreds of years in regions of the Middle East, Turkey, Africa, Spain, and India. (See Chapter 17 for more on East Indian architecture.)

Bow and Pray to Mecca

Mosques, Islamic meeting places for the faithful, were situated so that worshippers bowed and prayed in the direction of the holy city of Mecca. Because mosques were built for communal prayer, the buildings enclosed a large meeting space but didn't require long, covered sanctuaries for processions or places for mass (as do Christian churches).

The first mosques, built from the seventh to the eleventh centuries, were walled outdoor courtyards that were large enough to accommodate the Muslim communities they served. Open spaces were surrounded by rows of columns or piers supporting flat roofs. A decorated niche *(mihrab)* and the pulpit *(minbar)* and its protective barrier *(maksura)* were placed in the wall oriented to face Mecca, called the *qibla.* A fountain, or *meda,* in the center of the courtyard provided a place for washing before prayers. At the opposite end of building from the quibla was a tower called a *minaret.* The minaret was used for calling the faithful to five daily prayers. It may have been adapted from the design of lighthouses.

The teaching mosque, called a *madrasa,* was developed in the twelfth century. Student classrooms and lodgings were sometimes added to the mosque's prayer hall. In some madrasas, large domed tombs were added to create an imposing architectural complex. Porches with large vaults and arched openings, called *iwans,* replaced simpler porticoes around the courtyard. Elaborate doorways flanked by two minarets surrounded the entrance. By the fifteenth century, the courtyard was often enclosed and topped by a dome or wooden lantern.

Decoration that dazzles

Most of the elements that are characteristic of Islamic buildings were developed at an early date. Domes, pointed or *ogee* arches, and walls covered in stone carvings, inlays, and mosaics came into use by the end of the ninth century. But instead of using the domes and arches in a structurally expressive way, as in Roman or Gothic architecture, Islamic architects carpeted the surfaces of their buildings in fields of dazzling decorations so that worshippers could pray and meditate in a seemingly weightless, otherworldly environment.

Because figurative art is banned in Islam, artisans developed ornamentation based on plants, flowers, geometric shapes, and Arabic script. Glazed tiles patterned with this type of ornamentation have long played an important role in Islamic architecture, especially in Persia. The art of calligraphy was especially prized in conveying sacred verses from the Koran through architectural surfaces.

Dome of the Rock

Islam's oldest monument is the Dome of the Rock (688–692) in Jerusalem. Influenced by Byzantine architecture, the octagonal building is not used for public worship but as a shrine for pilgrims called a *mashhad.* At its center is the sacred rock from which Muhammad is said to have ascended to heaven. Though its octagonal form isn't typical, the Dome expresses a lightness that characterizes Islamic architecture. This graceful quality was not found in western European architecture until centuries later.

On the exterior, the shrine's walls are sheathed in colorful marble tiles and crowned by a gold dome (now paneled in aluminum). The dome is supported by a circular arcade of 16 piers placed around the rock inside the building (see Figure 18-1). Surrounding this circle of piers is an octagonal arcade of 24 piers and columns (see Chapter 8 for more on arcades and vaults). Four vaulted doorways lead into the passageways formed by the arcades. This geometric clarity is characteristic of early Islamic architecture. And you thought that geometry class was a waste of time!

Figure 18-1:
A drawing of the Dome of the Rock showing the interior structure.

Royal Calling Cards: Middle Eastern Mosques

In conquering foreign lands, Muslim Arabs adopted indigenous architectural forms in brick, stucco, and tilework to build hugely impressive mosques. These religious structures served as a place for prayer and as a symbol of the ruler and his reign.

In Persia (now Iran), the assimilation of local traditions led to the development of three important features of Islamic architecture:

✔ supports under the dome, called *squinches* (see Chapter 9)

✔ the "stalactite" decoration of icicle-like elements hanging from the ceiling

✔ glazed tiles on interior and exterior surfaces

Like a ton o' bricks: Great Mosque of Isfahan

Many of the important features of Islamic architecture are evident in the Great Mosque, or Masjid-i-Jami, of Isfahan. This teaching mosque was begun in the eighth century and expanded over centuries to reflect the latest styles in Islamic architecture. In addition to a courtyard covered in sumptuous mosaic tiles, its architectural glories include two domed chambers built during the eleventh century.

Some of the finest brickwork in the world is evident in the mosque's North Dome, which was built from 1088 to 1089. This structure might have served as a private chapel for the wife of the ruler, a women's mosque, a fountain house, or a library — no one is really sure. Inside its octagonal space, every surface is finely sculpted with reliefs. Carved into the walls and the base of the rounded dome are blank pointed arches. Supports between the angular walls and the curved base of the dome are hollowed out to form decorative recesses. This ornamental treatment makes the thick brick walls look as if they have been peeled back in layers. The delicate layered look is very different from the heavy masonry shells of the Romanesque churches from the same era.

Great Mosque of Samarra

The largest mosque ever built is the Great Mosque at Sammara, Iraq (848–852). Its vast prayer hall, measuring 787 x 512 feet, was constructed of brick and enclosed by rows of arches and a protective outer wall. Although the structure is in ruins today, the architecture of the Great Mosque is still impressive. Its most interesting feature is a huge, cone-shaped minaret encircled by a spiral ramp up which a horseman could ride (see Figure 18-2). Ancient Assyrian pyramids, called ziggurats (see Chapter 7), may have inspired this unusual design.

Mosque of Ibn Tulun: Simplicity at its best

The Ibn Tulun Mosque (876–879) is one of the finest surviving examples of classic Islamic architecture in Cairo, Egypt. It was constructed by Ahmad Ibn Tulun, who was the son of a Turkish slave and who eventually became ruler of Egypt and Syria. The mosque's powerfully simple architecture of interlocking spaces was inspired by the Great Mosque at Samarra in Iraq, where Ibn Tulun was born and educated.

Enclosing the mosque is a perimeter wall that forms an almost perfect square in plan. Inside this wall on three sides is an outer court with rows of pointed arches that lead to a *sahn,* or central courtyard, with a domed fountain house in the center. Muslims prayed in a dignified arcaded hall that faced the qibla — the wall oriented to face Mecca — and was marked by an ornate mihrab constructed of marble and mosaics and bordered by four columns with leaflike crowns. Other distinctive features include elegant stone carvings on the mosque's interior walls, inscriptions from the Koran carved in wood, and latticed windows. The mosque was used as a military hospital during the nineteenth century. It was then later used as a warehouse and a beggar's prison prior to its restoration in 1918.

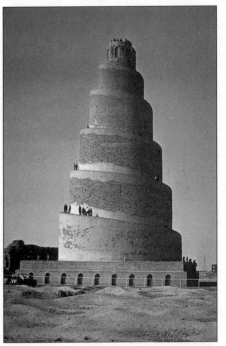

Figure 18-2: The minaret of the Great Mosque of Samarra.

© Media for the Arts. Used with permission.

In contrast to the stucco-faced brick of the mosque, the minaret was made of limestone — it was probably added in the late thirteenth century. The Samarra minaret influenced the structure's spiraling design.

Mosques for All Seasons: African Mosques

Over several generations, Arabian-invading dynasties built vast mosques on the southern coast of the Mediterranean, moving inland to the Sahara desert. The earliest of these dynasties was the Aghlabids, who ruled Tunisia and eastern Algeria from 800 to 909.

Spare and square: Tunisian mosques

Two of the Aghlabids' greatest architectural achievements are the Great Mosque (836) and the Mosque of Three Doors (866), both located in Qairouan, Tunisia. These structures featured the spacious courtyards common to early Middle Eastern mosques, but they were more utilitarian than their Islamic cousins. They were built according to local traditions, with stone and brick and few adornments. Minarets were square, and walls were shaped with arched openings. Later invasions of Morocco and Algiers resulted in more decorative mosques with horseshoe arches and sumptuous stucco ornamentation.

Keeping cool: Mali's mud mosque

One of the great wonders of Islamic — and African — architecture is the Great Mosque at Djenné in Mali. Djenné was once a center of trade and religion. In 1240, its ruler, the sultan Koi Kunboro, converted to Islam and turned his palace into a mosque. Very little is known about the appearance of this first mosque, which eventually fell into disrepair. The present mosque (1906–1907) was built of local materials — mud and palm wood — and its earthen architecture was designed in response to the hot climate of West Africa.

Raised on a platform, the Great Mosque is built of thick mud-brick walls that insulate worshippers from the sun's heat. Roof vents with ceramic caps also help the interior to stay cool. From the outside, the massive building resembles a mud castle with buttressed walls (see Chapter 9) and pointy towers. Projecting from the exterior walls are wooden spikes that are part of the framework supporting the mud bricks.

The Moors Create Their Own Style in Spain

While architecture was at a standstill in most of Europe from the eighth to the eleventh centuries, Muslims were constructing breathtaking buildings and lush gardens in Spain. This group of Muslims, known as the Moors, came to Spain from Syria via Northern Africa — these regions influenced their architecture. After they arrived in Spain, the Moors looked to ancient Roman structures as a source of inspiration. Structural systems and decoration were adapted from classical antiquity and combined with Islamic architecture to shape mosques and palaces. (What is old is new again!) Inside Moorish buildings, forests of pillars, shady courtyards, and ornately decorated ceilings convey a feeling of romance and mystery not associated with the logic and clarity of ancient Roman architecture.

Vision of beauty: Mosque of Cordoba

Begun in 785 and enlarged in several stages through the tenth century, the Mosque of Cordoba was the first monumental Islamic structure in Europe. It blends Eastern and Western traditions into architecture of distinctive beauty. The mosque is organized according to the traditional rectangular layout, with an open courtyard that is the same size as the adjacent covered prayer hall. Inside the sanctuary, rows of arches resting on columns (some looted from Roman structures; yes, it's true) are stacked into two tiers. This arrangement was unusual for a religious building; Roman aqueducts may have inspired it. While the upper arches are rounded, the lower arches are horseshoe-shaped. These horseshoe-shaped arches were used in Spain before the Arabian conquest and adapted by Moorish architects. Both tiers of arches are banded in brick and stone to create a striped effect.

Between 832 and 848, the prayer hall was expanded with eight more rows of arches to match those of the older section — except for the column capitals, which were carved with acanthus leaves following classic Roman models. In the adjacent sanctuary, scalloped arches support a dome with interlacing arches, rich stucco, and mosaics. This sumptuously decorated space, along with the prayer hall's forest of striped columns, dazzles the eye in a way not seen before in Islamic or European architecture.

Paradise on earth at the Alhambra

Set high on a hilltop in Granada, this fortress palace is one of the most ambitious and beautiful pieces of Islamic architecture ever built. The last Muslim rulers of Spain constructed it from 1238 to 1358. In addition to living quarters, the citadel housed state rooms, mosques, prisons, oasislike gardens, and even the royal mint. The sprawling walled complex included 23 towers and four gates.

The most celebrated portions of the Alhambra are its two main courtyards — the Court of the Lions and the Court of the Myrtles. Bordered by shady, covered walkways and pavilions, the open spaces are designed with water filled channels, pools, and fountains, and may have been at one time, planted with flowers, bushes, and small trees. This remarkable fusion of architecture and landscape, which had been unseen since ancient Rome, brought to life the descriptions of paradise in the Koran and Islamic poetry. It would later be developed in India in such Islamic influenced buildings as the Taj Mahal (see Chapter 17).

The star-shaped vaults (see Chapter 8) in the Alhambra's Hall of the Abencerrajes are unprecedented. They are covered with stucco ornamentation, called *muqarnas,* that resembles hanging icicles made of honeycomb. This cellular ornamentation is another example of the way Islamic architects hid their structures in layers of rich decoration to create an air of fantasy.

Sinan — The sultan of Islamic architecture

Sinan (1491–1588), a Turkish architect whose talents rivaled those of his Western contemporary, Michelangelo, was one of greatest innovators of Islamic architecture. Sinan began his career designing bridges and fortifications. In 1539, he was named court architect to Suleyman, the sultan of the Ottoman Empire. Over the next half century, he built more than 300 structures, from palaces and mosques to hospitals, schools, and bathhouses.

As the court architect, Sinan built three famous mosques: the Sehzade Mosque and the Mosque of Suleymaniye, both in Istanbul, and the Selimiye Mosque at Edirne. All three of the mosques developed the domed space first realized in the Hagia Sophia, the sixth-century masterpiece of Byzantine architecture in Istanbul (see Chapter 9). With his mosques, Sinan's idea was to impose the perfect circle on the perfect square. He wanted to express this geometric relationship both inside and outside of the building. He focused each mosque on a vast central dome and surrounded it with smaller domed structures and tapering minarets. Because Sinan emphasized structure and downplayed interior decoration, his buildings were closer in spirit to Gothic cathedrals than earlier Byzantine and Islamic architecture.

The largest of Sinan's mosques is the Suleymaniye, which was begun in 1550. Sinan based his design on the Hagia Sophia but made it even grander. The mosque sits on a plinth to provide a majestic view across the city of Istanbul down to the Hagia Sofia. Smaller domed spaces are clustered around the main dome, which measures181 feet high and 84 feet wide. This huge dome seems to float above a ring of light, which is projected through stained-glass windows at the dome's base. Its weight is actually transferred through buttress walls, half domes, and arches to the four gigantic pillars at its base.

Part V
Arranging the Present and Saving the Past

In this part . . .

No building is an island. A building relates to the land, the street, and the city around it. This part examines the ways that architecture — and the spaces around it — is connected into coherent settlements. A brief history of urban design illustrates this art of ensemble from ancient to modern times. This part shows how architecture is manipulated to form dense blocks and open spaces and to create new types of cities and towns in the process.

As the world has become populated with more and more buildings, the challenge of saving the architectural past — as well as constructing anew — has become increasingly difficult. This part defines the differences between restoration and renovation and presents various ways of refurbishing and adding onto buildings. If you want to preserve a landmark in your own backyard, consult the guide on listing a property on the National Register of Historic Places in Chapter 20.

Chapter 19

Understanding Urban Design

· ·

In This Chapter

▶ Remembering the world's first settlements

▶ Tracing the development of European cities

▶ Watching American cities take shape

▶ Seeing how urban growth leads to the city of tomorrow

· ·

Modern architect Mies van der Rohe once said that architecture starts when two bricks are put together. By extension, towns and cities start when two buildings are put together. The various placements of the buildings, streets, alleys, courtyards, squares, and parks give each city a distinctive rhythm, scale, and style. New York City's wide, straight avenues lined with tall buildings couldn't be more different than the narrow, winding streets of the medieval hilltop town of Siena, Italy. Understanding the basic building blocks of cities and how they evolved through history can strengthen your appreciation of architecture's *context,* or the relationships among individual buildings and their surroundings.

The First Cities of Humankind

Human settlements began thousands of years ago when people decided to live in one place and farm the land rather than move around and hunt and gather. The world's first cities were built along the banks of the Tigris and Euphrates rivers, in a lush area that is now part of Egypt, Israel, Iraq, and Iran.

Jericho and Catal Huyuk

Within this fertile valley, the earliest known urban settlement was Jericho, in what is now Jordan. Mud-brick houses were densely clustered together, beginning around 8000 B.C., and were eventually surrounded by defensive walls. Catal Huyuk, a town in southern Turkey that dates back to 6500 B.C. then followed Jericho. Its attached buildings were also designed to keep out enemies.

But instead of constructing a wall, the builders protected their settlement with a row of houses and storerooms that were accessible from the roofs rather than through doorways.

Mesopotamia's climate-friendly Ur

Early towns weren't planned in a deliberate sense: They grew according to the lay of the land and the local climate. A good example of this concept is the Mesopotamian city of Ur in present-day Iraq. Houses were arranged around courtyards with fountains and pools that provided natural air conditioning. Streets were narrow and winding to shield the buildings from the heat and windblown sand of the desert. This arrangement remained virtually unchanged in Middle Eastern and North African towns for thousands of years.

India's grid-iron plan

The first towns designed around a *grid-iron plan* — rectangular blocks bisected by straight streets at right angles — were built in ancient India around 2150 B.C. One of the best documented towns that followed this plan is Mohenjo-Daro on the Indus River. Large houses linked by courtyards and passageways were densely packed into "super blocks" off the main thoroughfares. A citadel of several civic and religious buildings, including a huge bathing pool, was raised above the residential district.

Ancient Greek and Roman Town Order: Hooked on a Classic

Grid plans similar to the one used in Mohenjo-Daro were adopted in ancient Greece. Hippodamus was the architect responsible for developing these geometric layouts. Considered the world's first urban planner, Hippodamus remodeled Piraeus (the port of Athens), planned the city of Rhodes (408 B.C.), and traveled with Athenian colonists to reconfigure the new city of Thurii in Italy (circa 440 B.C.). In 479 B.C., he drew up an orderly scheme for rebuilding the city of Miletus after the Persians destroyed it.

Miletus: A model Greek city

Hippodamus laid out his new cities with regularly patterned blocks and separate precincts for public and private functions. Civic buildings — a theater, gymnasium, and stadium — were placed next to an *agora,* the open public square or marketplace where political debate and self-government transpired. In front of the agora was a covered walkway, called a *stoa,* that contained shops and offices, and allowed people to carry out their business while staying protected from the sun and rain. Houses were spread out among three distinct neighborhoods. The planner's systematic layouts for Miletus and other cities emulated the republic of the Greek city-state.

Individual buildings and public spaces each had a role to play within the larger urban framework. This groundbreaking concept was adopted by the classical world of ancient Rome. It was then later adopted by Europe and modern America.

Roman camps and towns

As rulers of a vast empire, ancient Romans developed standardized plans for their settlements as a way of imposing and maintaining their authority. They built thousands of fortified military camps, known as *castra,* that were laid out in a grid pattern of buildings and streets, with walls around the perimeters.

Permanent towns were arranged according to plans that followed a similar grid pattern. At the intersection of the two main avenues was the *forum,* the Roman equivalent of the Greek agora. Placed near the forum were the main temple, a theater, and public baths. The amphitheater, which required sloping ground for seating, was located outside the town.

Rome: Capital of contrasts

Known as the City of the Seven Hills, the imperial capital of Rome grew up on the foundations of earlier settlements — in a less orderly way than the camps and towns scattered around the empire. At the center of the valley between the hills was the Roman Forum, with its market and public gathering areas.

Roman neighborhoods were linked by a system of streets: footpaths called *itineras,* a narrow street (wide enough for one cart) known as the *actus,* and wider roads called *viae* (one wide road is a *via*), which were wide enough for two carts, side by side. Most people lived in crowded blocks of mud-brick and timber apartments arranged around courtyards. These blocks of buildings were called *insulae.* After a fire destroyed much of the city in A.D. 64, a law was passed mandating that insulae had to be built of fireproof concrete walls and floors.

Rome continued to grow with the accumulation of self-contained buildings in contrasting geometric shapes. Circular arenas, elliptical circuses, rectangular temples, and linear colonnades were placed next to one another without following an underlying urban order. The mix of monumental buildings provided an element of excitement within the ancient capital.

Hadrian's Villa

A city unto itself, the 300-acre country estate built by the Emperor Hadrian near Tivoli (118–134) exemplified the visual surprise created by the juxtaposition of geometric buildings in ancient Rome. It included living quarters, libraries, baths, and garden pavilions strung out through more than two miles of gardens. Separate structures were unified by curved colonnades and rotundas, which provided hubs for paths leading in various directions throughout the complex. The villa's sophisticated arrangement of buildings, landscaping, and pathways has intrigued architects for centuries. In designing the Getty Center in Los Angeles, New York architect Richard Meier (see Chapter 15) looked to Hadrian's Villa as the inspiration for his hilltop campus of museums and research and administrative buildings.

Medieval Towns: Defense and Commerce

Informality and romance were the hallmarks of medieval towns and villages. The earliest medieval towns were walled military and government centers, called *burgs,* that were built by European rulers during the ninth century. These fortified towns were often built around a marketplace that was located close to a castle or monastery. Trading communities called *faubourgs* (from the Latin *foris burgum* — "outside the burg") grew up around the walled burgs and required defensive walls of their own. Magdeburg on the Elbe River in Germany is a good example of a faubourg.

Driven by commerce, later medieval towns were built so that trade could be conducted in streets and stores. Outdoor markets were often held in the open rectangular spaces in front of the cathedrals. Storefronts were an asset, so buildings were jampacked around narrow, winding roads. Upper floors often projected over the street, making it possible to shake hands between the windows of buildings located across from one another.

The Ideal Cities of the Renaissance

Beginning in the fifteenth century, formal arrangements of buildings and open spaces grew from the irregular plans of medieval towns. These formal arrangements originated in Renaissance Italy, as architects extended the calm, balanced architecture of individual buildings around a street or a square in an ordered, rational way. This concept is best shown in the famous painting by Piero della Francesca, hanging in the Ducal Palace in Urbino. Using the newly discovered technique of perspective drawing, the artist depicts three- and four-story classical buildings lining the sides of an open space with a round chapel in the center.

Della Francesca's calm scene represents several key concepts of the ideal city of the Renaissance:

- ✔ The wide streets have public squares called *piazzas* at their intersections.
- ✔ The individual buildings are unified into a coherent setting with the repetition of façades.
- ✔ Fountains, statues, or monuments are carefully placed as a focal point at the end of long, straight streets.

Leonardo's new town

Among the creations of the Renaissance genius Leonardo da Vinci (1452–1519) was a proposed ideal city, to be located outside Milan, that was way ahead of its time. Leonardo designed the city for Ludovico Sforza, the ruler of Milan, as a way of solving the overcrowded, unsanitary conditions — conditions contributing to the plague — within the city of Milan.

Da Vinci proposed dispersing 30,000 inhabitants into a low-density arrangement of 10 new towns, with each town having 5,000 houses. Vehicular and pedestrian traffic would be separated into different levels, with special routes reserved for the heaviest traffic. This same idea was taken up at the end of the nineteenth century by English planner Ebenezer Howard (see "Howard's garden city," later in this chapter), who proposed garden cities outside London. Howard was also influential in the design of the new American towns of the 1960s.

Scamozzi's star-shaped fort

Architect and theorist Vincenzo Scamozzi (1552–1616) proposed other schemes for an ideal Renaissance city. Scamozzi is usually credited with planning the fortified town of Palma Nova near Venice, which started construction in 1593. Like many Renaissance towns, Palma Nova was built with protective walls at its perimeter. But instead of arranging the fortifications into boring straight lines, Scamozzi used the ramparts as the basis of an ambitious geometric design. He shaped the plan into a nine-sided star with a hexagon in the middle. Radial streets lead out toward the perimeter walls from an open space at the center. Main buildings are grouped around the central square, and six smaller squares are formed in the centers of the housing blocks.

Scamozzi's plan influenced later fortifications, such as the French fortress city of Neuf Brisach on the banks of the Rhine River. Constructed from 1698 to 1720, it was designed by Sebastien Le Prestre de Vauban, the chief military engineer for Louis XIV. Inside its elaborate system of fortified walls, military barracks, civilian housing, and a church are grouped around a central square — much like the design of Palma Nova.

Nolli and his map

Many architects consider the huge map of Rome created by Giambattista Nolli (1701–1756) in 1748 (see sidebar figure) as the holy grail of urban cartography. Its 12 plates, which when put together measure nearly 6 x 7 feet, depict the city's network of buildings, landscape features, streets, squares, and even interiors, along with views of great monuments from the Renaissance and Baroque. The original purpose of the map was for tax assessment. But its aerial view of the city's layout came to be viewed as a valuable tool in revealing the relationships between private and public spaces. Nolli drew a clear distinction between solid building blocks, which were colored in dark tones, and open spaces, such as streets and interior public spaces, which were left blank. This urban mapping technique, which is used in a more abstract way today, is commonly referred to as *figure-ground*.

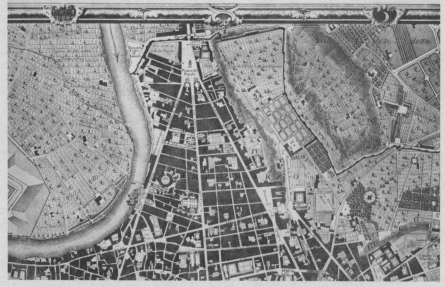

Photo lithograph by Veli Roth, 1966. Gift by Donald I. Foley to the University of Berkley. Used with permission.

Michelangelo's Campidoglio

Michelangelo was as good an urban planner as he was an architect, sculptor, and painter. (See Chapter 10 for more on Michelangelo's architecture.) One of his major contributions to the city of Rome is the redesign of Capitoline Hill, a government hub since ancient times. When an equestrian statue of Marcus Aurelius was moved to the site in 1538, Michelangelo was asked to create a fitting setting. He responded by creating the Campidoglio. He saved two old palaces and built new walls on three sides of a trapezoidal plaza to create a totally new effect. A grand, terraced ramp leads to the open space, and a star-patterned oval on the pavement focuses attention on the statue. To unify the façades around the plaza, he invented a giant classical order of two-story columns, which was widely copied throughout Europe.

Royal Bombast and Power: Baroque Grand Plans

In the seventeenth century, Baroque architecture, an urban style, stepped out into the street to fill cities with a new sense of drama (see Chapter 10). During this period, architects transformed piazzas and squares into stage sets for public spectacles. They surrounded the piazzas and squares with grandly curved façades and colonnades, and filled their spaces with fountains and sculpture. Royal palaces, town halls, and military structures gained even more prominence when they were integrated into a grand plan of avenues, approaches, and landscapes. This regimented planning technique symbolized the monarchy's power over nation and nature.

Versailles: Domination of nature

The palace and gardens produced by French King Louis XIV (1643–1715) at Versailles (outside Paris) is one of the most extravagant combinations of architecture and landscape in history. The Sun King, as he was nicknamed, expanded the hunting lodge built by his father into a huge complex that could accommodate his entire government. His model was Vaux-le-Vicomte, the grand estate built by his finance minister, Nicholas Fouquet. The king was so envious of its exquisitely planned buildings and gardens that he had Fouquet imprisoned and then immediately hired his design team to create an even more magnificent scheme.

I am the State

Beginning in the 1660s, architect Louis Le Vau, interior designer Charles Le Brun, and landscape architect Andre Le Notre transformed Versailles into an ordered stage set for courtly festivities. Le Notre's remarkable gardens were as highly structured as the palace architecture. The garden's formal designs were shaped by flower beds surrounded by clipped hedges *(parterres)*, radiating pathways lined with trees *(allées)*, and topiary, reflecting pools, canals, and outdoor theaters. In the center of the estate, a path stretched for miles, from the king's bedroom into the landscape, to create a seemingly infinite vista. At Versailles, the domination of man-made elements over nature physically represented the absolute monarch's motto, "I am the State."

Cities in the Age of Enlightenment

The eighteenth and early nineteenth centuries promoted rational order in European and American cities for increasingly urban societies. Architects revamped and consolidated cities with radial avenues, grand vistas, and monumental blocks of classical-style apartment buildings and townhouses arranged around public squares and gardens. Several of the most significant developments in urban planning of the eighteenth century were made in towns and cities that were located in remote areas away from European capitals such as London and Paris.

Merry old England: Bath's crescents and squares

Bath, which is a sleepy rural town in western England, rose to prominence in the 1700s as a health resort known for its springs. Its rapid expansion led to a new type of city block — a semi-circular row of townhouses, called a *crescent,* that would become a mainstay of British planning in the eighteenth and nineteenth centuries. Architects John Wood the Elder (1700–1754) and his son, John Wood the Younger, who redeveloped the medieval town from 1727 to 1781, were responsible for this innovative urban form. Their stately squares and crescents unified by classical façades created urban order from houses of various sizes. American historian Lewis Mumford called Bath's eighteenth-century plan as stimulating and restorative as the town's waters. Decades later, architect John Nash used many of Wood's ideas in redeveloping parts of London (see Chapter 11).

France: Nancy's grand boulevard

Stanislaus Leczinski, the ruler of Nancy — the capital of Lorraine in eastern France — devised an ingenious way of uniting the medieval and Renaissance sections of the city into a cohesive urban plan. Leszinski, the former king of Poland, collaborated with architect Here de Corny (1705–1763) to create two new streets at right angles to one another. One of the streets was an east-west route between the two parts of Nancy that connected the city to the surrounding countryside. The other street was a grand boulevard that extended through the medieval part of the city; instead of designing the boulevard as a straight street lined by uniform buildings, de Corny created an exciting series of interrelated spaces along a central promenade that extended from the city hall to the palace.

At one end of the boulevard, the architect placed a square in front of the city hall that featured a statue of Leszinski's son-in-law, Louis XV. He then extended the boulevard through a triumphal arch to a linear space lined by rows of trees in front of long buildings. The boulevard then led to a long public space with curved ends. Rounded classical colonnades called *exedra* framed the curves. De Corny's eighteenth-century plan of Nancy shows how a simple urban element such as a street can be shaped into a dramatic sequence of outdoor rooms and used to change the existing fabric of the city.

Magnificent distances in Washington, D.C.

The capital of the United States reflects many of the urban ideals of late-eighteenth-century Europe. It's no wonder: Washington, D.C., was designed by a Frenchman, Pierre Charles L'Enfant (1754–1825). L'Enfant was selected by President George Washington to design the capital in 1791. The son of a gifted painter, L'Enfant spent his childhood around the palace of Versailles. He then studied art in Paris before emigrating to America to join the Revolutionary army. He laid out the federal city of Washington by superimposing diagonal avenues, reminiscent of Versailles' grand axes, over a rectangular grid of streets. The diagonals united the capital's most important buildings — the Capitol, the president's "palace" (now known as the White House), the national bank, a church, and a market. The design allowed traffic to cut through the residential neighborhoods laid out on the grid without interruptions. At the intersections of the contrasting street patterns were squares and circles, which were to serve as focal points for the city's residential neighborhoods.

The scale of L'Enfant's plan was immense — 6,100 acres. He viewed his plan as the symbolic representation of the United States, which he called "this vast Empire." The major thoroughfares of the city were named after the states. The entire system of avenues and streets was designed to spread out toward the horizon. The English novelist Charles Dickens called Washington a "City of Magnificent Distances" after visiting the city in 1842.

Despite the brilliance of his vision, L'Enfant was fired in 1792, less than a year after he was hired. The friction that resulted from the architect's decision to demolish a new house that didn't conform to his plan led to his dismissal. Nevertheless, surveyor Andrew Ellicott and mathematician Benjamin Banneker, who laid out the city's streets, carried out L'Enfant's plan. During the 1800s, many talented architects continued to fill out L'Enfant's plan with government buildings, such as the U.S. Capitol and the Treasury Building. Much of what L'Enfant envisioned for the residential areas of Washington, D.C., also was realized.

American Cities: Growing on the Grid

In 1785, Congress established a national land policy for settling the country's territories west of the Ohio River. The policy allowed for an equal subdivision of property — the *grid-iron plan*. Townships were to be laid out in a 6 x 6 mile square that was to be divided into 36 sections, with each section measuring 1 square mile. This regular pattern of streets, blocks, and squares had already overtaken the older eastern cities as they grew from their impromptu beginnings. In deciding to extend uniform blocks over Manhattan, a New York state-appointed commission summed up the efficiency of the grid-iron plan by claiming that the right-angled houses within the plan were cheap to build and convenient to live in. While practical, the grid also inspired several elegant variations.

Philadelphia: Sitting fine between the lines

In 1683, Pennsylvania governor William Penn and surveyor Thomas Holme drew up a rectangular grid for Philadelphia that stretched between the city's two rivers, the Delaware and Schuylkill. Two avenues, crossing through a 10-acre public square at the center, divided the plan. Important civic buildings, such as a meetinghouse, a state house, and a school, were to surround the central public square. Four 8-acre public squares were dispersed within the grid. Residential neighborhoods were to be arranged around these smaller squares, which were to be landscaped as parks. But Philadelphia didn't exactly grow according to this geometric plan. By 1794, most of the city was concentrated to the east of the central public square along the Delaware riverfront. Civic buildings weren't built around the large public square — they were built on available sites as the need for them arose. Smaller streets were added to break down the size of the blocks formed by the original 1683 grid.

Savannah: Sweetheart of the South

James Oglethorpe, a member of Britain's parliament and a prison reformer, carried out a more elegant variation on the grid plan in Savannah, Georgia. The grid plan for Savannah was based on a system of neighborhood units called *wards*. The wards consisted of 12 blocks arranged around a square park. The blocks were divided into lots for 40 houses and four public buildings, such as the churches and stores that fronted the park. As the city expanded in the late 1700s and early 1800s, the wards were repeated around broad, shady streets. Oglethorpe's elegant checkerboard of buildings and open spaces proved that the grid plan could be gracious while allowing for speculative development and systematic growth.

Staying Connected: Urban Growth Explosion

As European cities mushroomed in the nineteenth century, new planning strategies emerged to deal with the overtaxed urban infrastructures — housing, streets, water supply, and transportation — that resulted from overcrowding. The new strategies were aimed at replacing the irregular blocks and winding, narrow streets of the medieval city with broad, well-lit thoroughfares that efficiently connected the inner city to the outer suburb.

Vienna's Ringstrasse

By the nineteenth century, the Austrian city of Vienna had developed into two distinct parts: The narrow streets, old churches, and palaces of the medieval city called the Altstadt were located at the city's center, while the suburbs, with large apartment blocks and spreading trees, were located on the city's outskirts. Between the two parts of the city lay a broad belt of open land and fortifications. French ruler Napoleon destroyed the fortifications when he captured the city in 1809 and the area fell into decline.

In 1857, Emperor Franz Joseph held a design competition to redevelop the derelict land between Vienna's Altstadt and suburbs into a new district of residential and civic buildings. The new district was to include the parliament, a university, a theater, and an opera house. The winner of the competition was Ludwig von Forster, whose scheme was approved in 1858 and implemented over the next decade. Von Forster's design focused on a broad avenue called the Ringstrasse ("ring street") that extended through the center of the newly developed area. The avenue, which was two miles long and more than 200 feet wide, wasn't circular like a ring but divided into straight sections and lined by imposing buildings.

Not everyone appreciated the Ringstrasse's strict, formal lines and monumental architecture: They were heavily criticized as establishing an inhumane barrier between Vienna's inner city and suburbs. Leading the charge was Austrian critic Camillo Sitte, whose influential book, *The Art of Building Cities,* was published in 1889. Sitte argued for a return to the type of curving streets and intimate spaces that were common in medieval cities all over central Europe.

Haussmann's Paris

Other grand plans to replace the medieval city were hatched in Paris. These plans, which were designed during the Renaissance, were characterized by a dignified open space called a *place* that glorified the monarchy (typically, a statue of the king on horseback was placed in the center). In 1612, French King Louis XIII established the prototype of the residential square, which would become popular in Europe and the United States, with the Place Royale (renamed Place des Vosges after the French Revolution). It was followed by the Place des Victoires (1687), the Place Vendome (1720), and the Place de la Concorde (1775). Napoleon continued the Parisian remodeling with new streets and his huge victory arch, the Arc de Triomphe.

Between 1852 and 1870, Paris underwent a much more radical transformation. Napoleon III (nephew of the first Napoleon), who wanted to turn the city into a modern metropolis, masterminded the transformation. He handed a map of the city, on which he had drawn new streets in four contrasting colors, to his chief planner Baron Georges-Eugene Haussmann. With ruthless zeal, Haussmann carried out his boss's plan by demolishing much of medieval and Renaissance Paris to make way for 85 miles of broad boulevards and traffic circles aimed at focal points such as the Arc de Triomphe. Bordered by new buildings with uniform façades, the gaslit streets efficiently carried high volumes of carriage traffic from the heart of the city to outlying areas. But Haussmann didn't stop there! He built great monuments, such as the new Paris Opera House (see Chapter 11), city parks, and an underground network of giant sewers.

The City Beautiful movement

Haussmann's sweeping plan for Paris (see preceding section, "Haussmann's Paris") had an enormous influence on other European capitals. It also inspired plans for American cities. The plan convinced generations of architects and city officials that efficient, coordinated planning of streets and buildings could impose order on chaotic urban slums and improve the lives of the inhabitants.

In the United States, the search for urban uniformity began in Chicago at the World's Columbian Exposition, which was held in 1893 to celebrate the 400th anniversary of Columbus's discovery of America. (The expo opened a year late.) Chicago architect Daniel Burnham (see Chapters 11 and 13) invited prominent architects to collaborate on a "dream city" of classical buildings arranged around a water-filled court of honor. This monumental grouping of white structures offered a serene, homogeneous alternative to the smoky, industrial city around it.

Soon other cities were copying the idea of arranging public buildings into a coherent district. This movement, called the City Beautiful movement, became part of the political agenda for municipal reform. Its concepts were first implemented in — where else? — Washington, D.C., where the federal government owned enough buildings to create several civic centers.

In 1902, the U.S. Senate adopted a plan prepared by Senator James McMillan of Michigan to revamp the Mall into a grassy carpet lined with museums. Wide axes linking the major monuments were to enhance L'Enfant's plan but be far more grandiose in design. Directing the project was Chicago's Burnham, who traveled to Europe to visit the great gardens and palaces of Paris and Rome for inspiration. Although the McMillan Plan wasn't entirely realized, its framework transformed Washington into the monumental city that it is today.

Burnham went on to advise Cleveland, Chicago, and San Francisco on building new civic centers. Later in the twentieth century, downtown government centers were also built in St. Louis, Los Angeles, and Boston. The centers were based on concepts that originated in the City Beautiful movement.

Modern Cities of Tomorrow: The 'Burbs

The desire to escape from the busy city to the peaceful suburbs has been a part of civilization for thousands of years. In ancient times, Pliny the Younger wrote of his commute from downtown Rome to his home 17 miles away, noting that the roads were "difficult and long."

Suburbs grew by leaps and bounds after the Industrial Revolution. Some followed a pre-established plan, such as Philadelphia and Detroit, while others, such as Llewellyn Park, New Jersey (1859), and Riverside outside Chicago (1868), sprung up beyond the city grid, with curving streets in park-like settings.

By the end of the nineteenth century, alternatives to both the gritty city and the far-flung suburb were proposed, as metropolitan areas sprawled in every direction. These visionary schemes focused on the idea of new self-sufficient towns that would provide both jobs and homes in a gardenlike setting.

Howard's garden city

Leading the way for the new designs was Ebenezer Howard, an English stenographer who had briefly worked in America. In 1898, he published the book, *Tomorrow: A Peaceful Path to Real Reform,* in which he proposed a "garden city." His plan called for replacing conventional industrial cities with smaller towns encircled by agricultural lands. "Town and country must be married," he explained, "And out of this joyous union will spring a new hope, a new life, a new civilization." In 1903, a version of his hybrid plan was carried out in Letchworth, north of London. Soon garden cities took root in Europe, as well as in places as far-flung as Japan and Australia. In the 1960s, new satellite towns, which followed Howard's garden city model, were built in the United States. The most famous of these new towns are Reston, Virginia, and Columbia, Maryland, outside Washington, D.C.

Wright's Broadacre City

Another hybrid of city and suburb was proposed by Chicago architect Frank Lloyd Wright (see Chapter 13). First described in his 1932 book, *The Disappearing City,* Wright's low-density Broadacre City was to be arranged as a grid of roads and highways connecting separate zones for houses, industry, farms, and recreation. Major intersections were to be built with markets, churches, and civic buildings. Wright eventually built a 12-x-12-foot wooden model that conveyed how his ideas might be applied to a 4-x-4-mile plot of land. He exhibited the model around the country. Though it was never built, Broadacre City anticipated many features of contemporary suburbia, including motels, malls, and highway overpasses.

Le Corbusier's towers in a park

Known for his stripped-down houses, Swiss-born French architect Le Corbusier applied his modern principles (see Chapter 14) to the design of entire cities. In such visionary schemes as La Ville Contemporaine (1922), the Plan Voisin de Paris (1925), and Villes Radieuses (1930–1936), Le Corbusier proposed highly ordered groupings of skyscrapers in landscaped open spaces connected by superhighways. He imagined his ideal city as a garden dotted with sparkling towers, where people could leave their apartments to enjoy sunshine and fresh air. Le Corbusier's radical tower-in-a-park designs were never built. But they did provide the inspiration for wholesale redevelopment of entire urban neighborhoods such as Stuyvesant Town in New York City.

Postwar Plans: From Sprawl to Smart Growth

In the decades after World War II, economic prosperity made it possible to adapt the city of tomorrow to postwar America. Suburbs grew, with developer-built houses and shopping centers that resembled Wright's Broadacre City.

The death of downtown

Meanwhile, the schism between city and suburb became more pronounced as millions fled old urban neighborhoods for new bedroom communities, leaving downtowns to decay and rot. Cities followed Le Corbusier's radiant city ideal as they tried to stem the deterioration by replacing slums with high-rise housing and office towers. (See the preceding section.)

By the 1960s, this destructive urban "renewal" had prompted a strong back-lash. Among the more eloquent critics was Jane Jacobs, whose 1961 book, *The Death and Life of Great American Cities,* argued convincingly for maintaining the close-knit vitality of old neighborhoods. This preservation movement gained momentum in the late 1960s and 1970s and became a part of mainstream architectural practice (see Chapter 20).

As the suburbs continued to grow in the 1970s and 1980s, they began to attract the type of department stores, hotels, restaurants, and office towers previously reserved for traditional downtowns. But instead of being neatly concentrated, these "edge cities" were spread out over several miles around highways and interchanges. Examples of this type of edge city include places like Tysons Corner, Virginia, outside Washington, D.C., and Irvine, California, near Los Angeles.

In the 1980s, a reaction against this sprawl had set in. By the 1990s, this anti-sprawl movement had a name — Smart Growth. Aimed at conserving open space and reducing dependency on the car, this approach calls for increasing the density of buildings and linking communities to public transportation. In other words, the approach is an attempt to make the suburbs more like a conventional city.

New urbanism

The inspiration for Smart Growth (see preceding section) came from a type of compact neighborhood design pioneered by Miami architects Andres Duany and Elizabeth Plater-Zyberk in the 1980s. Their design, called *New Urbanism, neotraditionalism,* or *traditional neighborhood development* (TND), replaces the typical suburban subdivision of cookie-cutter homes on cul-de-sacs with more diverse, closely-knit communities where people can live, work, and shop. The inspiration for New Urbanism is old urbanism — that is, the grid plans, mix of residential and commercial buildings, and charming atmosphere of historic towns such as Annapolis and Savannah (see "Savannah," earlier in this chapter).

Duany and Plater-Zyberk first experimented with New Urbanism at Seaside, a resort community in the Florida panhandle. In 1988, they were hired to apply their new planning ideas to a suburban development outside a major city — Kentlands in Gaithersburg, Maryland, near Washington, D.C.

In Kentlands, streets are laid out in a city-style grid, with sidewalks to encourage walking. A mix of single-family homes, townhouses, and apartment buildings are arranged closely together and near the streets. Homes are designed in a traditional style, with an old-fashioned porch in the front and a garage in the back.

Ever since Kentlands was completed, New Urbanist developments have sprung up around the country, most of them in the suburbs. Although the developments claim self-sufficiency, few incorporate services, workplaces, and connections to public transportation. The Disney-built town of Celebration, on the outskirts of Disney World in Orlando, Florida, is one of the most famous New Urbanist developments.

LINGO

Urban design dictionary

Architects and urban designers use special terms to describe their plans for cities and towns. Here are a few examples:

✔ **axis:** a directional pathway that connects places along a vista

✔ **context:** the setting around a building

✔ **edge city:** a large, urban-style development in the suburbs

✔ **figure-ground:** a technique of showing the relationship between buildings and open spaces through solid-looking objects sketched on a less distinct background

✔ **grid-iron, or grid plan:** a network of uniformly spaced horizontal and vertical streets and blocks

✔ **intervention:** a new building or addition inserted into an existing setting

✔ **perimeter block:** a large, doughnut-shaped building, with a courtyard in the middle, that extends to the edges of the surrounding streets

✔ **piazza, or plaza:** a paved open square

✔ **planned unit development:** a suburban cluster of buildings that is related to the landscape

✔ **radial plan:** a city or town arranged with diagonal streets that typically extend from a central square

✔ **street wall:** continuous façades on either side of a street

✔ **super block:** a collection of buildings, on a large parcel bordered by major avenues, that has its own internal pathways and open spaces

✔ **zoning:** dividing a city or neighborhood into sections dedicated to different purposes

Chapter 20

Historic Preservation: Saving the Past for the Future

• •

In This Chapter

▶ Understanding preservation

▶ Looking at the history of preservation

▶ Discovering the parameters of preservation

• •

During the prosperous postwar decades, the wrecker's ball swung to demolish historic structures and entire neighborhoods to make way for new buildings and towns in cities across the globe. From this destruction, a movement to preserve the world's architectural heritage was born. In the United States and Europe, it grew from earlier efforts to save individual landmarks by historical societies and citizen groups. By the late 1960s, historic preservation had become a federal law in the United States and a distinct discipline within the architecture profession.

Just How Far Should It Go?

Preservation presents architects who are used to building afresh with new challenges. Restoring and recycling old structures poses many questions about how much the existing architecture should be changed. Should the original be preserved in its found state or repaired to look like it did when it was first built? Should an addition resemble the historic architecture of the existing building or look completely different? Should a building that is falling down be stabilized, demolished, or rebuilt exactly as it was?

Answering these questions requires architects to grapple with the definition of "restoration," "reconstruction," and "rehabilitation" — not to mention the word "preservation" itself. In fact, architects have debated these terms for more than a century.

To restore or not to restore

Second Empire French architect Eugene Emmanuel Viollet-le-Duc, who enjoyed tampering with medieval monuments, defined restoration as the process of transforming a building into a completed state. Viollet-le-Duc believed that additions and alterations to great architecture could enhance the original design. English critic and social reformer John Ruskin, however, took an opposite view in arguing that old buildings should be left alone. Ruskin equated restoration with the total destruction of a building,

These views represent two opposite approaches to restoration, and there are many stages in between. Restoration varies in the degree to which it changes the original artifact. The alteration may enhance the exterior with a new coat of paint (like makeup) or radically disfigure the architecture forever (like bad cosmetic surgery). Understanding when, where, and how to restore or preserve a building requires a sensitivity to architecture as an artistic unit, not just a grouping of materials and spaces.

Knowing when to leave well enough alone

Some buildings are more easily altered and added onto than others. A rambling, informally arranged Victorian pile can more easily accept new wings than a compact, symmetrical classical building. Modern buildings in glass and steel may be even harder to expand. To move a wall or add a new wing to Mies van der Rohe's Barcelona Pavilion (see Chapter 14), for instance, would destroy the precise balance of this minimalist design. It would be like adding new brushstrokes to a Picasso painting.

But architecture is not painting. Buildings require constant repairs, from fixing a leaky roof to replacing a broken window. Alterations and additions are natural occurrences in the life of a building. The skill of the preservation architect is knowing how to change a structure without violating its essential identity.

The Gold Standards of Architectural Rescue

Today, American architects follow standards established by the secretary of the interior when preserving architecture. The following definitions are included in these standards.

Preservation

Sustaining the existing form, integrity, and material of an historic property is categorized as *preservation*. Preservation work focuses upon the ongoing maintenance and repair of historic materials and features rather than on extensive replacement and new construction.

One of the best preserved properties in America is Drayton Hall (1738–1742), a Colonial home near Charleston, South Carolina. Its brick structure has been maintained in its original condition without electricity or indoor plumbing.

Architects abroad often use different terms for preservation. Europeans often refer to it as "protection," while British architects use the word "conservation"; in the United States, "conservation" is associated with the cleaning and repairing of works of art and building materials, as well as with land preservation.

Restoration

Removing or replacing missing elements and accurately putting back the architectural form and details is called *restoration*. The goal is to re-create the historic building and its setting as it appeared at a particular period of time.

For example, the Pennsylvania State House (1732–1735), where the Declaration of Independence was drafted (the building is now called Independence Hall), was restored to re-create its appearance in 1776. A new steel structure was inserted to prop up its sagging roof. Some rooms were lacking floors, wood paneling, and furniture, so these elements were reproduced to look like the originals and added as well.

Reconstruction and replication

When an historic building has been destroyed, the reproduction of its architecture on the same site is referred to as *reconstruction*. Making an exact copy of the building is called *replication;* it is the most radical type of preservation.

Both of these techniques were used to resurrect European cities that were destroyed during World War II. After Warsaw was heavily bombed, the medieval center of the city was reconstructed — and in some cases, replicated. Existing fragments and archaeological research were used to help make it look just as it did before the war.

Rehabilitation

When an historic building is repaired, altered, or added to, the process is called *rehabilitation*. This process calls for upgrading the structure for contemporary use while preserving its historic and architectural character. Rehabilitation is also used interchangeably with renovation. It also may indicate adaptive use, which is the process of adapting a building for a different use.

One of the last great rehabilitation projects of the twentieth century was the overhaul of Germany's parliament building in Berlin, the Reichstag, after the seat of government was moved there from Bonn. Designed by architect Paul Wallot, the 1894 neo-Renaissance building, shown in Figure 20-1, was almost burned down by the Nazis in 1933, heavily shelled during World War II, and renovated into offices and a museum in the 1960s. In 1992, British architect Norman Foster won a design competition to renew the damaged Reichstag. He respected the history of the century-old structure (including damaged stonework and graffiti on the walls from Russian soldiers) while inserting a new glassy dome. Symbolizing the reunification of Germany, the large dome incorporates spiraling walkways and transmits daylight into the parliamentary chamber through skylights and a reflective cone at the center.

Figure 20-1: British architect Norman Foster renovated the Reichstag in Berlin (1992–1999) with a new glass dome.

Photo by Howard Davis © John A. Gascon.

The Upside of Preservation

Buildings are monuments to civilization. They represent who people are, what they have experienced, and what they value. With each building that's torn down, civilization loses a little bit of history and collective traditions. Unfortunately, America has lost much of its architectural tradition. Frank Lloyd Wright's prodigious outpouring of buildings, for example, has already been reduced by 20 percent. Several of his most groundbreaking designs are gone, including the Midway Gardens in Chicago and the Larkin Building in Buffalo. Many Wright houses have been pillaged for their stained glass windows, light fixtures, and furniture. (For more on Wright, see Chapter 13.)

Some architectural landmarks have survived only to have been altered beyond recognition. One recent preservation technique, for example, is to demolish the guts of a building and save only the façade, behind which a new interior is inserted. While some preservationists claim such a "façadectomy" is preferable to total demolition, others claim it only prolongs a superficial image of the building rather than its architectural essence.

The debate underscores the fact that preservation is not an exact science but an art as subjective as any architectural design. The styles for new buildings change, and so, too, do the styles for restoring and recycling old ones.

During the nineteenth and early twentieth centuries, for example, it was common for architects to replace historic architectural elements with new ones that reflected their own personal tastes. Viollet-le-Duc, for example, restored the walled city of Carcassonne and the cathedrals of Laon, Amiens, and Notre Dame based on his admiration for the Middle Age's "rational" structures. See Chapter 11. The worn appearance of these restored structures has caused many to mistake his nineteenth-century alterations for the medieval originals.

Today, such historical ambiguity is frowned upon. Architects are encouraged to distinguish new from old rather than to blur the boundary between the two. When historical evidence is lacking, they are called upon to interpret the lost architecture through a different material or design. Philadelphia architect Robert Venturi, for example, designed a stark metal frame to outline the site and mass of Benjamin Franklin's original house instead of trying to reproduce its architecture from insufficient information. Visitors can immediately tell that Venturi's structure is new, not old. Yet, at the same time, they understand the size and location of Franklin's house through the metal frame of Venturi's design.

In historic buildings where some old materials survive, sophisticated conservation techniques have made it easier to repair original elements and reproduce accurate facsimiles. Paint analysis, for example, has revealed that colors applied to eighteenth-century interiors were much brighter than the muted tones that were first associated with Williamsburg.

Patriotism Saves the Day (And a Few Buildings, Too!)

In America, where progress means newness, preservation caught fire in the 1960s after grassroots groups protested — and took legal action — against the destruction of historic buildings in the name of urban renewal. One of the most important legal cases fought by preservationists was over Grand Central Terminal in New York City. The Penn Central Railroad wanted to build a 55-story tower over the Beaux-Arts train terminal, but preservationists went all the way to the Supreme Court to argue for transferring development rights to adjacent sites. The preservationists won, and the tower (as well as several other high-rises) was built on blocks adjacent to the train station. The case provided the constitutional basis for landmark legislation throughout the country.

Early preservation campaigns

The first preservation campaigns, however, go back much further. For example, patriotic efforts to enshrine significant landmarks of the American Revolution led to the purchase and restoration of Philadelphia's Independence Hall in 1816. The Mount Vernon Ladies' Association was formed in 1853 to preserve the decaying home of President George Washington. The Paul Revere Memorial Association was organized to renovate patriot Paul Revere's house in Boston, which opened to the public in 1908.

These private initiatives were followed by two government programs: the Antiquities Act of 1906, which was created to prevent looting of prehistoric sites built by North American Indians in the Southwest, and the National Park Service, which was created in 1916 to protect federal property. Although these programs were aimed at land conservation, they sparked building preservation programs under President Franklin Delano Roosevelt's New Deal.

In 1933, the Historic American Building Survey was established to create a national architectural archive. Out-of-work architects were hired to draw and photograph the country's historic buildings. (This program still continues today, although most of the architects participating in it are students.) Two years later, the Historic Sites Act was passed, allowing the secretary of the interior to survey, purchase, restore, and interpret historic properties. By the end of World War II, Congress had chartered the National Trust for Historic Preservation, a quasi-public organization that began buying old estates and turning them into house museums.

HISTORICAL NOTE

America's first preservation project

When Thomas Jefferson died in 1826, he was in debt, and his mountaintop home, Monticello (see the color insert), was put on the market. Monticello sat empty until 1831, when a Charlottesville druggist bought it for $7,000. Three years later, Monticello was sold to the country's first Jewish naval officer, Uriah Phillips Levy, who had made a fortune in real estate. Although he didn't live at Monticello, Levy undertook major repairs and opened the home to visitors. His preservation efforts preceded those at Washington's home, Mount Vernon, by two decades.

After Levy died, his nephew, New York congressman Jefferson Monroe Levy, bought out the other heirs and continued the restoration project. The younger Levy spent nearly $1 million restoring and repairing the house as a weekend retreat. After being pressured to turn the property into a government-run shrine, he eventually sold Monticello to the newly formed Thomas Jefferson Memorial Foundation in 1923. By then, Monticello had been in the Levy family for 89 years — far longer than the Jeffersons had owned it.

Preservation goes national

In 1966, preservation gained even more public stature when Congress passed the National Preservation Act and established historic preservation offices in every state. The act also created the National Register of Historic Places, an inventory of properties that are at least 50 years old, and provided tax incentives for fixing up historic properties. Reinforcing the effectiveness of this legislation was a growing interest in the architectural past as a source of inspiration for the design of new buildings. In fact, some claim that preservation, not new imitations of the past, constitutes the real postmodern movement in architecture. See Chapter 15.

The Face of Preservation Today

Preservation has grown from saving the historical, "Washington-slept-here" type of landmark to salvaging drive-in restaurants, modern high-rises, and bustling waterfronts. It has even inspired a backlash of its own, as historic neighborhoods are spruced up into chic, upscale enclaves — a process referred to as *gentrification*. It is often criticized for displacing poorer residents and restricting architectural change.

But overall, preservation has breathed new life into dying cities. Its revitalizing benefits extend from individual landmarks to neighborhoods and entire towns. The following sections cover some of the parameters that shape preservation projects today.

Historic districts

A protected grouping of buildings is known as an *historic district.* Charleston, South Carolina, was the first American city to designate part of its downtown as an historic district. In 1931, the city set up an architectural review board to review and approve any changes to buildings within the designated 22-block area. New Orleans followed in 1937 with the Vieux Carré Commission, which had power over all work done — from replacing shutters to beginning new construction — within a 260-acre area in the city. Today, there are hundreds of historic districts, from New York's cast-iron SoHo neighborhood to an entire postwar suburb outside of Denver.

Architects working in these areas are often called upon to place a new building between historic landmarks and create what is called *infill.* The design may be contemporary, but careful attention must be paid to scale, proportions, and materials so that the new structure harmonizes with its historic surroundings. The architect is often limited in his or her choice of materials, paint colors and the number and type of windows and doors.

Let's do the time warp again! Historic towns

Did you think you were at the midnight movies again? Well, even buildings can do the time warp! Thanks to the designation of historic districts, the original settlements in cities such as Santa Fe, New Mexico, and Savannah, Georgia, are now preserved as historic towns. But freezing an entire town in one moment of time is rare. Preserving large-scale historical settings to present a time warp of authenticity requires strict design controls.

The best example of an historic town is Williamsburg. Settled in 1633, it served as the capital of Virginia until 1780. When the government moved to Richmond, the town of Williamsburg began a long decline. In 1926, a local minister, William Archer Rutherford Goodwin, convinced millionaire John D. Rockefeller, Jr., to restore Williamsburg back to its Colonial heyday. To help restore the town, all buildings completed after 1790 were torn down — 720 in all. Surviving landmarks were restored, and more than 300 structures were built from scratch to look old. People dressed in period costume and wandered the streets to add to the Colonial atmosphere.

Another preserved town is Deerfield, Massachusetts. The preservation project began in 1945 when Frank Boyden, the headmaster of Deerfield Academy who had restored old houses for the school, convinced New York lawyer Henry Flynt and his wife Helen (their son had attended Deerfield Academy) to invest in preserving the New England village. Deerfield is not as well known as Williamsburg, but it has a fine collection of houses from the eighteenth and nineteenth centuries, as well as a museum exhibiting artifacts from 1650 through 1850.

Outdoor architectural museums

Atmospheric re-creations of historical settings were nothing new in Europe. In 1891, an outdoor museum called Skansen opened in Stockholm. Its collection of 150 buildings included log cabins, a sod-roof farmhouse, and Lapp dwellings complete with reindeer. To heighten the atmosphere, guides in folk costumes performed activities appropriate to the buildings, such as making cheese and baking. Skansen was followed by similar outdoor museums in Norway and Denmark.

Greenfield Village in Dearborn, Michigan, is one of the oldest outdoor museums in the United States. The museum, which opened in 1933, was the brainchild of the pioneering automobile maker, Henry Ford, who wanted to re-create a typical American small town. Ford began putting together the museum by moving the school that he had attended as a child. He then set up the Illinois courthouse where Lincoln had practiced law, as well as Thomas Edison's laboratory and Orville Wright's bicycle shop. Other additions included slave cabins, a railroad station, a post office, a farmhouse, and a carding mill. Ford also imported a couple of English cottages and a London jewelry shop, where he displayed his collection of clocks and watches.

Some other collections of historic properties that have been removed from their original sites are exhibited at the Farmer's Village in Cooperstown, New York, and Sturbridge Village in Sturbridge, Massachusetts.

Adaptive use

Another way of preserving a building is to adapt it for a new purpose. House museums such as Mount Vernon and Monticello are the earliest examples of adaptive use. The architects involved in such projects try to make the building practical and comfortable while preserving its historic flavor.

The 1956–1964 renovation of the medieval Castelvecchio in Verona, Italy, into a museum by the Venetian architect Carlo Scarpa is one of the most striking modern-day conversions of an old building. Rather than copying the original, Scarpa designed fresh details that contrast with the old.

Another interesting adaptive use project is the Gare d'Orsay, a Beaux-Arts-style railway station in Paris that was turned into a museum in 1986. Italian architect Gae Aulenti added new side galleries that respect the grand procession of the vaulted terminal.

Larger scale examples of adaptive use can be found in successfully preserved urban areas such as the Warehouse District in Cleveland or the Fan in Richmond. These historic districts rely on adaptive use to stimulate commercial activity by turning abandoned structures into stores, restaurants, and apartments.

Historic museum rooms

When a building can't be saved, the last resort for preservationists is to take one of the building's rooms and put it into a museum. Before Frank Lloyd Wright's Frank Little House in Wisconsin was torn down, the Metropolitan Museum of Art in New York acquired its living room and put it on display with its early American period rooms. The demolition of the Chicago Stock Exchange, designed by Louis Sullivan, led the Chicago Art Institute to build a new wing around the stock exchange's salvaged trading room. The interior re-creates Sullivan's dazzling wall patterns through a combination of original canvas panels and new stenciling.

How to get a property listed on the National Register

To get a property listed on the National Register, you should start by doing some preliminary research to make sure that the structure is eligible. Keep in mind that it must be at least 50 years old and possess most of its original features — this is referred to as *architectural integrity*. You must also prove the "significance" of the property, or its association with important historical events, people, or architectural trends. Consult your local historical society or a preservation consultant for help. After you research and photograph the property, contact your local or state historic preservation office for a preliminary review; they can also help you fill out the National Register nomination form. When the nomination is completed and approved by the state, it is sent to the National Park Service in Washington, D.C., for a final review and decision.

Part VII

The Part of Tens

The 5th Wave   By Rich Tennant

"I like the marble vanity and the wall sconces, but I think the Eurostyle fixtures on the whirlpool take away some of its simple country charm."

In this part . . .

*I*n this part, you can find out about the most fascinating architects designing buildings today. You can also pick up a few facts about architecture to impress your family and friends. You may be surprised to discover how much scandal architecture — and architects — have stirred up.

If you're planning a trip abroad, you may want to consult the list of ten architectural masterpieces and include a few on your itinerary. Visiting these monuments will convince you just how powerful architecture can be.

Ever wonder just how high a building can rise? Flip over to the list of the ten most impressive skyscrapers, and you'll get a good idea.

Chapter 21

The Ten Most Fascinating Architects Working Today

Architecture has been called an old persons' profession. And it's no wonder: Most architects don't see their first building constructed until they are well past age 40. Many don't do their best work until they are in their 50s or 60s. The really good ones keep working into their 70s, 80s, and even 90s, until they drop dead at their drawing boards. Frank Lloyd Wright, for instance, was commissioned to design his most famous house, Fallingwater, when he was 68 and the Guggenheim Museum when he was 76. He continued designing into his 80s, and he died at age 92.

Mastery of architecture takes diligence, persistence, and time. Patience is clearly a virtue for architects who spend years waiting for their designs to get built. Daniel Libeskind, for example, won the competition to design Berlin's Jewish Museum in 1990, but it was a dozen years later before the building finally opened. Frank Gehry has waited even longer to see his Disney Concert Hall in downtown Los Angeles, which was conceived in 1989 and still isn't finished.

Few architects become famous, as the following list can attest. With the possible exception of Frank Gehry, none of these talented designers are household names. Most are in their 50s and 60s and have spent years creating interiors and small buildings in preparation for larger masterpieces.

Tadao Ando

The simple and serene buildings designed by Japanese architect Tadao Ando possess a spiritual quality that sets them apart from much contemporary architecture. Ando, self-taught in architecture, was born in 1941 and began his career as a carpenter's apprentice. He traveled abroad extensively to study buildings of Alvar Aalto, Frank Lloyd Wright, Louis Kahn, and Le Corbusier before opening his own office in Osaka, Japan.

Ando combines western modernism with Japanese esthetic traditions to create spare, geometric spaces that have been compared to the work of American modernist Louis Kahn (see Chapter 15). Ando's favorite material is concrete, which he leaves unfinished to serve as both structure and surface. Many of his buildings forge a strong link to nature through the use of reflecting pools, light shafts, and framed vistas.

Ando has won international recognition for his many buildings in Japan and Europe. In 2001, he completed his first American building, the Pulitzer Foundation for the Arts in St. Louis. He has also designed the Modern Art Museum of Fort Worth, completed in 2002, and the Calder Museum in Philadelphia, scheduled to open in 2005.

Elizabeth Diller and Ricardo Scofidio

The wife-and-husband team of Elizabeth Diller (1954–) and Ricardo Scofidio (1935–) is associated with visionary designs that incorporate electronic media. They are considered the darlings of the architectural avant-garde.

Diller was born in Poland. She met Scofidio in the 1970s at New York's Cooper Union, where he still teaches. The two began their practice as "guerilla architects," staging art installations on vacant land. In 1999, they became the first architects to receive a "genius" grant from the MacArthur Fellows Program.

Diller and Scofidio have only recently turned their theories into built projects. In 2000, they completed the Brasserie restaurant in Mies van der Rohe's landmark Seagram Building (see Chapter 22). As patrons walk through the revolving door, video cameras capture their photos and broadcast the images on monitors above the bar. The restaurant reflects the pair's continuing exploration of how architecture defines social behavior, as well as space.

At the Swiss Expo 2002 in Yverdon-les-Bains, Switzerland, the architects completed a lakeside pavilion called the Blur Building. Shrouded in a mist fed by 13,000 high-pressure water nozzles, the structure is meant to create an inhabitable cloud.

Their first major building will be the Institute of Contemporary Art in Boston. The building, a cornerstone of the city's Fan Pier waterfront development, is scheduled for completion in 2004.

Frank Gehry

Frank Gehry is one of the most brilliant architects working today. With the completion of his titanium-clad masterpiece, the Guggenheim Museum in Bilbao, Spain, Gehry has achieved the fame that he has long deserved. He may not be as well known as Frank Lloyd Wright, but "the other Frank," as Gehry is known, and "the other Guggenheim" have sparked as much controversy as Wright and his Guggenheim.

Although Gehry is considered an American original, he was born in Canada in 1929 and moved to Los Angeles at age 17. After studying architecture at the University of Southern California, he joined the Army, studied urban planning at Harvard, and lived briefly in Paris. Gehry opened his own firm in 1962. It took another two decades for him to develop his signature collages; this new direction in his work stemmed from a long-held interest in the relationship between art and architecture, and was fueled by his friendship with painters and sculptors.

In projects such as the Loyola Law School in Los Angeles (1981–1984) and the Winton Guest House in Wayzata, Minnesota (1983–1986), Gehry divided the functions of the buildings into separate, dissimilar volumes that he called "a village of forms." In the 1990s, his designs became looser and more sculptural, as in the Frederick R. Weisman Art Museum in Minneapolis (1990–1993). Sophisticated computer software, borrowed from the aerospace industry, helped translate the irregular, curved shapes of his architecture from sketches and models to built form.

Gehry has completed buildings in Japan, Europe, and the United States and designed several lines of furniture. He has won numerous prizes, including the Pritzker (1989), the Praemium Imperiale (1992), and the first Lillian Gish Award for Lifetime Contribution to the Arts (1994). His Guggenheim Museum has drawn millions of tourists to Bilbao and has been featured in everything from car commercials to pop music videos.

Zaha Hadid

One of only a few woman architects to achieve superstardom, Zaha Hadid designs boldly angular architecture that seems to defy gravity. Born in Baghdad, Iraq, in 1950, Hadid studied mathematics before attending the Architectural Association in London. She burst onto the international scene in 1983 after winning the design competition for The Peak sports club in Hong Kong. Her first completed building was a fire station for the Vitra furniture company in Germany. With its trapezoidal walls and soaring canopy, the building looks as though it could explode in several directions at any moment — like firemen about to be called into action.

Hadid is one of the first architects to work in the Deconstructivist style (see Chapter 15), which emerged in the late-1980s and 1990s and is inspired by the early-twentieth-century modernism of the Russian Constructivists (see Chapter 14).

She is renowned for her colorful, futuristic drawings and paintings that capture the dynamic energy of her architecture. The drawings and paintings have convinced many design competition judges to award her important commissions, such as the Cardiff Opera House (never built) and a cultural center (under design) in downtown Barcelona. Hadid's first building in the United States, the Contemporary Arts Center in Cincinnati, is due to be completed in 2003.

Jacques Herzog and Pierre De Meuron

Jacques Herzog (1950–) and Pierre De Meuron (1950–), who have been friends since childhood, have practiced architecture together in Basel, Switzerland, for more than two decades. They are known for stripped-down buildings that inject an element of the unexpected. In comparing their work to the Pop paintings of artist Andy Warhol, Herzog explains that he and De Meuron use familiar images and ordinary materials in new ways. A good example of this approach is the Swiss duo's Dominus Winery in the Napa Valley. Instead of building conventional stone walls, the architects filled wire cages with loose rocks to create a thick, textured perimeter that insulates the interior from extreme temperature changes.

The highest profile project by Herzog and De Meuron is the Tate Gallery of Modern Art in London. The architects took advantage of the huge industrial spaces of the original building (a power plant designed by Sir Giles Gilbert Scott in 1947) on the south bank of the Thames River and turned them into lofty galleries for displaying contemporary art. One of their latest projects is a new building for the de Young Museum in San Francisco, scheduled to open in 2005.

Rem Koolhaas

Dutch architect Rem Koolhaas is as well known for his books as he is for his buildings. Born in 1944, he made his debut in architecture in the 1970s with *Delirious New York,* a manifesto declaring the relevancy of Manhattan's "culture of congestion." This thought-provoking account was followed in 1995 by an architectural bestseller titled *S, M, L, XL*. In between writing books, Koolhaas completed several buildings, including a dance theater in The Hague, a house outside Paris, and a convention center in Lille, France.

Although no two of his designs are alike, Koolhaas uses jagged shapes, industrial materials, and inventive ways of traversing a building. A home he designed in Bordeaux, France, for example, has an enclosed glass room that moves up and down like an elevator, allowing the disabled owner to maneuver easily through the three-story house.

While many architects decry the ugliness of shopping malls, airports, and casinos, Koolhaas maintains that this "junk space" must be studied and even used as inspiration for new architecture that recognizes the clashing realities of contemporary life. To prove his point, the architect has designed several American stores for Italian fashion designer Miucca Prada, and a branch of the Guggenheim Museum in Las Vegas.

Daniel Libeskind

Daniel Libeskind is one of the most radical architects working today. His fragmented designs explode out in every direction, as if to symbolize the energy and alienation of contemporary life. Libeskind first won international attention for the Jewish Museum in Berlin, a zigzag-shaped building that has been compared to a broken Star of David.

The museum has special meaning for Libeskind, who is the son of Holocaust survivors. Born in Lodz, Poland, in 1946, Libeskind became an American citizen in 1965. He has practiced in Berlin ever since he won the Jewish Museum competition in 1990.

Among his controversial projects is the Spiral, an extension to London's Victoria and Albert Museum. The design, compared to a collapsing house of cards, created so much criticism that it was denied public funding and shelved. Libeskind is also responsible for the Imperial War Museum North in Manchester, England. The museum resembles a shattered globe to show the impact of war on the twentieth century. In the United States, he has designed the Jewish Museum in San Francisco and an addition to the Denver Art Museum. The addition is scheduled for completion in 2004.

Jean Nouvel

French architect Jean Nouvel enjoys playing with transparency and light to make the solid boundaries of architecture seem to disappear. One of his earliest buildings, the Arab Institute in Paris, is faced in glass with metal apertures that open and close, like the irises of the human eye, to control the level of daylight entering the building. Another of his Paris creations, the Cartier Foundation, is layered with glass screens that obscure where the building begins and ends.

Nouvel was born in 1945. He was educated at the École des Beaux Arts in Paris. He has been awarded with many prizes and honors since completing his first buildings in the 1980s, including the 2001 gold medal from the Royal Institute of British Architects.

Among Nouvel's more recent projects is his 1993 remodeling of the Lyon Opera House. The nineteenth-century music hall, representing a fusion of old and new, is topped by a large glass-and-steel barrel vault. His 1999 Cultural and Congress Center in Lucerne, Switzerland, also demonstrates his skillful manipulation of light-reflective surfaces. The building, paneled in aluminum under a sweeping roof, appears to merge with the distant mountains.

Renzo Piano

Italian architect Renzo Piano is known for pushing the limits of building technology into high art. Like Renaissance architects before him, Piano believes the architect must maintain control over the building process from design through execution. All his projects reflect a keen attention to materials and craftsmanship, which is not surprising given that his father, uncles, and grandfather were builders.

Born in Genoa in 1937, Piano first gained fame in the late 1970s for the Centre Pompidou in Paris, a high-tech extravaganza designed in collaboration with British architect Richard Rogers. Since then, his work has grown more subtle and varied. The Menil Museum (1981–1987) in Houston is a prime example of this shift in Piano's work. The boxy building is subdued from the outside, and the high-tech gadgetry is limited to a dramatic roof of movable concrete "leaves" that allows daylight to filter into galleries. Another Piano museum is the Beyeler Museum (1993–1997) in Switzerland. It shows the same mastery of space, light, and form.

Piano is a versatile architect who adapts building technologies and materials to the particulars of place and purpose. His steel-clad Kansai International Airport Terminal — the world's largest — in Osaka, Japan, is completely different from his wood-ribbed, environmentally sensitive structures for the Tjibaou Cultural Center in New Caledonia.

Piano's restless search for inventive structures has earned him many honors, including the Praemium Imperiale (1995) and Pritzker Prize (1998).

Antoine Predock

The buildings created by New Mexican architect Antoine Predock are often shaped like an abstract mountain or mesa, as they are inspired by the rugged landscape of the West. Predock typically begins a project by analyzing the topography, climate, and cultural history of a place. He then distills these site-specific influences into forms that are bold, primal, and austere.

Predock was born in 1936 in Lebanon, Missouri. He received his architecture degree from Columbia University. He opened his Albuquerque office in 1967, and a branch office in Los Angeles in 1989. Predock was thrust into international prominence for his innovative design of the Nelson Fine Arts Center at Arizona State University in Tempe (1989). The art center's sculptural spaces and passageways, accented by sunlight and water, achieve a sense of movement and mystery that has become a hallmark of his architecture.

In recent years, Predock has branched out to create buildings all over America. Some of his most notable commissions include the volcano-shaped American Heritage Center in Laramie, Wyoming (1993); the Museum of Science and Industry in Tampa, Florida (1995); the Arizona Science Center in Phoenix (1996); and the museum and art gallery at Skidmore College in Saratoga Springs, New York (1999).

Chapter 22

Ten Architectural Masterpieces

In This Chapter

▶ Discovering ten great masterpieces

▶ Understanding the genius behind the innovations

*N*arrowing a list of the greatest buildings down to ten is an almost impossible task. This chronological list serves only as an introduction to the most brilliant creations from ancient times through the post–World War II era. Think of these structures as signposts to design shifts within the history of architecture. They are meant to whet your appetite for learning more about a specific period and style.

Selected on the basis of their originality, beauty, and influence, all of these buildings still exist and are accessible to the public for tours (some require an appointment in advance). In most cases, time has only enhanced their original appeal. For anyone serious about architecture, these 10 buildings are definitely worth the trip.

The Parthenon

The Parthenon is one of the greatest achievements of Western civilization. This supreme example of classical architecture forms the centerpiece of the Athens Acropolis, a hilltop cluster of temples built by the great Athenian general Pericles. It was inspired by the Greek defeat of the Persians after 40 years of war. It was built from 447 to 438 B.C. to honor Athena, the goddess of wisdom and the patron of Athens.

Designed by architects Ictinus and Callicrates, the Parthenon advanced classical architecture by incorporating both Doric and Ionic traditions (see Chapter 8). From the outside, its fluted columns, simple capitals, architrave, and sculpted pediment solidly follow the Doric order. But instead of having six columns across the façade, as in the Doric, the Parthenon has eight columns, as was common in earlier Ionic buildings such as the Temple of Artemis at Ephesus (Selcuk, Turkey). A second row of columns at each end also gave the impression of an Ionic colonnade. The Ionic influence was also expressed in the decoration of the friezes both inside and outside the temple.

Combining Doric and Ionic traditions created a powerful symbol of the Athenians' rule over the Greeks and *Ionians,* inhabitants of Greek cities on the coast of Asia Minor and the nearby islands. The scenes of battles and processions, created by the sculptor Pheidias, that fill the pediments and architraves reinforced the message of Athenian rule. These scenes also underscored the religious role of the Parthenon as the destination of the yearly procession from the city to the Acropolis on Athena's birthday.

Like many Greek temples, the Parthenon was originally painted in vibrant colors of red, blue, and gold. The architecture was meant to create a bright ceremonial setting that was far more lively than the somber, white structure that we see today.

Even in ruins, the perfect proportions of the Parthenon are still discernable. One of the most superb buildings ever constructed, it has played an influential role in architecture through modern times.

The Pantheon

The emperor Hadrian in A.D. 118–128 built this temple to all the gods to express the political and religious ideals of ancient Rome's Golden Age. A synthesis of Greek and Roman forms, the Pantheon is one of the most beautiful and influential buildings ever created (see Chapter 8).

Constructed on the site of an earlier temple, the Pantheon was conceived in two parts: a pediment-topped porch and a circular rotunda. The Corinthian columns of the porch are inspired by Greek architecture, while the rotunda is a purely Roman invention. This hybrid became the model for later buildings by such architects as Renaissance master Andrea Palladio (see Chapter 10) and American Thomas Jefferson (see Chapter 11).

The Pantheon achieves a milestone in both architectural design and structural engineering. Crowning its rotunda is a concrete dome — the largest constructed in antiquity. At the top of this curved structure is a 30-foot-wide round opening that lights the interior and connects the religious space to the heavens. On the floor, disks and squares of granite, marble, and colored stones called *porphyry* are set into a grid, aligned with the ceiling coffers overhead.

Part of the Pantheon's appeal is the perfect harmony of its proportions. The domed rotunda is exactly equal in height and diameter — 142 feet tall and 142 feet wide. If doubled in size, the dome would form a sphere that would fit into the space of the rotunda.

Chartres Cathedral

All the majesty of Gothic architecture can be summed up in one building: Chartres Cathedral. Flying buttresses, pointed arches, towering spires, and jewel-like stained glass windows display all the elements of Gothic architecture's structurally and spiritually expressive style (see Chapter 9).

Chartres was begun in 1194 after a fire destroyed most of a Romanesque cathedral built on the site. The earlier church had been constructed to house one of the most sacred relics of Christianity — the tunic worn by the Virgin Mary when she gave birth to Christ. Working within the length set by the western façade, which had partially survived, and the eastern choir, the architects set about raising the height of the new Chartres to honor Mary with a more impressive structure.

They extended the walls of the nave with arcades topped by low *triforiums* — passageways over the slanted roofs at the sides of the church. Above the arches of the triforium, rows of monumental stained-glass windows called *clerestories* reached as high as the arches on the ground floor. *Rose windows* — round openings traced in stone — were added to the west façade and the projecting wings, or *transepts,* of the cathedral. Filled with luminous blue-and-red glass, the stained-glass windows — 130 in all — are the cathedral's most glorious achievement.

The lightweight feeling of the architecture continues with graceful piers made of four thin columns. Rising to support the ceiling vaults, the piers create uninterrupted lines that direct the view heavenward. Reinforcing the vertical lines are hundreds of thin, columnar statues (placed along the doorways) that are skillfully integrated into the architecture.

The rebuilding of Chartres created a soaring space full of energy and light. The large space was made possible by structural braces called *flying buttresses* that absorbed the increased loads of the higher walls. The buttresses, first used at Notre Dame in Paris, were placed on the outside of the building so that they didn't take up room inside.

While other cathedral designs of the period may be more consistent, Chartres symbolizes the collaborative struggle that made the glory of the Gothic possible. Stonemasons, carpenters, sculptors, glassblowers, and other artisans worked at a feverish pace for 30 years to create this masterpiece. Even after it was finished in 1220, building continued so that the cathedral would reflect the latest architectural developments. Part of the charm of Chartres is its two different towers — the simple, early Gothic spire on the south and the more flamboyant late Gothic design on the north, which was completed in the 1500s.

Tempietto di San Pietro in Montorio

The towering achievement of the early Renaissance is a tiny, round building in Rome designed by architect Donato Bramante for the Spanish king and queen in 1502. It is tucked within the cloister of the church of Saint Peter in Montorio to mark the spot where St. Peter was believed to be crucified (he was hung upside down so as not to imitate Christ).

Bramante borrowed the concept of a little temple or "tempietto" from Temple of Vesta, built in the second century B.C., which is located only a mile away. He obviously knew this Roman ruin. But instead of copying it, Bramante used its classical architecture as a point of departure. Around the base, he designed Doric columns — rather than the ancient temple's Corinthian columns — and raised the building on a stepped platform to separate it from the surrounding buildings and give it height. Pilasters on the walls of the cella repeat the Doric order of the colonnade.

Above the frieze — the first in Renaissance times to use the correct classical language — Bramante departed from antique precedents by extending a tall dome from the top of the building. It is a brilliant move that gives this 15-foot-wide, one-room building a grand presence, in spite of its small size and cramped site.

The dome, in turn, would become a model for later buildings, including St. Peter's in Rome, St. Paul's in London, and the U.S. Capitol in Washington, D.C.

A sculpture in the round, the Tempietto was a clear departure from the flattened walls of earlier buildings by Bramante's contemporaries. Its reinterpretation of the antique classical tradition and powerful illusionism marked a new stage in Renaissance architecture.

Katsura Palace

Sometimes referred to as "Katsura Villa," this country estate in Kyoto is regarded as the quintessential example of Japanese architecture. More importantly, it is the perfect example of the integration of building and landscape that would later become common in the West.

Set in extensive gardens, the Katsura Palace provided a retreat for the enjoyment of nature. It was built in the early seventeenth century by Imperial princes, and the architecture evolved over several decades. The first building is called the Old Shoin, or writing hall, and it was constructed by the eldest family member, Toshihito Hachijonomiya, in 1616. His son, Toshitada, expanded this structure with the Middle Shoin around 1641, while the Music Room and New Palace are thought to have been added in the 1660s by Yasuhito, the third in the Katsura line of princes.

The villa marked a new informality in Japanese architecture called the *Sukiya*, or *Sukiya Shoin*, style. Rough-hewn posts, open verandahs, and understated decoration created a rustic style appropriate for the countryside.

The landscaping was designed as carefully as the buildings. Trees were artfully manicured and stones were carefully placed to be visually pleasing in all seasons. Located on the grounds were a pond for boating and five teahouses, where the imperial family and their guests would consume delicacies while contemplating the cherry blossoms and brilliant autumn leaves. Landscape views could be enjoyed from porches fitted with sliding and removable screens.

The interaction of interior and exterior spaces, the simplicity of the architecture, and the sparing use of natural materials influenced many Western architects in their development of modern architecture. Frank Lloyd Wright was inspired by the Katsura Villa's style of Japanese architecture when designing his early Prairie houses. Wright may have visited the villa during his 1905 trip to Japan. German architect Bruno Taut highlighted the Katsura Villa as exemplifying the best of modernist principles in his 1938 book, *Houses and People of Japan*.

San Ivo della Sapienza

All the energy and movement of the Baroque is boldly displayed in the San Ivo della Sapienza. This church is located at the end of a courtyard belonging to the University of Rome. Francesco Borromini, a troubled genius who revolutionized architecture with his flowing designs, designed it in 1642. This building further develops many of the ideas introduced by Borromini in his previous work, the tiny, oval church of San Carlo alle Quattro Fontane. See Chapter 10 for more details.

At San Ivo della Sapienza, the architect carves mass and space as if sculpting stone. On the exterior, he repeats the pilasters and moldings of the adjacent two-story buildings and compresses them on a façade that curves inward. Above the façade rises a six-sided drum with curves that push outward and seem barely contained by bunched pilasters. This drum supports a lantern that terminates in a spiral supporting a bulbous pinnacle made of wrought iron.

Borromini shaped the interior to be equally dynamic. It is formed by two equilateral triangles superimposed to create a hexagonal room with contrasting, curving sides. By shaping the hexagonal space so that the opposite sides don't match, the architect further emphasizes his theme of restless movement. Above the space, he placed a faceted, six-sided dome — a startling shape that no one had ever seen. Windows set within its base bathe the sanctuary with abundant, even light.

San Ivo della Sapienza's luminous, rounded spaces sharply contrasted with the heavy, static forms of the Renaissance to achieve a new vitality in architecture. Its fluid curves had a far-reaching effect that can still be felt today in the work of Frank Gehry and other contemporary architects.

Altes Museum

Since his youth, Prussian architect Karl Friedrich Schinkel had dreamed of building a great museum. Schinkel finally got his chance in 1823, when King Friedrich Wilhelm III tapped him to design a large gallery for the royal art collection in the heart of Berlin. The Altes (old) Museum not only presented the architect with the opportunity to create rooms for display, but it also gave him the chance to connect the building to its surroundings.

Schinkel's monumental Greek Revival edifice achieves both goals through a well-orchestrated procession. Visitors enter the building by climbing up a broad flight of steps through a grand portico marked by 18 Ionic columns. The stairs continue inside and are visible from the adjacent public square, which was also designed by Schinkel. The stairs, in turn, lead to a landing that offers a view back through the façade to the square.

One of Schinkel's master strokes was to surprise visitors with an enormous rotunda, modeled on the Roman Pantheon (see Chapter 8), in the center of the building. He inserted a courtyard on each side to emit light into the innermost galleries. Originally, sculptures were displayed on the lower floor, while paintings were exhibited on the upper level where wall panels placed perpendicular to the windows provided glare-free lighting. Schinkel even designed the picture frames to correspond to the styles of the paintings.

Deceptively simple, the Altes Museum was dedicated in 1830. It set a precedent for later public museums in the nineteenth and twentieth centuries. A place to contemplate the treasures of the past, its architecture is both uplifting in its recall of antiquity and practical in its clear organization. The museum succeeds in reflecting Schinkel's comment to the king that the architecture was intended to delight visitors first, and then instruct them.

Thomas Crane Library

Boston architect Henry Hobson Richardson was a big man who liked big buildings. His late-nineteenth-century architecture was robust. It made even the smallest building seem weighty.

Though the Beaux-Arts-trained architect started out copying Romanesque architecture from southern France and Spain, he quickly developed his own personal style. The most sophisticated example of what came to be known as Richardsonian Romanesque architecture is the Thomas Crane Library (1880–1882) in Quincy, Massachusetts, outside Boston.

Like all of Richardson's work, the library is asymmetrically arranged with the main room and book stacks flanking either side of the entrance hall. These spaces are indicated on the façades by contrasting windows outlined in sandstone trim. Inside, all the woodwork and furniture was designed by Richardson to create a total look in every detail.

But unlike the architect's earlier buildings, the library subordinates each different element to the strong granite walls and broad, sheltering roof, which incorporates curved, projecting windows called *eyebrow dormers*. The architecture conveys a forceful unity, rather than a picturesque assembly of parts.

With its Romanesque-inspired arches and streamlined horizontal lines, the Thomas Crane Library looks backward and forward at the same time. Its inventiveness marked a turning point in American architecture, from academic historicism to bold individuality.

Villa Savoye

This luxurious house in Poissy, France, is *the* icon of early twentieth-century modernism. An austere white box raised on stilts, it was designed by the Swiss-born French architect Le Corbusier to embody his slogan, "a house is a machine for living in." Le Corbusier designed the country retreat from 1928–1929. He designed it around the car so that the owners could park right under the house. Instead of climbing the stairs (they were provided for the servants), the Savoyes ascended ramps to reach the main living spaces on the second floor and the bedrooms on the top floor. On the roof, metal railings and a smokestacklike enclosure create the look of a steamship.

All of these elements skillfully embody Le Corbusier's five points of modern architecture, which influenced architects for decades. Sleekly enclosed by smooth white walls, the house is lifted off the ground on columns, or *pilotis,* to help it appear lightweight. The thin, rectangular enclosure exemplifies his free façade, which acts as a screen rather than a load-bearing structure. Long, horizontal openings cut within the exterior show his preference for elongated, "ribbon" windows.

Inside, the house is divided by partitions arranged independently of the building's structure — what Le Corbusier called the *free plan.* Even the master bathroom is designed as an open space, with a blue-tiled recliner where Madame Savoye could rest after exercising. The roof serves as a garden, with the curved walls enclosing a solarium. Although Le Corbusier experimented with these ideas previously, the vacation house offered him the opportunity to implement them in a freestanding building with unobstructed views on all four sides.

The Villa Savoye is an inventive example of early modernism that alludes to great buildings in history. Its proportions and white columns reflect Le Corbusier's interest in the Parthenon and other ancient classical monuments, while its raised living quarters recalls the second-floor arrangements of formal rooms (called the *piano nobile*) in Renaissance villas. These echoes of the past ground the architect's abstraction within the canon of architecture. At the same time, this house, aptly nicknamed "Les Heures Claires," or "bright hours," turns its back on tradition. It maximizes light and space to express the liberation of the modern age.

Seagram Building

The Seagram Building, a masterpiece of skyscraper design, was created by the German-born Chicago architect Mies van der Rohe, one of the directors of the Bauhaus (see Chapter 14). Its elegant tower and urban plaza established a powerful model for the corporate office tower of the 1950s and 1960s.

In 1954, Mies van der Rohe was selected to design the New York headquarters for whiskey distiller Joseph E. Seagram and Sons on Park Avenue between 52nd and 53rd Streets. Instead of building the skyscraper directly on the street, he separated the tower from the avenue by a plaza. The plaza acted as a plinth for the tower and made Mies's architecture seem monumental. Its open public space, flanked by fountains, created an island of calm within the busy city, and an unprecedented gap in the urban grid.

The exterior walls of the Seagram Building are constructed of unusually luxurious materials for a skyscraper — bronze-tinted glass panels held in place by exposed bronze supports. Just like Louis Sullivan and Chicago architects before him, Mies van der Rohe designed his sophisticated curtain wall to express the idea of the structure underneath. Although the Seagram Building was widely copied in the postwar decades, very few architects succeeded in achieving the refinement of Mies's seemingly simple architecture.

Chapter 23

Ten Amazing Items of Trivia That'll Impress All Your Friends!

In This Chapter

▶ Headlines from the annals of architectural history

▶ A couple of real shockers!

▶ The fact-filled stories behind the headlines

Do you want to impress friends and strangers at parties? Read this chapter for some interesting facts about architecture through the ages.

One of the Seven Ancient Wonders of the World Is Still Around!

The Great Pyramid of Khufu (or Cheops) of Giza near Cairo, Egypt, is one of the oldest and best-known Wonders, as well as the only Wonder to survive to the present day. Built by the pharaoh Khufu around 2560 B.C. to serve as his own tomb, the structure consists of about 2 million blocks of stone. The structure was originally covered in a smooth casing. It rose to a height of 481 feet but has since lost about 30 feet off the top.

Ancient Greeks included the Great Pyramid in a list of the Seven World Wonders compiled around the second century B.C. A few centuries later, historian Herodotus referred to them in his book *History*. The final list was drawn up during the Middle Ages and interpreted in sixteenth-century Dutch engravings. By that time, many of the Wonders had already disappeared. (See Chapter 7 for more about the Seven Wonders.)

French Gothic Cathedral Collapses!

Soaring to a height of 157 feet, the Cathedral of St. Pierre in Beauvais, France, represents the vertical expression of Gothic architecture taken to the extreme. But it took more than 400 years before this ambitious structure could stand up.

Construction of the cathedral began in 1225. By 1272, part of its vaulted interior (see Chapter 9 for more about vaults) was higher than any other Gothic cathedral. But in 1284, the exterior wall supports buckled unexpectedly, and the central vault came tumbling down. After the structure was repaired, the work on the cathedral continued over the next two centuries. By the mid-1500s, a 502-foot-tall stone spire, rivaling the dome of St. Peter's in Rome, crowned the building. Disaster struck again when the tower collapsed in 1573. By 1600, work on the cathedral was abandoned, and a wall closed off the unfinished part.

Far from stable, the Beauvais cathedral is still at risk from flaws in its original design. Stresses from strong winds have caused the buttresses to move back and forth and the weakened roof timbers to shift. In the 1990s, a system of ties and braces was installed to help prevent another collapse. Experts are still debating over how to keep this Gothic wonder standing.

World's Largest Art Gallery Is Russian!

The Hermitage Museum in Russia covers more ground than the Metropolitan Museum of Art and the Louvre — visitors have to walk 15 miles to view nearly 3 million works on exhibit. The museum's origins can be traced back to Peter the Great, who purchased artworks during his travels and brought them back to St. Petersburg, the capital he founded on the Neva River.

Peter's daughter, Empress Elizabeth, elaborated the city started by her father, adding grand monuments in the latest Baroque and Rococo styles (see Chapter 10). Chief among the architecture added by the empress is the Winter Palace (1754–1762). Italian-born architect Bartolommeo Francesco Rastrelli (1700–1771) created it as the first building in the Hermitage Museum complex.

Elizabeth's successor, Catherine the Great, was even more of an architecture buff. Catherine the Great added onto the Winter Palace with the newer, more restrained neoclassical style (see Chapter 11). She hired German architect Yury Veldten to create a gallery wing to accommodate a collection of art acquired from Berlin in 1764. The wing is known as the Little Hermitage. When more space was required for her growing collection, she tapped French architect Vallin de la Mothe to expand the gallery with another pavilion to the north. This pavilion is known as the Old Hermitage. Catherine continued to enlarge the palace complex in the late 1700s with neoclassical buildings, including the Hermitage Theater designed by Italian architect Giacomo Quarenghi.

In 1837, the palace was ravaged by fire. Emperor Nicholas I undertook the renovations. He expanded the royal art collection further. He also wanted to build a museum as part of the palace complex. After visiting two royal museums in Munich, the Alte Pinakothek and the Glypothek (see Chapter 4), Nicholas hired the German architect who designed the royal museums, Leo von Klenze, to create a gallery for the palace. The New Hermitage was completed by a Russian architect according to von Klenze's design and then opened to the public in 1852. After the Russian Revolution in 1917, the government transferred its capital to Moscow, and the Winter Palace complex was turned into the state-run Hermitage Museum. Today, the Hermitage is undergoing a major restoration.

Disney Steals Design from Bavarian Castle!

When Walt Disney decided to put a storybook castle in the center of his California theme park, he looked to Neuschwanstein in Bavaria, Germany, for inspiration. The mountaintop palace was built between 1869 and 1892 as a country getaway for King Ludwig II. The swan in Richard Wagner's *Lohengrin* opera (the name Neuschwantstein means "new swan stone") inspired its fanciful architecture of white turrets and spires, dreamed up by set designer Christian Jank. Like a Disney creation, the building was equipped with the latest technology, including a central heating system. On the outside, a mixture of Romanesque, Byzantine, and Gothic elements creates the image of a fairy tale castle.

King Ludwig, however, didn't live happily ever after. An eccentric who loved opera and architecture (he built two other castles), the Bavarian ruler was considered mentally deranged by his family and politicians who conspired to have him deposed. In 1886, just three days after being declared legally insane, "Mad King Ludwig" was found drowned — most likely a suicide, though some believe he was murdered.

Women Join All-Male Architecture Profession!

In 1888, the American Institute of Architects accepted Louise Blanchard Bethune, its first female member. Seven years earlier, Bethune — then Jennie Louise Blanchard — announced the opening of her own architecture office in Buffalo, New York, at the Ninth Congress of the Association for the Advancement of Women. Later that year, she married former colleague Robert Bethune, who became her business partner. Although her specialty was schools, Louise Bethune designed a variety of buildings, including

Buffalo's 225-room Hotel Lafayette. She believed that pioneering woman architects must be able to tackle every aspect of a building project, from design to site supervision.

Another pioneering female architect was Julia Morgan (1872–1957). The first woman to graduate from the École des Beaux-Arts in Paris, Morgan ran her own office from 1905 to 1940. She designed more than 700 homes in the San Francisco area. She is best known for designing the lavish mansion of publishing magnate William Randolph Hearst. Known as San Simeon, the Hearst castle incorporates architectural fragments from ancient classical temples and European palaces.

Architect Murdered by Jealous Husband!

One of the most successful architectural practices of the Gilded Age was McKim, Mead, and White. From 1870 to 1906, this New York firm designed 900 structures — from mansions to university campuses — in a stately neoclassical style. Among their best known buildings was Pennsylvania Station (demolished in 1963), an ingenious blend of modern engineering and Roman architecture.

The youngest, most boisterous member of the trio was Stanford White (1853–1906). He joined the firm in 1879 after an apprenticeship with Boston architect Henry Hobson Richardson and travels in Europe. Best known for his interiors, White skillfully mixed styles, colors, and textures to rich effect. This fondness for sensuousness extended to his personal life, as well. White partied with his rich clients and carried on affairs with young women, including teenage actress Evelyn Nesbit.

In 1906, Nesbit's new husband, Harry K. Thaw, shot and killed White on the roof garden of Madison Square Garden, a building completed by the architect 16 years earlier. The murder created a scandal, and, for months, stories circulated about White's marital indiscretions. Thaw was found not guilty by reason of insanity and committed to a mental institution.

Hotel Survives Worst Japanese Earthquake of the Twentieth Century!

The Imperial Hotel in Tokyo, Japan, was one of Frank Lloyd Wright's masterpieces. Wright's mentor, Chicago architect Louis Sullivan, went so far as to call its architecture a noble prophecy. In fact, the hotel set the standard for the type of earthquake-proof "floating" foundation that is now used all over the world.

Wright spent six intensive years on the project, which he began in 1916. He traveled to Japan frequently from 1919 to 1922. Wright's H-shaped building was to replace an older hotel with a more modern facility. Guest rooms were contained in 500-foot-long wings, with public functions — theaters, a banquet hall, and a dining room — placed at the center to overlook Japanese gardens. Wright lavished attention on every detail, from the architecture and furnishings to the notepaper and plates.

The biggest challenge of designing the huge complex was anchoring the structure in soft soil and mud to resist Japan's frequent earthquakes. Wright developed a foundation system of concrete posts under the floors that allowed each section of the hotel to move independently during an earthquake. To keep the center of gravity low, he made the walls thicker at the bottom. The roofs were covered in copper rather than traditional Japanese tiles, which could fly off during a severe tremor.

In 1922, Wright's design was put to the test when Tokyo received the worst earthquake in 30 years. His unfinished building stood unscathed, and the architect noted that the work had proven itself. But that calamity was mild compared to the great Kanto earthquake that struck on September 1, 1923, just minutes before the opening ceremony for the hotel was to begin. The quake and its aftershocks destroyed three-quarters of the city and cut off all communication with the outside world. About 150,000 people were killed, and 1.5 million residents were displaced. Wright's hotel, however, survived with only slight damage.

But the Imperial was far from safe — fire bombing of Tokyo during World War II destroyed the banquet halls and the south wing. In subsequent decades, the remaining portions were altered beyond recognition. In 1968, the hotel was demolished. Only the lobby was saved as part of the Meiji Mura outdoor museum near Nagoya.

New York City Home to the World's Largest Gothic Cathedral!

At 601 feet long and 146 feet wide, the Cathedral of St. John the Divine in upper Manhattan is bigger than any Gothic church in Europe. Yet its history is as long and complicated as any medieval cathedral.

Begun in 1892 according to the Romanesque-inspired designs of G.L. Heins and C. Grant La Farge, the plans for St. John the Divine were altered in 1911 to follow a French Gothic scheme proposed by architect Ralph Adams Cram. By 1941, the length of the cathedral was completed. But construction was halted during World War II. Construction of the architecture picked up again in the 1980s until funds were depleted and the church decided to concentrate on preserving the existing structure. In December 2001, a fire destroyed the cathedral's gift shop and a pair of seventeenth-century tapestries originally woven for Pope Urban VIII.

Famous Architect Disqualified for Using the Wrong Ink!

In 1927, the Swiss-born French architect Le Corbusier (see Chapter 14) participated in a design competition for the League of Nations headquarters in Geneva. His proposal for the new political organization was not a neoclassical temple but a grouping of modern buildings sited to overlook gardens and nearby Lake Geneva. Rectangular office blocks extended from an angular assembly hall, which radiated outward as if broadcasting the League's mission to the world. This groundbreaking scheme later influenced the design of the United Nations headquarters in New York.

Though it appeared to be the front-runner, Le Corbusier's design was eventually eliminated on the grounds of not having been drawn in India ink as specified in the competition rules. A conservative Beaux-Arts building was chosen as the winning scheme instead. The scandal that arose from Le Corbusier's disqualification brought the architect to the forefront of public attention as a leading proponent of avant-garde modern design. In 1928, he cofounded the International Congress of Modern Architecture (CIAM) to defend the progressive architecture defeated in the League of Nations competition.

Skyscraper Resembles Chippendale Furniture!

When New York architects Philip Johnson and John Burgee unveiled their design for the AT&T Building on Madison Avenue in 1978, many people were shocked. The 37-story pink granite tower didn't look like the typical, flat-top skyscraper. It looked like an eighteenth-century *highboy* — a tall chest of drawers — crafted by English furniture-maker Thomas Chippendale. The building's top was shaped into a broken pediment with slanted sides and a scooped-out center — what Chippendale called a *bonnet-top*.

Behind the mammoth entrance arch was an open lobby designed to display the large golden statue, *Genius of Electricity* that formerly stood atop AT&T's previous headquarters in lower Manhattan. The interior was vaulted and paved in black-and-white marble after a pattern designed by English architect Edwin Lutyens (see Chapter 17). (AT&T eventually sold the building to Sony. The lobby is now enclosed for retail space.)

The AT&T tower became one of the most celebrated icons of postmodern architecture (see Chapter 15). It was featured on the front page of *The New York Times* and the cover of *Time* magazine and hotly debated in architectural circles. By the 1980s, office towers with sculpted tops were all the rage.

Chapter 24

The Top Ten Skyscrapers

*T*he skyscrapers listed in this chapter represent design and engineering innovations that changed the nature of the skyscraper — and skylines — all over the globe. Many of these buildings started out as the tallest towers in the world, but they were eclipsed by subsequent structures. To learn more about the early development of the skyscraper, check out Chapter 13.

Chrysler Building: Art Deco Fantasy

For what was to be the world's tallest building, automobile tycoon Walter Chrysler wanted a structure that was bold and used all of the best that the modern age had to offer. He got what he wanted in the Chrysler Building (1928–1930), a 77-story New York skyscraper with hubcaps, mudguards, and hood ornaments (just like his cars). Designed by architect William Van Alen, the 1,048-foot-tall building and its automobile-inspired decorations were part of a strategy to turn the structure into a 3-D advertisement for Chrysler. (Ironically, Walter Chrysler never used the building as his headquarters. He refused to pay Van Alen for his work because he believed the architect had taken bribes from the building contractor.)

Van Alen designed his ArtDeco–styled skyscraper in white and dark brick, with curved setbacks rising to a stainless-steel spire decorated with sunburst motifs. The rounded metal pieces for the 27-ton spire were mounted on wooden forms that were prepared in a shipyard and assembled on the 65th floor. From there, the metal pieces were raised in just one and a half hours to add nearly 122 feet to the building's height. An observation space, a private men's dining room and gym called the Cloud Club, and a duplex apartment for Walter Chrysler were all located just below the spire.

On the ground floor, the triangular lobby was finished in colored marbles and onyx, an ornate ceiling mural, and dramatic lighting. All the building's elevators were lined in different patterns of exotic wood paneling. Although it was derided by a critic for its "inane romanticism," the Chrysler Building — with its quirky spire — has become one of the most beloved skyscrapers in the world.

Empire State Building: New York's Highest

In 1931, only months after the completion of the Chrysler Building, the title for the world's tallest building was claimed by an even higher structure, the Empire State Building. At 1,250 feet high, it surpassed the Chrysler Building by 204 feet and broke every previous construction record.

The base of the Empire State Building covers 2 acres, and its 85 floors contain 2.1 million square feet of offices. Its construction required 60,000 tons of steel, 200,000 cubic feet of Indiana limestone and granite, 10 million bricks, 730 tons of aluminum and stainless steel, 70 miles of water pipes, 2,500 toilets and sinks, and more than 3 million light bulbs.

Despite its staggering size, the Empire State Building was planned and built with lightning speed. It took just 20 months from the time the contracts were signed with the architecture firm Shreve, Lamb and Harmon until construction was completed and the first tenants moved into the building in April 1931. Because of the Depression, however, it was difficult to rent office space, so the skyscraper was nicknamed the "Empty State Building."

In 1945, a plane crashed into the 79th floor of the Empire State Building, but the building suffered only minor damage. Because of the devastation that destroyed the World Trade Center towers, the Empire State Building is once again the Manhattan skyline's tallest skyscraper.

Lever House: Cleaning Up the Avenue

Give up the ground floor of your headquarters to the public? Not many corporations would do that. But Lever Brothers thought differently. When the world's largest manufacturer of soap and detergent decided to relocate from Chicago to New York in 1951, it decided to elevate its glassy new headquarters on stilts over a landscaped plaza where people could walk, sit, and enjoy the outdoors. The elevated skyscraper wasn't a new idea; modern master Le Corbusier first proposed it (see Chapter 14) back in the 1920s. But it took postwar architects working for corporate America to carry out Le Corbusier's concept.

Lever Brothers hired architect Gordon Bunshaft of Skidmore, Owings and Merrill (known as SOM) to design the tower on Park Avenue. Bunshaft pushed the 24-story skyscraper to the side of the site and turned the building so that its narrow side faces the avenue. He set the tower onto a low, horizontal structure that acts as a podium. This horizontal structure contains offices, stores, and exhibition spaces that flank the public plaza (it also has a rooftop terrace for employees).

The vertical slab of Lever House was covered in shimmering panels of blue-green glass set into a stainless steel frame. At the top of the slab, opaque glass was set into the exterior to conceal machinery. (The glassy, washable surfaces of this curtain wall were certainly appropriate for a soap maker!) By dividing the building into a podium, transparent slab, and opaque top, Bunshaft followed earlier skyscraper designs of mirroring the base, shaft, and capital of a classical column (see Chapter 13).

Completed in 1952, Lever House set a precedent for postwar corporate high-rises and urban planning (see Chapter 19). The skyscraper's early use of a ground-floor public plaza was echoed across Park Avenue at the Seagram Building, designed by Mies van der Rohe, and in cities across America. For more on Mies's skyscraper, turn to Chapter 22.

John Hancock Center: "Big John"

The John Hancock Center, located on North Michigan Avenue along Chicago's "Magnificent Mile," is a dark, 100-story tower that was designed by the architecture firm Skidmore, Owings and Merrill for the John Hancock Mutual Life Insurance Company. "Big John," as it is called, clearly expresses how its structure deals with the wind in the Windy City.

Steel columns and beams are concentrated in the skyscraper's perimeter to create a super-tall structural tube that is crisscrossed by gigantic diagonal braces on the building's exterior. To give it extra wind resistance, the 1,127-foot-high tower is tapered in shape and rises from 40,000 square feet at the base to 18,000 square feet at the top. The entire structure rests on giant caissons that reach 191 feet below the ground to bedrock — the deepest foundations ever sunk in Chicago.

Apartments occupy the top stories of the building, while offices are located on the lower floors. The tower also includes restaurants, a health club, and an ice-skating rink. The cross-braces completely block the view from two windows on each floor; the rooms in these sections are considered status symbols and cost more to rent.

Sears Tower: Office in a Tube

The Sears Tower, currently the second-tallest building in the world, is one of the most efficient wind-resistant skyscrapers ever created. The tower is made up of a bundle of nine tube structures. Each tube measures 75 feet square in plan; as the tower rises to 110 stories, the tubes drop off in height to create a series of setbacks at the 50th, 66th, and 90th floors.

Skidmore, Owings and Merrill designed this innovative structure when Sears Roebuck and Company decided to consolidate its operations in downtown Chicago. The retailer determined that it needed 3 million square feet of office space to accommodate its 13,000 employees and then decided to build an even taller building with upper floors for tenants.

Constructed from 1970 to 1974, the Sears Tower is sheathed in dark tinted glass and black aluminum to create a distinctive stepped silhouette on the Chicago skyline. Inside, it contains enough steel to build 50,000 cars, and enough telephone wiring to wrap around the world almost twice. Although Sears Tower is no longer the tallest building in the world, it still boasts the highest occupied office floors and the longest elevator ride. On a clear day, it is possible to see four states — Illinois, Indiana, Wisconsin, and Michigan — from the visitor skydeck.

Boston's Hancock Tower: Blowing in the Wind

The Hancock Tower, the 60-story building designed by New York architect I.M. Pei in the heart of Boston, is sculpted into a parallelogram shape and appears to be the opposite of the John Hancock Center in Chicago. Its structure is completely hidden behind sleek walls of identical, reflective glass panels supported by thin metal supports. Like a person wearing mirrored sunglasses, the exterior offers no clue to the internal expression of the building.

When glass windows started dropping off the building in 1973 while it was still under construction, people were puzzled. Executives believed that the windows were falling because the skyscraper was swaying too much in the wind. Others believed that wind forces were sucking out the windows because of the tower's sharp angles. The culprit turned out to be a simple detail: The reflective chrome that was placed on the glass panes to give them a mirror effect was bonded too tightly to the window frames. The windows couldn't move with the wind or the changes in temperature, so the glass cracked. All 10,344 of the Hancock Tower's windows were eventually replaced.

But that wasn't all that was wrong. The Hancock Tower was found to be twisting in the wind as it moved a few inches forward and back. To fix the problem, a device called a *tuned mass damper* was installed at the top of the building. The tuned mass damper consists of two weights that tug in opposite directions to stabilize the tower when it slides and twists.

In 1975, a Swiss engineer discovered that the Hancock Tower could fall over on its edge under certain wind conditions. The problem wasn't its unusual angular shape but its uninterrupted length of almost 300 feet. If the tower shifted even a few inches out of line, the force of gravity would pull it down even farther until it fell. To stiffen the thin tower, diagonal steel braces were placed along the walls of the interior elevator cores. Boston's Hancock Tower eventually became more like Chicago's John Hancock Center — only no one could see the change from the street.

Hong Kong Shanghai Bank: High-Tech Beauty

By selecting British High-Tech architect Norman Foster (see Chapter 15) to design its headquarters in 1979, the Hong Kong and Shanghai Banking Corporation achieved a milestone in contemporary skyscraper design. Although the Hong Kong Shanghai Bank is not the tallest or the sleekest building, it is a structurally expressive, super-expensive tower that adds a futuristic note to the Hong Kong skyline.

The 47-story bank, which was reputed to cost $1 billion, fronts one of Hong Kong's few open green spaces and offers spectacular views of the waterfront. The building is made up of three vertical slabs that become narrower as the building rises. From the side, they look like very thin towers sandwiched together.

Instead of extending the floors from a central core, Foster moved the supporting structure to the outside to create unobstructed floor space. The silvery network of trusses and columns (see Chapter 6 to find out how these work) gives the tower façades a machinelike appearance that also extends inside.

At the bottom of the building, the main banking hall rises nine stories on either side of a central open room framed by large X-shaped braces. A specially designed sun scoop with computer-controlled mirrors reflects daylight into the hall. Elevators, also located at the perimeter, take people up to the main floors where they ride escalators to their destinations.

Much of the building was designed like an Erector Set. Components were manufactured outside of Hong Kong and then brought to the site, where they were connected together. The structure itself was fabricated in England, and the aluminum exterior panels were made in the United States. Prefabricated capsules containing bathrooms, electrical wiring, and other systems were assembled in Japan.

Petronas Towers: The World's Tallest

The highest occupied floor of the Sears Tower rises more than 200 feet above the topmost office floors of Malaysia's Petronas Towers. The Sears Tower's antennas extend higher still. But the Petronas Towers, completed in 1998, are considered the world's tallest buildings because their spires reach higher than the top floor of the Sears Tower (antennas don't count, according to tall building experts).

Built as a monument to the commerce and culture of Kuala Lumpur, the twin skyscrapers house more than 8 million square feet and include shopping and entertainment facilities, a concert hall, a museum, a mosque, and a conference center. A bridge links this pair at the 41st floor that creates a dramatic gateway to the capital city.

Central 75-foot-square cores and an outer ring of super-columns support the slender, 88-story structures, constructed of high-strength concrete. The design provides column-free office space, ranging from 14,000 to 22,000 square feet per floor.

The structurally efficient towers were designed by American architect Cesar Pelli to reflect Kuala Lumpur's Muslim culture. Each building's floor plan forms an 8-pointed star, and the curved and pointed bays suggest the interlacing geometric ornamentation of Islamic architecture (see Chapter 18).

World Trade Towers: An Icon Destroyed

The twin towers that rose above a complex of seven buildings known as the World Trade Center were the highest buildings in New York City until hijacked airplanes destroyed them on September 11, 2001. When the twin towers were completed in 1972, they were the world's tallest and largest buildings until the Sears Tower surpassed them in 1974.

The twin towers were designed by architect Minoru Yamasaki and were considered innovative for their day. Instead of using internal bracing for the towers, the architect used closely spaced steel columns and a light glass-and-steel facing on the outside of the buildings. The columns (61 on each side) gave the towers most of their stiffness and support. This type of structure is known as a *hollow tube*. It has become a common structure design for holding up skyscrapers.

The elevator system was the first of its kind. Extending elevator shafts from the lobbies straight up through to the top of the 110-story buildings would have consumed half the area of the lower stories. So instead, the engineers developed a system of local and express service elevators. Visitors changed elevators at lobbies on the 44th and 78th floors, reducing the number of elevator shafts by half.

Although the twin towers were designed to withstand impact from hurricane winds and a jet crash, they were unable to survive the direct hit of a fully fueled 767 for very long. The south tower collapsed after 56 minutes. The north tower fell after 1 hour and 40 minutes. An intense fire, fed by the jet fuel, weakened the steel columns, causing the external walls to buckle outward and the floors to collapse.

Experts agree that no skyscraper could have withstood the terrorist attack. They also point out that a steel-reinforced concrete structure would have lasted longer. But back in the late 1960s, when the World Trade Center was being erected, a 110-story concrete building would have required massive, unwieldy piers to support the towers. Since then, higher strength concrete has been developed to support more weight with slimmer structural elements.

Index